The Indu
pottery inc
power all
ground the
newly settled American West, teeming with an ever growing number of inhabitants, there was one pottery center that rose to pre-eminence because of its favorable location, ready supply of excellent clay and, most importantly, eager capitalists and craftsmen who applied their ingenuity and skills to carload after carload of the most excellent ware. That place and that ware were known by one name, "Red Wing."

For three quarters of a century they made stoneware pottery: jugs and jars, churns and bowls, baking pans and milk pitchers. The Red Wing potteries are gone now, first converted from utilitarian stoneware to domestic dinnerware because of the changing needs of modern times, brought about by the same progress which had made them great, and finally closed forever by a labor dispute.

Red Wing Potters and Their Wares tells the story of the stoneware years. Extensive original research has gleaned the answers to their history's many riddles and supplied an insight into the pottery industry that will be of interest to historians and students of Americana as well as to pottery collectors. The photo catalog of their wares is the most complete and well organized display ever presented.

On the Cover:
A potter applies the handle to a jug in the shop of the North Star Stoneware Co. 1892-1896.

i

Red Wing Potters
&
Their Wares

by Gary and Bonnie Tefft

Gary & Bonnie Tefft

ISBN 0-9606730-6-7
Library of Congress Catalog Card Number 81-82729

Published by:    Locust Enterprises
                                          W174 N9422 Devonwood Road
                                          Menomonee Falls, Wisconsin 53051
                                          (414) 251-1415
                                          E-mail Address: locustent @ aol.com

Additional copies of this book may be obtained through book sellers or directly from the publisher.
Send $18.95 (include $2.00 for postage and handling)

Also, be sure to order the latest revision of the companion publication: *Price Guide to Red Wing Potters
& Their Wares* which lists the current collector value of each of the items displayed in this book.
$1.50 (Include $.60 for postage and handling of
price guides ordered separately.)

Dealer Discounts available.
Inquiries and correspondence with the authors may be made through the publisher, Locust Enterprises.

Table of Contents

ACKNOWLEDGMENTS

There are several individuals and organizations who have been helpful in making the preparation of this book possible by allowing us to photograph collections and helping us discover information. The difficult jobs of photography and research were made more enjoyable by their hospitality and interest.

Willis and Lois Ackerman
Frances Anderson
Dan Barry
Helen Bell
Adolph Bender
Bob and Mardell Blank
Roger and Doris Blohm
Delores and Morris Callstrom
Dom and Karen Colonna
Bob and Nancy Costa
Andy and Mary Hebenstreit
Carl and Rosa Larson
Bob and Teri Leitz
Karl and Curt Leitz
David Lindblom
Craig and JoAnne McNab
Vi and Royce Malmquist

Joy Martz
James Norine
Orville Olson
Ray Pahnke
Jim Paul
Gordon and Pat Ray
Jewell and Bob Peterson
Larry and Pauline Peterson
Carol Schaffer
Steve and Phyllis Showers
Nancy Splitstoser
Mary Sweeney
Lyndon and Ann Viel
Jim and Joan Walter
Mary and Bob Warth
Mary and Lou Whitman
Dennis Yaeggi

The staffs of:
The Goodhue County Historical Society
The Minnesota Historical Society
Red Wing Public Library
Maude Shunk Public Library; Menomonee Falls, Wisconsin

INTRODUCTION
To Third Edition

When we started collecting Red Wing in earnest, nearly 20 years ago, we longed for a source of reliable information on the history of the companies and the breadth of their product lines. Interest in Red Wing had blossomed, but confusion and speculation still clouded the true story. We soon became as much collectors of information as of jars and jugs. In 1981 we put together the fruits of our historical research and photo sessions and published the 1st Edition of *Red Wing Potters & Their Wares*. We designed it as the book that we would have liked to have had available when we started collecting — complete and reliable.

While the collectors' catalog of ware photos has proven to be definitive of the product line, the 2nd Edition allowed us to include some wonderful information on early Red Wing potters and historical photos which had come to light in the intervening years. We have been deeply gratified by the reception given our book. Readers have appreciated that it is put together with a collector's zeal. It is appropriate that we issue a 3rd Edition of *Red Wing Potters & Their Wares*. Interest in Red Wing's pottery industry has never been greater and new information has been discovered, without which no book can claim to be complete.

We introduced the 1st Edition with the pledge: "Beyond what we have accumulated as collectors or compiled as researchers, there is one more thing which we have gained. That is a deeper and more appreciative understanding of the pieces we collect, because we feel that we have come to know the people who made them. The story of Red Wing's potters is a fabric woven of human elements and mineral, of events both calamitous and triumphant. It is something we hope that we can help the reader to share."

Red Wing

Red Wing, the City

Red Wing's village 150 years ago. The white pyramids in the foreground are Indian tepees.

Goodhue County Historical Society photo

The recorded history of Red Wing does not become continuous until near the middle of the 1800's. From our present day vantage point we sometimes forget that only a little more than a century ago any lands beyond the Mississippi River were "the west" or maybe more appropriately "the wild west." Herds of buffalo grazed the prairie, fat trout choked the streams, the rich soil had never yielded to the cut of the plow and pioneer settlements were only beginning to appear on the frontier.

At the time of the arrival of the white man, the native residents, the Mdewakanton Dakota Indians, had occupied the site of the city or its surrounding area for several hundred years. They called their people the Dakota; the white man has designated them the Sioux. They had been preceded by earlier, prehistoric Indians who were the makers of the numerous earthen mounds and "cairns," piles of stone, which were found on nearly every hilltop in the region. Only from these mounds has any knowledge been determined of their culture.

Of the several expeditions of French explorers Father Louis Hennepin is the first to give definite record of being in the immediate vicinity. His trip up the river in 1680 led to capture and near execution at Lake Pepin. He was taken to a village a few miles above the head of the lake where he met their leader. The chiefs of this tribe inherited the title Koopoohoosha which is the phonetic spelling of the words describing a "swan's wing dyed scarlet" which was a symbol of their chiefly status. Each chief also had his own personal name.

By 1800 the French names L'aile Rouge (red wing) for the chief and his village and Mont La Grange (the barn mountain) for the huge hill abutting the river and overlooking the site had become commonly applied. The Indians called the place Remnicha which connotes

hill, wood and water. (The origin of the name of the bluff, which resembled a barn to the French explorers, has been lost to most present residents who mistakenly call it Barn's Bluff. The confusion occurs, most likely, because a neighboring bluff is named Sorin's Bluff after Matthew Sorin, an early settler; the correct name is Barn Bluff.) Lieutenant Zebulon Pike of Pike's Peak fame used both the French and English language words for the village in the log of his journey up the river on behalf of the U.S. government in 1805 and his return the following spring. The chief at that time was Talangamane, Walking Buffalo. It was this "Chief Red Wing" after whom the city was named.

In 1837 a mission station operated by a Calvinistic church out of Basle, Switzerland was established. Talangamane had died in 1829 and was succeeded by Wacouta. His exact relationship to Talangamane is unclear because in their language the same word was used for father's brother as for father. The village was inhabited at this time by between one and three hundred Indians and half-breeds and was located at the foot of Barn Bluff on the plateau overlooking the river. The population and location varied as they were seminomadic, raising corn and fishing near the village, then breaking into smaller groups during the hunting

"Chief Red Wing" printed at the 1915 Minnesota State Fair by Red Wing Advertising Co. from a retouched photo of a descendant of the chief.

1

This 1848 painting by Henry Lewis shows the log cabin of the missionaries among the tepees and huts of the native Dakotas.
Goodhue County Historical Society photo

season. At times their "permanent" village had been located a few miles upstream where the Cannon meets the Mississippi.

The summer of 1849 brought the first permanent white settler in the person of Rev. J.W. Hancock who came as a missionary but lived out his life serving as postmaster, register of deeds, minister and historian until his death in 1907. The village consisted of some dozen or so bark houses, roughly half as many buffalo skin tepees and the two log dwellings erected by the Swiss missionaries who had now departed. A painting done in 1848 depicts this scene faithfully; what a contrast with the skyline of today still dominated by the majestic bluffs and footlighted by the river's bay.

Beginning in 1851 the white settlement grew to more than a mission station. Wacouta and Wabasha who were the two most prominent leaders of the "Lower Sioux" signed a treaty which, although neither leader favored, gave over their lands to the government. It was 1853 before the treaties were ratified but several settlers, notable among them Calvin Potter, did not tarry. Potter and an associate established a trading post near the river. It is after him that Potter Street was named, years before the first pottery was made here.

The city's proclivity for industry was evident as early as 1851 when a lime kiln was begun. This venture, however, soon failed. The first frame houses were put up at this time although not more than four white dwellings were counted by one visitor. After the treaty ratification, push finally came to shove and in the spring of 1853 while the Indians were still away at their winter hunts, their bark lodges were burned to the ground. It was really quite unnecessary because the Indians were soon officially displaced to a reservation along the Minnesota River under the provisions of the treaty. There they stayed until "The Sioux Uprising" of 1862. This battle, caused by the withholding of the annual annuity payments to the Indians, resulted in the death

of 500 whites and the expulsion of the Sioux to Nebraska. In the 1880's some of the original tribe returned to Prairie Island, about 8 miles upstream from the center of town where their descendants reside to this day.

The first settlers were, for the most part, U.S. born; not coming out of desperation but in search of a place where fortunes could be won. With the official opening of the land a great influx of new immigrants and second generation Americans took place throughout the Northwest. Red Wing, with its location at the gateway to the rich farmland of central Minnesota, became a major debarking point if not the home of these newcomers.

Promptly, businessmen took up position along Main Street; two stores were opened in 1853 and a millinery store, a dry goods and grocery and a shoe store were among the next commercial improvements. Several hotels were built in a short while; Calvin Potter's trading post being enlarged into the Metropolitan Hotel on the bank above the levee at Main and Potter as one of them. The clay industry started in 1855, but not in a way remembered by most pottery collectors. George Wilkinson established a brick works for the purpose of constructing the buildings of Hamline University which was located on the present site of Central Park. The brickyard of Barnes and Van Houten was begun in 1856 on the site which later accommodated the stoneware works. Presumably, it was one of these brickyards which supplied the bricks for James Lawther's magnificent octagon house which was built in 1857. Red Wing brick found much favor and was used in the construction of the old capitol building in St. Paul.

Sawmills, a sash and door factory, a tannery, and a small flour mill were in operation by 1857 and in the next year a small brewery was started. Fourteen stores, two millinery shops, five real estate offices, five saloons, three banks and four lumber yards were in business by the end of the decade. Industry and commerce became bywords of the little city. Because of its location of prominence in the middle of rich farming territory and its access to river navigation it became important in the wheat and lumbering industries. Early-on the growing of wheat proved to be a profitable venture in the fertile soil of the prairie. Just as soon, the profit to be had in storing, milling and shipping the wheat was seen. Until the building of the railroads in the 1870's Red Wing was the hub of this activity. Farmers brought their grain on wooden wheeled wagons and sledges from as far as 50 miles to be shipped by riverboat. In 1873 Red Wing was recorded as the largest wheat shipping center in the world. The city was well endowed with entrepreneurs to exploit these characteristics to their favor and supplied with an able, persevering corps of workers to provide the manpower.

July of 1855 saw the publishing of the *Red Wing Sentinel* edited by William Colvill. The *Minnesota*

The Mississippi forms a large bay as it bends around Barn Bluff, the city is situated on a plateau elevated from the water. This photo was taken at the turn of the century near where Jackson Street meets the river. In the water is a log raft headed for the Chas. Betcher Saw Mill.

Gazette began the next year after the original *Sentinel* failed. In less than a year it was sold and its name changed back to the *Red Wing Sentinel* with Colvill again as editor. In 1857 the first copy of the *Red Wing Republican* was issued by Lucius Hubbard expounding the principles of the recently formed Republican party in competition with the Democratic political leanings of the *Sentinel.* Such was the flavor of the newspaper business in those days. Words were not minced and emotions seldom checked. From those days forward Red Wing has always had at least one and often more papers in publication at any given time. This fact has been crucial to the researching of the pottery industry for this book.

When the Civil War began in 1861 Minnesota, having received statehood just three years earlier and eager to display its loyalty, was the first to offer troops in aid of the Union. Red Wing and Goodhue County men were quick to answer the call. Even after the war became unpopular as it suffered on through four vicious and bitter years, the number of volunteers always exceeded the quota, and the draft was never employed locally. Colvill and Hubbard both served with distinction and each was promoted to brigadier general by war's end. Their steadfastness in editorial matters was matched by their actions on the battlefield. Each saw combat in several key battles of the conflict and

each suffered wounds in the process. In all, 122 Goodhue County men died in the war of nearly 400 who served.

After the war a new burst of immigration and building was felt and the importance of Red Wing as a center of business and industry in the West grew as well. A second lumber mill was begun in 1867 and lumber and millwork continued to be important until after the turn of the century. Several wagon makers were in production at various times. Benjamin and Daniel Densmore took over a fanning mill factory at the foot of Bush Street in 1866 and added a foundry which became the Red Wing Iron Works. This company manufactured much of the machinery and equipment used in local factories including the clay industry. Silas Foot and G.K. Sterling were making boots, shoes and "shoe pacs," rough buffalo hide moccasins. In 1872, they built a tannery along Trout Brook; although their shoe operation was later discontinued the S.B. Foot Tannery remains in operation today near its original site. Erickson and Swanson furniture manufacturers set up shop in 1874; it became the Red Wing Furniture Company in 1880. A second furniture company, Red Wing Manufacturing Co. started in 1882. The milling of flour was taken on in larger proportions with the founding of the Bluff, Diamond, and LaGrange mills. A number of quarries were worked in the bluffs around town to extract limestone. There remain several sturdy and beautiful examples of buildings made from blocks of this material and Memorial Park atop Sorin's Bluff is built in the remains of some of these quarries. More extensive than building stone was the production of lime. When heated in kilns the stone decomposes into lime powder which was used to make mortar when mixed with sand and water.

By the year 1900 the clay industry had become the largest employer in town. The Red Wing and Minnesota Stoneware factories continued to turn out utilitarian stoneware and the John H. Rich and Red Wing Sewer Pipe Companies produced sewer pipe and related goods. In the twentieth century the city continued to progress and change, although the advantages it once held due to its access to river navigation and capitalistic opportunities became less of an attraction for new-comers and the population growth settled significantly. Nevertheless, new business and manufacturing firms continued to be developed as the times changed. Everything from felt hats and cigars to boats and marine engines have been produced in Red Wing. The market for her products has always been more than local. Manipulator arms for the remote handling of radioactive materials are made at Central Research Laboratories, the leading producer of this nuclear industry equipment. Meyer Industries, now a division of ITT, started as a small machine and repair shop in the 20's. They are the makers of the graceful, high voltage power transmission poles seen throughout the country and the tubular steel floodlight towers found at many sports stadiums. Red Wing Shoe Company, founded in 1905, is perhaps the city's most famous firm today. Their sports boots and work shoes enjoy national recognition. Crushing of flax to extract linseed oil used in making paints and varnishes was begun here in 1901. Another industry started at the turn of the century, making malt from barley, is carried out by the Red Wing and Fleishmann Malting companies, the former being housed in the converted factory of the North Star Stoneware Company. Red Wing is once again important as a shipping terminal for grain products. Corn, soybeans, wheat and oats are trucked in from southern Minnesota, northern Iowa, eastern South Dakota and western Wisconsin to be shipped by river barge from Red Wing.

The city today is every bit as unique and beautiful as it ever was. The contrasts between the designs of nature and man provide a panorama of uncommon variety and wealth. The bluffs now stand sentinel over homes and shops and grain terminals as they have for centuries over the eternal, winding river; yet eagles still circle above them and nest along the banks. The poignant, midwestern charm of the park in the square and the municipal auditorium, built by gifts from men made rich exploiting the natural bounty, speak of the pride of its inhabitants. When settlers first arrived, the townsite was barren of trees. They soon transplanted seedlings from the forests across the river to make the place look more like the homes they had left behind. The scene today belies that stark past with trees lining nearly every curb and many streets having cathedral arches of towering branches. It is certainly true that the people who came here were deeply devoted to this place and put down roots in a very real and lasting way.

Engravings published in 1891 by Red Wing Printing Co. show views of the city. At top is scene from College Bluff looking toward Barn Bluff. Lower is view from Barn Bluff looking west.

History of the Red Wing Pottery Industry

The distinguishing characteristic of Red Wing potters was the way that they applied the tenets of American capitalism and industrialization to the stoneware pottery industry. They lived in a time of industrial revolution, applying steam power, specialization and technology to activities that had previously occupied only individuals. Whereas the country potter could set up his shop, dig and prepare the clay, fashion and sell, let's say, 500 jugs in a season, the factory potter had only to bend over his wheel to turn out that number in a week.

Red Wing by no means "invented" the pottery factory. The idea had come quite into its own in Europe and back east, more well developed in the production of tableware and crockery than stoneware, but, for the most part, the country potter was being displaced. If transportation had been up to modern standards, it is unlikely that a pottery industry would have ever been started in Minnesota.[1] But, because of the fortunate combination of circumstances existing at that place and time, the Red Wing factories became the largest single stoneware producers in the nation.

These were, you see, different times; what was well developed and industrialized in the civilized East was still pioneer fashion on the frontier which was pre-Civil War Minnesota. To this vicinity came John Paul, a German potter, who settled in Goodhue County in 1861 on the site later to become the clay pits of the Red Wing stoneware industry. A first person account of his activities was recorded in an essay by Mrs. Carrie Morgan for the Goodhue County Historical Society.

"He operated the bench which he made by a treadle. He worked the clay with a paddle until it became soft and pliable so he could mold it into the shape of the articles

"Turk's head" baking pan by John Paul.
Goodhue County Historical Society collection

The donor of this coffee pot recalled, from when she was a little girl, this pot being presented to her mother by John Paul.
Goodhue County Historical Society collection

which he intended to make. The glazing he prepared in a small vat.

We went by the place everyday on our way to and from school and often stopped and watched him at his work. It was very interesting to see him prepare a lump of clay, weigh it and place it on a disk or table, put the wheel in motion and proceed to shape a jar or jug, dipping his fingers in a nearby vessel of water to make the article smooth and shapely. He was very skillful and knew his trade well. He could also make fine drawings of various articles he made. He fashioned toys of several kinds, whistles, dishes, animals like dogs, cats, monkeys and chickens. The larger articles were jugs, milk crocks, plates, pitchers, cups, jars and bowls.

Coal was at that time practically unknown in this section and Mr. Paul experienced much difficulty in getting his product properly burned as he had to use wood for this purpose, and as it required from 36 to 48 hours of time to effect a proper burning, it was hard to stay awake for that length of time to secure an even heat. Much ware was spoiled because of improper burning."

Paul continued at this location until at least the fall of 1871, after which he moved to Shakopee where, by 1880, he became a brick mason.[2] State Geologist

---

0

---

[1] Heinrich Reis & Henry Leighton, *History of the Clay-Working Industry in the United States* (1909). Production figures and state by state analysis show that Ohio had at least 130 potteries in 1860.

[2] John Schwartau, *Red Wing Collectors Society Newsletter* (October 1995). Census and real estate records show John Paul. (A Joseph Pohl farmed in Featherston Township beginning after the Civil War.)

Newton Winchell misidentified him as "Joseph Pohl" in his 1888 *Geology of Minnesota,* an error which was repeated in several other early publications and previous editions of this book. There are only two known examples of Paul's work, both at the Goodhue County Historical Society Museum.[3]

There are no details available of any other pottery activity in the area until 1866. But late that year a newspaper article gave a brief announcement that Mr. Philleo of Red Wing intended to start a factory the next season to manufacture earthenware from a large bed of "the best pottery clay."[4] Nearly two years after this first notice:

> "Mr. F.F. Philleo, after two years experiment and trial, has finally had his labors rewarded, by succeeding in producing a sample of earthen and glazed ware, which in all respects is as durable and complete as any manufactured in the country … The result is the product of a large and varied assortment of crocks, jars, pickle-jars, flower crocks, hanging baskets, of all sizes and dimensions, and of as good a quality and of as tasty a style and appearance as any made in the country.
>
> Mr. Philleo says he intends to commence manufacture of this ware on an extensive scale at once, as this is the first bed of clay as yet discovered in the state, so far as he knows."[5]

Francis F. Philleo was a prominent Red Wing citizen. He had come to town in 1856 and served as mayor in 1858. He was best known for his building on Main Street called Philleo's Hall which housed Olson & Bush's general store on the first floor and a popular meeting room upstairs where that first display of Red Wing factory-produced pottery was presented. The factory, however, was not his own; it belonged to his son William.

William M. Philleo was the eldest son of F.F. and Mary L. Philleo. After serving as a sergeant in the Civil War he returned to Red Wing and set up the small pottery on land he later purchased from his parents just outside the southern city limits. He used the final pages of a diary he had kept during the war as a ledger book for the factory. He recorded wages for Daniel Larson, L.P.W. Bowman and Jonas G. Swahn.

The prices listed were: 1 & 2 gallon jugs and 1, 2, 3 & 4 gallon butter jars with lids @ 12½¢ per gallon; ½ gallon jugs and butter jars @ $1.25 per dozen and ½ gallon covered jars @ $1.75 per dozen. The Board of Trade of Red Wing listed "…stoneware — 2 crates" among items shipped from town during 1869.

That notice and occasional ledger entries for "1 bushel of salt" seem to indicate an attempt at producing salt-glazed stoneware. The clay being used, however, was not able to withstand the firing temperature necessary for stoneware. Much bloated and melted ware fragments were found among the shards on the factory site. Of the utilitarian ware shards exhumed, all were of glazed or unglazed earthenware, the latter being most numerous. The glazes, where used, were browns on interiors and cream, pale yellow, or yellow-green on the exterior. Spectrographic analyses indicate that tin compounds produced the white, manganese the brown, but there was neither chromium nor copper to account for the green. All the glazes were lead based. The dangers of lead glazes were becoming well known and this might explain the favor given unglazed ware. The inability to produce stoneware might also have been the impetus for Philleo's most successful product line: architectural terra cotta.

On May 5, 1870, the *Goodhue Country Republican* reported:

> "We are pleased to notice the success which William Philleo seems to have attained in the manufacture of terra cotta at his grounds a short distance from this city. (The original shop was along Hay Creek Rd., at the southern city limits, two miles from downtown and, at that time, quite isolated.) Mr. Philleo lately showed us a sample of the terra cotta arch which is to ornament the second story windows of Gen. Hubbard's magnificent residence which is a model of beauty and elegance, and made at much less cost than if iron or wood. The arches for the windows of the first and third stories will be of different patterns and are not yet done . . . Mr. Philleo has recently secured the services of Mr. Morley, an experienced and skillful English workman, and with the facilities at his command there can be nothing but success in the future.
>
> In the establishment we noticed a good amount of pottery, hanging baskets, vases, wall brackets, flower pots and a large number of useful and substantial articles."

But, on July 21:

> "At 2 p.m. on Sunday, Wm. Philleo's pottery was destroyed by fire. The plaster of Paris molds were destroyed, and some of the patterns for the terra cotta intended for Gen. Hubbard's house was spoiled … The fire is believed to have originated from the chimney."

The pottery was rebuilt and the moldings for the Hubbard house completed and installed. At this time the factory was known as Philleo and Williams Pottery.[6] Williams was Philleo's wife Celeste's maiden name. She, or another family member, was likely the "Williams" part of the partnership. In 1871 the shop was moved closer to downtown to a lot at Main and Jackson and the trade was devoted exclusively to architectural forms, statues and flower pots. T.B. McCord and Philander Sprague, Red Wing businessmen, became Philleo's partners. There

─── 0 ───

[3]William C. Ketchum Jr. included Pohl (Paul) among Minnesota redware producers in his *Pottery & Porcelain Collector's Handbook* (1971). Redware is a term generally applied to lead-glazed earthenware. It often has a reddish-brown color when given a clear glaze, though the unglazed body may be lighter.

[4]*The St. Paul Daily Press,* Sunday, November 18, 1866 quoting from an article in the Red Wing *Argus.* No copies of the *Argus* of that date are available at the Minnesota or Goodhue County Historical Societies, or at the Red Wing Public Library.

[5]*Goodhue County Republican,* July 31, 1868.

[6]*Goodhue County Republican,* February 9, 1871 in reporting on building activity the preceding year listed, "Philleo & Williams, pottery on Hay Creek Road...$700."

Office of RED WING TERRA COTTA WORKS,

WM. M. PHILLEO,

PROPRIETOR.

Above: Letterhead from an 1877 correspondence.

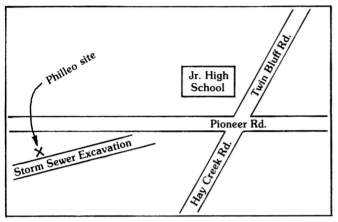

Philleo's original pottery was along a branch of Hay Creek Road which followed a valley southwest from the present intersection of Twin Bluff, Pioneer and Hay Creek Rds. Within the last 20 years Pioneer was built along the southern city limit. An 1877 plat map shows a symbol for a building and another labeled "Brick Kiln" at the location indicated on the map above. A storm sewer excavation in 1981 uncovered the shards shown below and the charred timber fragments and old square nails above which appear to be rubble from the 1870 fire.

Jar fragments display crude handles, impressed capacity numbers and various glazes. Also shown are flower pot bottom with inscribed size identification, jug and bottle necks, a small jar lid, wafers used in kiln stacking and decorative buttons from architectural terra cotta. Philleo's diary contained a price list and ledger of expenses.

was an attempt at forming a stock company in 1872, but the effort did not catch on. In 1874 David Hallum, Philleo's foreman, and worker Henry Mitchell bought out McCord's interest. The company, while listed officially as Philleo & Sprague, was known as The Red Wing Terra Cotta Works. The firm employed from seven to ten men and achieved a fair share of success.[7] In 1880 Philleo moved the business to St. Paul where it operated as Stillman and Philleo Terra Cotta Works until his death at age 45 in 1885.[8]

Accounts from the turn of the century make confusing references to early pottery activity in Red Wing. The 1902 *Red Wing Yearbook* speaks of "Swan's [sic] kiln on the southern edge of town" and states that Ezekiel Harrison and F.L. Morley coming from East Liverpool made terra cotta. We now know that these were all Philleo employees working at his two sites.[9] Swahn took over the St. Anthony Pottery near St. Paul in 1876 and supplied flower pots to Red Wing's Minnesota Stoneware Company until that firm began making its own. Other references were made to Lyman Boynton, who was a lawyer. We have not learned any specifics of his contribution.

——————— O ———————

[7]*The Grange Advance*, February 18, 1874 and *The St. Paul Daily Press*, August 6, 1874.

[8]G. Hubert Smith, "The Manufacture of Pottery in Minnesota," *The*

Minnesota Archaeologist, volume 36, number 4, December 1977.

[9]*The Red Wing Advance*, September 15, 1877.

When Lucius Hubbard built this house in 1870, he chose window caps and moldings made by the Red Wing Terra Cotta Works. The house was purchased in 1903 for use as St. John's Hospital. After several expansions the original structure was razed in the 1960's for a new hospital addition; unfortunately the arches were not salvaged.

Red Wing Terra Cotta Company

"The Red Wing Terra Cotta Company take pleasure and the liberty of saying to the people of Red Wing and the country generally that they are making a thing of beauty, economy and durability which supercedes any other material for building purposes in this or any other country, viz: Window and Door Caps and Cornices, Brackets for buildings; also Garden Vases and Urns for the adornment of public & private grounds and cemeteries."

Goodhue County Republican January 12, 1871

Above and left is the house of Philander Sprague. Sprague was a backer of Philleo in the Terra Cotta Works. His house is still standing; its window moldings representing some of the oldest remaining examples of the Red Wing clay industry.

"Mr. Sprague is ornamenting his beautiful residence with window caps, etc., from the terra cotta works in this city. They are far cheaper and better finished than stone caps, and are more durable than brick."

Goodhue County Republican, May 21, 1874

8

Englishman David Hallum* had come to Red Wing by way of East Liverpool, Ohio around 1872 to work at the terra cotta works. He and coworkers Henry Mitchell and L. Bowman went into business for themselves in the backyard of Hallum's residence on the corner of 3rd and Minnesota Streets in April of 1875 according to *The Red Wing Argus* of April 22nd that year. There they made utilitarian stoneware of the highest quality using clay from the Goodhue beds.[10] Their firm was named Mitchell and Hallum in the city directory but the pieces of their work which have been displayed bear the stencil "Minn. Pottery — D. Hallum." Wm. Colvill, who among other things was interested in geology, told

Minnesota Pottery's products like this 2 gallon jar were the first known to bear the brand "Red Wing."

geologist Newton Winchell in a letter concerning the use of Goodhue clay, "Hallem was a very ingenious man and enthusiast. He had to learn kiln-making and burning by his own experiments. He was really broken down by the Akron folks who, after he had succeeded in making good ware, put the price of their ware down one-half to our dealers who were fools enough to buy, thus destroying his market and their own local enterprise."[11]

This 3 gallon butter churn from the Goodhue County Historical Society collection was produced by the Minnesota Pottery between 1875 and 1877. This company, which was formed by former Philleo employees David Hallum, Henry Mitchell and L. Bowman, demonstrated the suitability of local clay for stoneware and led to the formation of the larger Red Wing factories.

Hallum's products display the precision and stark form characteristic of factory made utilitarian ware. Yet the old traditions were honored by the circumferential trim lines scribed into the clay with a wooden form tool. The discoloration on the 4 gallon jar is from absorption of the product stored inside, probably lard.

——————— 0 ———————

*Hallum's name was subjected to various spellings. On his products it was spelled Hallum; elsewhere it was represented as Hallem, Hallen, Hallam and even Harem. We will spell it as he did on his ware, except where quoting from other sources.
[10]*The Advance Sun* of January 9, 1889 gives a history of the local

pottery industry up to that time including the statement that " . . . A farmer from the town of Goodhue . . ." brought a sample of clay to the terra cotta pottery which Hallum tested and found suitable for stoneware. Could this "farmer" have been Paul?
[11]Newton H. Winchell, *The Geology of Minnesota, 1884-1901*, p. 55.

Hallum's work was not unappreciated by all local businessmen, however. On Thursday, February 1, 1877, C.C. Webster called together a meeting of several local businessmen in his office to view some of "Mssrs. Hallam's" work and to discuss the organizing of a company to manufacture stoneware on a large scale.[12] The result of this meeting was the Red Wing Stoneware Company, incorporated on February 9, 1877. Hallum sold his interests to the new company and was retained by them to aid in the experimentation leading to the building of their first kilns. He didn't remain long in their employ. In February of 1879 the pottery of William Winkelmann in New Ulm, Minnesota was sold to a "Mr. Hallem." One year later, however, the contract for the deed was defaulted and Winkelmann bought it back at the Sheriff's sale.[13] It is not confirmed that this was David Hallum of Red Wing, but it is known that about this time Hallum moved back to East Liverpool and worked in the pottery industry there.[14]

Early in August of 1877, grading began in preparation to set the foundation stones of the factory. By January 1, 1878 the 40 x 70 foot brick building and the necessary attendant buildings, kilns, clay sheds and warehouse were nearly ready for operation. This was a full-fledged factory; the men who owned and managed it were businessmen, not potters. They began with two large up-draft kilns fired with wood and coal. Four lathes, or potter's wheels, were located on the second floor against the east wall and behind them a drying frame. The mill for preparing the clay was nearby the lathes so that it was convenient to the potters (clay was never hand mixed in these factories). With these four lathes it was stated that 1000 gallons of ware per day could be turned. Milk pans, which we know today as shouldered bowls, were made by molding on three presses; each with a capacity of 400 gallons per day. Power for the plant came from a 24 horsepower steam engine made locally by the Densmore Bros.[15] The factory was run by E.T. Howard, a local businessman of admirable reputation, and the foreman was a Mr. S. Lee who was hired from Akron, Ohio where he had 25 years of experience.[16] Glazing was done with Albany slip and salt.

By August of the first year the new company was gaining notice as a story appeared in the *St. Paul Globe* finding that 6000 gallons per week of the most excellent stoneware were being produced with plans being made to increase the capacity to 10,000. Milk pans, churns, jars and jugs, water coolers, flower pots and "other

Front and rear views of a miniature jug made for Mrs. E.T. Howard, the wife of RWSCo.'s first superintendent. Dated July 15, 1878, this jug was made within the first six months of production.

useful and beautiful wares" were counted.[17] After the first year of production $40,257 worth of business involving 270,000 gallons had been conducted on a capital investment of $25,000.[18]

The Red Wing Stoneware Company was making a good name for itself and its ware soon was preferred over the respected Ohio product. The thought got around in 1883 to an additional company in town and within 24 hours all $30,000 of the capital stock of the

Hand turned jug, personalized "Robert Jeffrey; Red Wing; Aug. 4th, 1884."

Goodhue County Historical Society collection

———————— 0 ————————

[12]*The Grange Advance*, February 7, 1877.
[13]George Tyrrell, *Potters & Pottery of New Ulm, Minnesota* (1978), p. 24.
[14]Private correspondence.
[15]*History of Goodhue County*, Wood Allen & Co., (1878).

[16]*The Advance*, January 23, 1878.
[17]*St. Paul Globe*, August 3, 1878.
[18]*St. Paul & Minneapolis Pioneer Press*, February 15, 1879.

Red Wing Stoneware Company's second plant, built in 1884 after the original workshop was destroyed by fire. Absence of clay storage shed behind office dates this picture prior to June of 1885. These buildings remained until 1900 when they too were burned to the ground. The Red Wing Pottery Salesroom is on this site today.

Goodhue County Historical Society photo

new firm was taken up. The Minnesota Stoneware Company was incorporated on May 11, 1883; again by local interests including many of the same men who were stockholders of the older company.[19] This no doubt accounts for the spirit of good will which always existed between the companies.

A technical advantage that the new company employed from the beginning was the use of down-draft kilns, the first ever constructed in the Northwest.[20] They provided an economy of fuel and a more even temperature throughout their interior resulting in a higher quality yield. The layout of the shop and the design of the kilns was on plans purchased from industrial architects in Ohio.[21] The plant consisted of a 60 x 120 foot shop, a coal shed, two kilns, a 40 x 100 foot warehouse, a straw barn and the horse barn all built at a cost of $22,000. After their first several months of operation their output was 18,000 gallons of stoneware per week from 44 employees. At this same time the Red Wing Stoneware Company had 60 employees and produced roughly 18,500 gallons of stoneware and 2000 flower pots per week.[22] Although smaller, the Minnesota Stoneware Company was clearly

more efficient, due, no doubt, to its better layout and employment of knowledge gained through the operation of the Red Wing Stoneware Company.

A little before midnight on Saturday, February 16, 1884, a fire coming from the kiln shed around the newly installed down-draft kiln of the Red Wing Stoneware Company was detected by a Mr. Carlson who lived nearby. Fire protection being what it was, the shop, the warehouse and the clay shed were lost. The company had established a warehouse in St. Paul the previous fall so the business was not interrupted.[23] The Board of Directors decided almost at once to rebuild on an improved and larger scale. The new workshop would contain 18 lathes, two clay mills, a new engine and two additional down-draft kilns to replace the two old up-draft kilns damaged in the fire.[24]

The Red Wing Stoneware Company reorganized and reincorporated itself, appointing John H. Rich as president.[25] Rich had come to Red Wing in 1876 and left after three years to pursue the banking business. In 1882 he returned to town and became involved in the clay industry serving as superintendent and later president of RWSCo. The company continued under

——————— 0 ———————

[19]*Red Wing Republican*, May 12, 1883.
[20]*The Advance*, November 14, 1883.
[21]Information from early business letters of the Minnesota Stoneware Company on file at the Goodhue County Historical Society.

[22]*Red Wing Republican*, February 2, 1884.
[23]*The Advance*, February 20, 1884 also *The Sun*, Feburary 21, 1884.
[24]*Red Wing Republican*, February 23, 1884.
[25]*Red Wing Republican*, March 1, 1884.

This early photo of Minnesota Stoneware Company's first factory was taken sometime after the office building was erected late in 1885. This shop, with several expansions served until the fire of 1900. The plant that replaced it is still on this site and was in production until 1967.

his direct management until 1892 when he devoted his attention to the J.H. Rich Sewer Pipe Works though retaining his position as president. His brother Horace then looked after the stoneware business.

The new works were ready by the end of June 1884. The shop was now two stories throughout and measured 65 x 150. A separate building, 44 x 60, housed the 100 hp. engine, boiler and clay mills. Three down-draft kilns for stoneware and one up-draft kiln for flower pots served to double the previous capacity. Twelve turner's wheels were located on the first floor and six more on the second. Also on the second floor were three jollies for molding milk pans and flower pots at the rate of 1200 per machine per day.[26] The improvements proved worthwhile, for in the year 1888 the state geologist reported that the Red Wing plants were the largest stoneware establishments in the United States.[27]

Minnesota Stoneware Company, meanwhile, had also been doing well for itself over these years. They matched improvement for improvement with the older company and stayed just behind them in total output until about 1889 when they finally pulled ahead. The capacity of each company at that time was nearly 2 million gallons, each utilized four down-draft kilns for stoneware and a separate terra cotta kiln for flower pots. The work force of each was 100 men and they

consumed a total of 5000 tons of clay yearly which was now brought in on the Duluth, Red Wing & Southern Railroad.[28] Their product lines were identical even down to the hand applied decorations on the large jars. Very few items were made exclusively by one company or the other. The shapes of the tops of the molded jugs were one of the only differences, but even here there are exceptions now and then when a Minnesota style top is found on a base marked Red Wing Stoneware Co. or vice-versa.

Early attempts were made at diversification into other grades of pottery. The Red Wing Stoneware Company made their own fire brick for a new kiln which they added in May of 1879 according to the *Red Wing Advance*. In 1890, the Minnesota Stoneware Company built a separate kiln intended exclusively for the production of fire brick.[29] It was later generally noted that clay suitable for fire brick did not exist in large quantities in the surrounding area, contrary to the frequent earlier enthusiasm. This enterprise likely never supplied more than the local needs.

Yellow ware, Rockingham ware† and white ware‡ lines were also experimented with as early as 1886.[30] Most work in these lines is an unknown because the earliest advertising literature available displays only the salt-glaze or slip-glazed stoneware or unglazed terra

─────────── 0 ───────────

[26]*The Republican*, June 28, 1884.
[27]G. Hubert Smith, "The Manufacture of Pottery in Minnesota."

[28]*The Advance Sun*, January 9, 1889.
[29]*Red Wing Daily Republican*, May 27, 1890.

Rockingham glazed dogs are a pottery tradition carried over from England. This one, in yellow ware was produced in the 1890's and presented to Miss Tina Seiz by Lou McGrew. It was used as a doorstop.

A white ware saucer; evidently part of a complete table service. The Minnesota Stoneware Company signature dates it certainly before 1906; perhaps as early as the mid 1880's. How much of this was produced or how much remains is anybody's guess.

cotta ornaments. Only two attributable examples and one "possible" have been displayed.

Another enterprise which did have a major and lasting effect was the beginning of the sewer pipe industry in 1891. On September 28, the Red Wing Sewer Pipe Co. incorporated and soon purchased the factory of the Red Wing Wagon Factory on Main and Jackson where Wm. Philleo's shop had been. Presently, a second plant, the J.H. Rich Sewer Pipe Works, was formed and their factory built on Featherstone Road; the unveiling of which was celebrated with a gala grand opening attended by hundreds of people. These firms were able to make use of lower quality clay which overlay the fine stoneware grade. The industry continued in Red Wing until the 1970's.

Early in 1892 newspaper reports rumored the imminent formation of a third stoneware factory. On March 5,

the articles of incorporation were signed and the North Star Stoneware Company was proudly born. Once again the names of the owners were familiar ones in the local business scene and included those with a long history in the two established firms. One hundred thousand dollars in capital stock was bought up at once; this sum represented roughly twice the capital investment of either of the other firms. Grading of the new plant site was begun in April and contracts to set the foundation were let in May. But, in July the company received its first setback with the sudden death of its president F.W. Hoyt. Hoyt had been on the original board of the Red Wing Stoneware Company; A.J. Meacham, another former RWSCo. officer, took his place the following year. By November 1892 the factory began production. It boasted a three story brick building 62 x 210 feet with the engine house and clay

——————— 0 ———————

†Rockingham ware is pottery done in a particular style of mottled brown glaze. It gets its name from the Marquis of Rockingham on whose estate it was first produced in England. The Bennington, Vermont potteries made many famous items in Rockingham glaze; this has led many people to mistakenly refer to any mottled brown pottery as "Bennington." Rockingham ware was first produced in this country at East Liverpool, Ohio, in 1836; it was produced by several potteries well into the twentieth century.

‡See section on Technology of Pottery for a discussion of white ware vs. white-glazed ware.

[30]Newton H. Winchell recorded in his report *The Geology of Minnesota* that the Red Wing Stoneware Company was just beginning to manufacture Rockingham and yellow ware. Also, "President John H. Rich is of the opinion that it is simply a question of time when white ware will be produced in this state." These statements were recorded in approximately 1886. The *Red Wing, Minnesota Annual Calendar for 1887*, Red Wing Printing Co. (printed in 1886) and several other references speak of "... yellow and white ware of the finest finish and most exquisite coloring, suitable for table ..." made by the Red Wing Stoneware Co.

This 1893 photo shows the third story which was added to the original Minnesota Stoneware Company building in 1892 which brought the entire shop to three floors. The company had boasted since 1888 of being the largest stoneware factory under one roof in the country.

Goodhue County Historical Society photo

shed extending an additional 100 feet beyond that. Six kilns were put in at once with plans for more to be added later.[31] The first firing was a failure but the second was up to the usual Red Wing standard. The city now referred to itself as "the Akron of the West."

North Star could hardly have chosen a worse time to begin business. The early 1890's saw a serious economic downturn which affected the stoneware business severely and prevented North Star from attaining its place in the market. Where RWSCo. and MSCo. had never before been forced to closed down except for those days in the spring when clay was still being hauled by horse cart and the roads were impassable, now they too found themselves idle. In September of 1893 MSCo. announced that they were willing to start up the shops the second week in October provided the employees would take a 10 percent cut in pay. No mention was made of how long they had been idle, but the *Red Wing Journal* reported on Sept. 22 that North Star was about to reopen after being idle for about three months; Red Wing Stoneware Co. had also been idle for several months that summer.

The companies found themselves in a common situation and settled on a common solution. A separate corporation was formed, the Union Stoneware Company on September 10, 1894. This company became the sales outlet for all three of the stoneware firms, the intent being to reduce shipping and distribution expenses, and presumably to avoid competition. Orders for stoneware were received by the Union and distributed among the member firms. If there was a fly in this

Evidence of the hard times befalling the economy in the early 1890's was this scrip issued by the Red Wing Stoneware Company to pay wages. Other Red Wing industries also issued similar scrip in lieu of cash. Goodhue County Historical Society collection

ointment for North Star it was that they held a minority of the stock in the Union; less than either of the other two firms.[32] Since it was a provision that participants would receive orders proportionate to their share of the Union it is clear that North Star was at a disadvantage with but 24 percent compared with MSCo.'s 42 percent and RWSCo.'s 34 percent. Presumably, it was viewed as making the best of a bad situation. It is our opinion that regardless of the provisions of the Union arrangement North Star would have survived if business had been healthy enough to allow them to operate their plant at nearer its full capacity. The trouble was that business was just not there. North Star's light flickered in the fall of 1896 when seven-eighths of their capital stock was bought out by the leadership of the other two

———————— 0 ————————

[31]J.W. Hancock, *Minnesota Past and Present,* (1893). Also, *The Red Wing Daily Republican,* March 30, May 27 and July 19, 1892.
[32]Minutes of Meetings, Union Stoneware Co. 1894-1909, Minnesota

State Archives, Minnesota Historical Society. Also, James Norine, "Union Stoneware Catalogs," *Red Wing Collectors Newsletter,* Vol. 2 No. 1, February, 1978.

The North Star Stoneware Company, 1892-1896. This factory was intended to have twice the capacity of the other two companies; "The Panic of 1893" prevented it from realizing that goal. The building was converted to a malt house in 1900 and continues in that function today.

Goodhue County Historical Society photo

Above is an 1894 ad for North Star Stoneware Company. North Star substituted the star symbol for the word on their ware as well as in this ad.

At left is a newspaper ad from 1896 for the Union Stoneware Company, a separate corporation which acted as the sales outlet for the three member companies.

companies.[33] No further news reports spoke of production there and late the next year the building had been stripped of its clay working equipment.

Thus ended the most enigmatic period of Red Wing's clay working history. Few items have been more misreported than the birth, life or death of North Star. Accounts of its relationship with the Union have been in error for so long and repeated so often that the "official" story makes out that the two older companies alone formed the cooperative and then, fortified, drove the "outsider" from business.[34] An even more bizarre charge has more recently been constructed holding that a disgruntled former North Star employee was responsible for the fires that destroyed the MSCo. and RWSCo. factories in 1900.[35] We have found no evidence or suggestions that this was the case. Nor do we believe that it is logical.

Prosperity had returned by 1900. Minnesota Stoneware Company had expanded to a level that necessitated employing nine kilns. Advances in ceramic technology had resulted in a change-over about three years earlier from the old salt-glazed, hand decorated to white-glazed, rubber stamp decorated wares. Both companies had converted in the mid 90's to oil firing.[36] Then, early on the morning of February 15, during a heavy snowstorm, the entire MSCo. factory was reduced to ruin by fire spreading from kiln #2. On the evening of November 21 that same year a similar fate befell the Red Wing Stoneware Company plant. Each was rebuilt on its original location and was back in operation within a few months.

The companies merged completely in March of 1906 taking the name, The Red Wing Union Stoneware Company with a capital stock of $750,000. It was under the leadership of E.S. Hoyt who had been the driving force behind MSCo. since the previous decade. Hoyt had a proclivity for keeping a large cash reserve in the company coffers as a hedge against changes in the market. Perhaps he foresaw what was eventually to happen to the stoneware business as modern times caught up with their primitive earthen vessels. Equally

frightening was the realization that the Goodhue clay beds, though possessing pockets of clay perfectly suited for pot making with little more preparation than digging and adding water, were definitely limited. The entire deposit covered only about 160 acres 10 to 45 feet thick and it was being consumed at a rate of 75 tons per day. A washing plant was built to refine the gravelly or silty grades of clay which had previously been passed over or used for sewer pipe.[37]

Art pottery increased in importance to the company's trade and kitchen and household utensils of every imaginable form were spawned. Hand turning was abandoned in about 1917[38] and all save jug handles became molded or pressed by machine. Around 1930 a continuous tunnel kiln joined the time honored fire domes which had been brought to their final state of perfection but could not match the relentless pace of the new method. As had been predicted for nearly fifty years, the company began to make wares from other than stoneware clay and before long entered the dinnerware field. In recognition of the changing nature of their business the company changed its name to Red Wing Potteries, Inc. at the beginning of 1936.

As the country emerged from the Second World War it was a foredrawn conclusion that the stoneware production would be eliminated. The RWSCo. building, which had served only as a warehouse for several years was razed and a salesroom built on the site. The route of highway 61 which used to follow West Main Street out of town curving between the pot shops was rerouted and modernized. In the process, the lot upon which David Hallum had tossed his defects 75 years earlier was excavated, disturbing shards bearing his proud Minnesota Pottery trademark.[39]

The post war period and on through the 50's and into the 60's saw dozens of designs in dinnerware, flower vases and ash tray lines. Most of the dinnerware was decorated with hand applied patterns; painted in an assembly line process with each "artist" adding a few strokes of one particular color to plate after plate. Changing tastes and increased competition from foreign

———————— 0 ————————

[33]*Red Wing Daily Republican,* September 22, 1896.

[34]The relationship of North Star to the Union was misreported by Christian A. Rasmussen in his *History of Red Wing, Minnesota,* (1933). Under events of the year 1894 Rasmussen reported that a partial combination of the Red Wing and Minnesota Stoneware Companies had been effected under the name the Red Wing Union Stoneware Company. Rasmussen made three errors in this statement; first, the Union Stoneware Company was not a partial combination but a separate sales corporation; second, he omitted North Star and third, Red Wing Union Stoneware Company was the name taken after the remaining companies formally merged in 1906. This error was repeated by numerous writers who used Rasmussen's book or later works based on it as their sources.

[35]This speculation was first made by Richard S. Gilmer, *Death of a Business,* (1968). In fairness, Gilmer labeled this theory as speculation. The theory was repeated by Lyndon Viel, *Clay*

Giants, (1977).

[36]Oil firing had been tried by the Red Wing Stoneware Co. in May of 1887 but was abandoned because of the imperfection of the system, though it was predicted that petroleum fuel would become standard once improved. The March 26, 1895 *Red Wing Daily Republican* reported that the Minnesota Stoneware Company had been burning ware by the oil method for ten days. The *Daily Republican* of June 16, 1897 gave the first indication of white-glaze replacing salt-glazing.

[37]Frank F. Grout, *Clays & Shales of Minnesota,* (1919).

[38]Sarah Mellinger Schouweiler wrote in a *Golfer and Sportsman* magazine article in 1947 that C.L. McGrew did hand turning for the trade as late as 1917. Large jugs were probably the only pieces still made this way. Churns, water coolers and crocks were all jigger molded by that time.

[39]Sarah Schouweiler, Red Wing Potteries' 75th anniversary pamphlet.

sources and plastics took an ever increasing toll of the market and profits. The company, no longer possessing Elmore Hoyt's cache of reserves, was unable to modernize the plant which centered around the same old brick building which MSCo. had built in 1900. Their options were limited as they had never been before. R.S. Gilmer in *Death of a Business* gives management's view that the corner could have been turned by changes that had been made in the mid 60's.

It is interesting to speculate what might have been; what kind of company might have emerged and what manner of wares they might have produced if they could have stayed in operation. The governmental regulatory mandates of the 1970's and the high-cost energy age of the 1980's would have added burdens which might have been fatal. As it was, a labor strike in the summer of

1967 brought a relatively quick end to production. Many former employees bitterly characterized it as a sweat-shop. It had been built and grown up in a less enlightened age and the image remained.

R.A. Gilmer, the last company president, bought out the entire holdings of the firm and continued operation of the Red Wing Potteries Salesroom on the old RWSCo. site. The salesroom now trades in the products of several other potteries, both foreign and domestic and in fine crystal, gift and collector items. Their supply of original Red Wing dinnerware has been reduced to a few odd pieces of some of the later patterns, but it has been years since whole place settings have been available. Their garden shop carries crocks, jars and water coolers of other companies in the old stoneware style.

After their fire in 1900, Red Wing Stoneware Company built this three story wooden building. It became known as "Factory R" of Red Wing Union Stoneware Co. but diminished in importance as years went by and was relegated to storage use in the 30's. It was torn down shortly after W.W. II and the Red Wing Pottery Salesroom built on the site.

Minnesota Historical Society photo

Minnesota Stoneware Company's 1900 building was four stories and of brick. Its size was soon doubled by an addition on the far end. It remained in use until 1967 and then served as a warehouse. It has now been rehabilitated with specialty and retail outlet stores and an antique shop on the lower floors and office and residential condominiums above. The old office building houses a restaurant.

Goodhue County Historical Society photo

In the "as found" state, the clay was dry, compacted and hard as rock. It had to be broken up with picks and shoveled into carts. All done by hand until the 1900's.

Goodhue County Historical Society photo

Once at the factory the clay was pulverized and mixed with water to the proper moisture. The first clay used was suitable with little other preparation than this.

The American Thresherman Vol. 8 No. 4, 1905

A boy stood beside each potter to measure out a lump of clay of the proper size and work out the air bubbles.

The American Thresherman Vol. 8 No. 4, 1905

Large ware, like this 50 gallon jar, was turned out by machine. This worker is merely smoothing and finishing it; a job called fettling.

The American Thresherman Vol. 8 No. 4, 1905

Potters at work in the Minnesota Stoneware Company turning out 3 gallon jugs.

Red Wing, the Desirable City, 1903

Worker "jiggering" a bowl. Clay placed in the revolving plaster mold is shaped by a template on the hinged lever.

Goodhue County Historical Society photo

The Technology of Clay and Pottery

Clay is primal stuff. A finished piece of pottery is the culmination of a series of events transversing the entirety of both human and natural history. The chemical analysis of an average clay would reveal the same proportions and kinds of ingredients as make up the whole of the earth's crust. Geologist Heinrich Ries defined clay as "... one of the most widely distributed materials and one of the most valuable commercially... a fine-grained mixture of the mineral kaolinite (the hydrated aluminum silicate) with fragments of other minerals, such as silicates, oxides and hydrates, and often organic compounds, the mass possessing plasticity when wet and becoming rock hard when burned to at least the temperature of redness."

Without going too deeply into geology or chemistry the kaolinite to which Ries refers is a mineral resulting from the natural decomposition of feldspar or feldspar-bearing rocks such as granite by wind, water and other natural elements. Clay's unique property is its plasticity; its ability to take and hold any shape given to it. This is due to its extremely fine particle size, many times smaller than the finest grains of sand. The difference between clay and common soil is that clay is only one of the constituents of soil along with sand and decayed vegetable matter. When fired, the clay particles fuse together to form a continuous solid. To be useful to the potter the clay must be relatively pure; however, pure kaolinite would not be very versatile due to the high firing temperature necessary and its shrinkage upon drying. All clays contain some degree of extraneous material in the form of fragments of undecomposed rock, limestone, sand, iron ore or organic matter. These impurities change the clay's color, its plasticity and its reaction during firing. This is why there are so many different types of pottery that have been made.

The reason for going into this discussion is to form a background for an understanding of the different types of clay and the various classifications of ceramics made from them. Some definitions will help in understanding the historical implications.

EARTHENWARE—Also known historically as red ware or yellow ware because of their color upon firing. These clays comprise the majority of all clays found in nature. Their color and low maturing temperature, below 1950°F, are due to the presence of impurities which act as fluxes. They do not fuse completely upon firing and if heated to higher levels will blister and distort before melting.

Much country pottery was red ware; a red, brown or pink burning earthenware clay. A well known midwestern example is pottery from the Galena, Illinois area.

Yellow wares often used a clear glaze leaving the yellow body to show through. An example of this is Red Wing Saffronware, which, though produced in many of the same molds as their stoneware kitchen lines is a softer, lower firing and porous earthenware. That is the reason that this line of articles is often stained from use.

White-burning earthenwares are not common in nature but can be blended by adding talc or other fluxes to reduce the maturation temperature of a normally higher firing, white-burning clay. Such clays are widely used for gift ware pottery.

STONEWARE—These clays are fired at higher temperatures, from 2100 to 2300°F, and become fully vitrified. Because of this more complete fusion they are much stronger than earthenware and are more nearly nonporous. They are generally grey, tan or buff when fired, again due to impurities, principally iron compounds. Because the fluxes and most of the colorants used in earthenware glazes will not withstand the higher temperatures; stoneware glazes are limited in color selection but are always free of lead poisoning danger.

PORCELAIN & WHITEWARE—These clays are high firing and vitrify completely, sometimes to the point of becoming translucent. They differ from stoneware principally in their freedom from iron or other discoloring impurities. Porcelains sometimes fire as high as 2700°F. They are often glazed with a clear glaze; not requiring a colored coating to be pure white.

It should be noticed that none of these distinctions are clearcut but rather the classifications overlap. Additionally they are often used in a non-technical manner which can add to confusion. For instance, in 1897 the Red Wing papers carried an article describing the fact that the stoneware works were producing "white ware." After analyzing the article and verifying dates from other sources it is clear that what is meant is that the companies had begun making white-glazed stoneware, replacing the older, tan salt-glaze. This dating is important in determining the age of pieces in a collection. Earlier, in the 1880's, there were reports that the companies made yellow or Rockingham ware and whiteware. This was evidently an early attempt at producing finer grades such as tableware in addition to the utilitarian stoneware. There are repeated references to such experiments by the Red Wing firms in the early days but all were apparently shortlived because few attributable examples have been recorded.

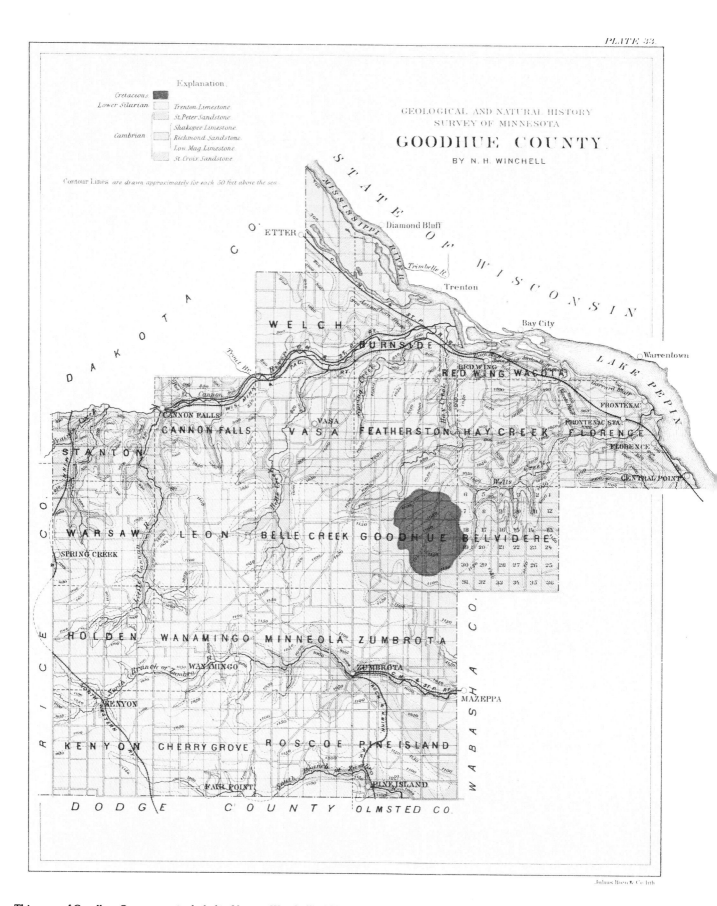

This map of Goodhue County was included in Newton Winchell's 1888 *Geology of Minnesota*. The dark area in Goodhue township represents the clay deposit.

20

The stoneware clay used by the factories, found in sections 3 and 10 of Goodhue township, was deposited in the Cretaceous period of the Mesozoic era five million years ago. Later, glacial action transported it to its final location before it was discovered and mined. On March 7, 1877, less than a month after the Red Wing Stoneware Company was formed, the *Grange Advance* reported:

"On last Friday a committee of the Stone Ware Company went into Goodhue township, to examine the clay beds in that vicinity, and at their invitation we accompanied them. We found clay of a very fine quality in several places, at depths varying from four to twelve feet below the surface, and the beds varying from seven to twenty feet in thickness. In some places the clay is mixed with ingredients that render it unfit for the stone ware, but leaves it still suitable for flower-pots, terra cotta ornaments, etc. . . . The beds extend over an area four or five miles in extent in one direction and, perhaps, two or three miles in the other; and the different qualities of the clay are found occasionally in the successive layers in the same bed and in other places in beds slightly separated from each other . . . "

Much clay suitable for earthenware, sewer pipe and bricks was found in the more widely spread locations; but the stoneware clay suitable for pottery was found nowhere else in appreciable quantity. Some of this clay was usable as dug; requiring only to be mixed in a pug mill to the proper consistency and moisture. The others were reduced to a slush in blunger mills and passed through a sieve, then run into settling tanks where the excess water was decanted off. Filter presses squeezed out more water and the clay was then pugged to prepare it for use.

When finer grades of art pottery and ultimately tableware began to be made, the local stoneware clay was not suitable and various clays from other states were shipped in and blended. Shortly after World War II, faced with a seriously dwindled market and the depletion of the better grades of clay, utilitarian stoneware manufacture was discontinued entirely in favor of dinnerware, vase and ashtray lines. Some of the dinnerware lines, notably Hearthstone, were stoneware body but not local clays. A few other lines were made in high firing china clay and touted as "True China by Red Wing" for a touch of class.

GLAZES

Pottery glazes serve to smooth and seal the ceramic surface as well as to decorate the article. A glaze is fundamentally a glass differing in that it must be viscous enough to hold its position over the surface when melted. Ordinary window glass is made from sand, which is essentially silicon dioxide (silica), with some type of flux added to lower the melting temperature. In ceramic glazes the source of the silica is more often flint, quartz, clay or feldspar. To add toughness, a refractory element, aluminum oxide (alumina) is added; a glaze formed solely of silica would be rather soft and susceptible to shock.

The compounds employed as fluxes are generally metallic oxides or alkaline earths. For example: Lead oxides, sulfide or carbonate, calcium carbonate and zinc oxide, to name a few. They are used to cause the silica to melt and, in general, do not form a glaze if used alone. Each reacts in its own way with the other ingredients in the glaze which explains the large variety of materials employed for this purpose.

The most widely used glaze fluxes historically have been lead compounds. Discovered in Syria or Babylonia, their use spread to China around 500 BC. They were widely used in this nation on red ware by country potters. Galena, which is the common name for lead

A rare photo of the clay pits shows the stratified nature of the deposits. Alternating layers of sand and various grades of clay had been deposited glacially.

U.S. Geological Survey — *Clays & Shales of Minnesota*, 1919

Clay was broken out of the earth with hand power and hauled to the factories in horse drawn wagons over dirt roads. A large crew was employed, many of whom were put up in a boarding house at the pit.

Goodhue County Historical Society photo

sulfide or lead ore, gave the lead mining and pottery town of Galena, Illinois, its name. It, as well as litharge and red lead (lead oxides) and white lead (lead carbonate), was also used. A well known hazard of lead is its poisonous nature; this is suffered by the person mixing or applying the glaze if precautions are not taken and also by those using the resulting utensil if the ware has not been fired highly enough to lock the lead inside the glass of the glaze.

At higher temperatures, those above earthenware firings, lead compounds become volatile and cannot be used. Fortunately, at these temperatures it is easier to melt the glass forming constituents and fluxes are less critical. It had been noticed centuries ago that bare pots fired in wood fueled kilns frequently had a glaze on one side where the ash blew onto them. This resulted in glazes prepared from ashes and clay. Wood ash contains a good deal of sodium and other alkaline fluxes in addition to some silicon.

Clay itself forms an important ingredient of many glazes as a source of silica, alumina and flux. When the melting temperature of the glazing clay is slightly lower than the maturization temperature of the body clay, a glaze can be made of clay alone. Such glazes are applied as thin, soupy mixtures of clay and water called slip. Until just recently, Albany, New York was an important source of slip clay in the U.S. Albany slip is an opaque brown, varying from deep chocolate to tan in color. It

was used in utilitarian stoneware, Red Wing included, to seal the inside of large jars and jugs and as an all-over covering on smaller pieces.

An ingenious method traditionally employed in glazing large stoneware pieces was to shovel rock salt into the kiln at the peak of firing. The salt vaporizes in the intense heat and the vapors fill the interior of the kiln, mingling with the glowing pottery. Common salt is comprised of the chemical elements sodium and chlorine; the sodium combines with the silica in the clay to form sodium silicate compounds which become an intimate part of the surface of the piece. The chlorine is released as a gas. Good, even draft is necessary in the kiln to provide an even coating. Down-draft kilns are most successful for this purpose. Salt-glazing has two notable drawbacks: It also glazes the interior surface of the kiln, the fire bricks being formed of clay; and the chlorine gas is corrosive and deadly. The kiln has to be relined frequently due to erosion and dripping of viscous globs from the ceiling onto the ware.

The white, opaque glazes used on Red Wing stoneware after about 1897 were made from clay and feldspar with a considerable amount of zinc oxide as a flux. Such glazes are called Bristol glazes after Bristol, England, where they were developed, first for earthenware as a replacement for lead glazes, but by adjusting their chemistry can be used on stoneware as well.

Coloring agents in glazes are usually metallic oxides

FIGURE 25.—Geologic section at Clay Bank.

4′drift
3′clay
1′sand
1⁺′clay
1′sand
6′clay
1′sand
1′clay
2′sand
14′clay
1′sand
1′clay
10⁺′sand

Analyses of materials from Red Wing.

[F. F. Grout, analyst.]

	Chemical analyses.			Mechanical analysis (sample 1)	
	1	2	3		
Silica	69.92	69.26	64.98	Fine clay	26.7
Alumina	17.39	18.57	11.38	Coarse clay	16.0
Iron oxide	1.68	1.93	12.03	Silt	49.8
Magnesia	1.11	.62	2.51	Fine sand	6.5
Lime	.60	.45	.68	Coarse sand	1.0
Soda	.07	.06	.00		
Potash	2.25	2.41	1.93		100.0
Ignition	5.45	5.58	5.28		
Moisture	1.10	1.10	1.08		
Titanium oxide	.63	.77	.71		
	100.20	100.75	100.58		

1. Clay as shipped to the stoneware plant, ready for washing.
2. Washed clay; sampled at the plant.
3. Refuse of washing; sampled at the plant.

Cone No.	Color.	Shrinkage.	Absorption.
		Per cent.	*Per cent.*
010	Cream	1	15
06	....do	2	12
02	Buff	3	9
3	....do	4	7
6	Gray	6	4
10	....do	7	....

Geologic studies and analyses published in U.S. Geological Survey Bulletin 678 — "Clays & Shales of Minnesota," 1919 by Frank F. Grout. The cone numbers in the lower table refer to pyrometric cones relating to firing temperature.

Shown here in actual size are "side stamps" from the two older factories. It could be assumed that North Star would have had a similarly applied mark, though none have been displayed. These stamps, hand applied in the clay, were used until the end of the salt-glaze period.

such as iron oxide, manganese oxide, cobalt oxide and copper oxide to name a few. They are used in small percentages because their effect is very powerful; they do not act as pigments would in a paint. Some of them, notably most of those giving the brightest reds and yellow, burn out at the higher firing temperatures. For this reason stoneware pottery has an earthy quality more subdued than the sometimes gaudy splashes on lower firing grades.

DECORATION and IDENTIFICATION

By its very nature, clay is a medium allowing an infinite creativity of form. The things that can be done to further glorify pottery are equally myriad. In the types of wares Red Wing potters produced, a good number of these decorating methods were used. John Paul dipped his creations in a vat of glazing materials which he prepared himself. From the two attributable examples of his work, two different colors are displayed. The first is a cake mold in a translucent, yellowish cream color, slightly speckled and homespun; the other is a coffee pot in a thin, light brown. They show a highly developed skill in their execution. The ingredients could only be guessed at but are most likely lead glazes.

William Philleo's diary/ledger listed purchases of manganese, cobalt, lead and salt. No salt-glazed stoneware was found on his factory site and the clay he used was probably not reliably suited for stoneware. In laboratory analyses we had performed on shards dug there we found tin and manganese as the coloring oxides and lead as the flux. A great deal of the utilitarian ware and all of the architectural ware was unglazed. In the case of the architectural terra cotta, the fired clay's resemblance to finely carved stone suited the purpose perfectly without adornment.

Hallum's ware was stoneware using the fine clay from the Goodhue beds. It was glazed in the traditional manner with a brown slip, probably Albany, applied inside and salt-glazed outside. He identified his pieces with dark blue lettering daubed on through a stencil. The blue is contributed by cobalt oxide which is mixed with some kind of base to make it usable as ink or paint would be. Cobalt is a powerful and versatile coloring agent usable at all firing temperatures.

Before the turn of the century, the later Red Wing factories relied upon identification stamped or molded into the clay body. Rare examples of stenciled identification have also been displayed. A tradition that was well developed by the start of the industry in Red Wing was decorating utilitarian stoneware with bold drawings of flowers, animals, birds or geometric designs. This was done in blue from cobalt oxide mixed with clay or powdered sand in linseed oil or gum arabic and painted on with the thumb, brush or trailed out the way it used to be done with contrasting colored slip on country redware plates. This "slip trailing" method was the most favored in Red Wing. The fluid mixture is poured through a spout or feather quill from the "slip cup." By the practiced tipping of the cup and drawing with the quill, graceful designs could be quickly applied by the skillful decorator. The articles were then salt-glazed overall except for Albany slip applied on the insides. The insides were slipped because when stacked for firing the salt vapors could not reach their interiors.

Decorations on signed* RWSCo. and MSCo. pieces are identical. Much has been said of how the decorations were the "signature" of an individual potter or decorator and finding the identical decoration on wares of the different companies shows that the potter was hired away by the competing firm. We do not believe this to

——————— 0 ———————

*When we say that a piece is signed, we mean that it bears the name or initials of the company which produced it. Pieces bearing the name or signature of the actual craftsman who turned it out are prohibitively rare.

have been the case because of the large volume of ware produced over such a span of years. It could not have all been the work of one decorator and no factory can be credited with "exclusive" use of the most often seen decorations. We feel that the individual hand drawn designs were well practiced, standard forms learned and applied with little variation by several workers. Although no signed North Star Stoneware Company decorated pieces have been displayed, the dump into which they cast their discards has yielded shards decorated with the familiar geometric squiggles used on ware from the other two companies and variations of the leaf and "lily" decorations as well.

After salt-glazing was replaced by white, just before the turn of the century, the decorations and company signature were applied in the glaze with a rubber stamp. Leaves in two major varieties were the stamped decoration. The usually blue or black coloration showed up brilliantly against the smooth white background. The companies took advantage of this in offering custom lettered lots of jugs or jars to firms using them to contain their products for sale. Pitchers and mixing bowls bearing the advertising slogan of the local hardware or grocery store were used as premiums to valued customers. Occasionally a piece will be found with the company signature both in the clay on the bottom and in the glaze on the front, evidence of its relative age.

Around 1909 a red colorant was devised that wouldn't burn out at stoneware temperatures. The red glaze was reportedly an "old world formula" perfected by one of the old-timers. It contained uranium ore. An interesting note from Heinrich Ries' *Economic Geology* published in 1910 concerned the industrial importance of the mineral uranium: "Uranium is of comparatively little practical value. Uranium minerals are radio-active, and the oxide is used to some extent as a coloring agent in pottery glazes and iridescent glass." A red coloration on utilitarian stoneware was elsewhere unheard of; it allowed Red Wing to identify its wares with the city's time-honored symbol and to produce some of its most well-known and collectible lines. Bidders at country auctions where both Red Wing leaf and wing stamped crocks were being sold have been overheard commenting that they wanted the one with the wing because . . . "that is a Red Wing crock and that is the best kind." Outside of collector circles the "wing" crocks outsell the "leaf" crocks with no regard that the leaf is older, rarer and made at the same place.

PRODUCTION METHODS and CHARACTERISTICS

The potter's wheel is predated only by the kiln in its historic origin. But, while the kiln has seen much technical advance, the potter's wheel or lathe has remained fundamentally unchanged save for the source of motion. The descriptions of Paul's wheel given by

A kiln of ware has just been opened and unloaded onto iron wheeled carts to be taken to the warehouse or shipping area. The gentleman second from left can be seen again in the photo on the next page. The ware is decorated with red wings and large ovals.

Photo from Mark Knipping collection

24

The tall columns at left are stacks of shouldered bowls, in front of them are churns. On both sides of the aisle are jars and in the loft at right are more churns.

U.S. Geological Survey — *Clays & Shales of Minnesota*, 1919

Carrie Morgan could apply to those of potters practicing hundreds of years previous in far flung corners of the world. "Kick wheels" propelled by pushing a pedal attached to a crank were displaced in the Red Wing plants by wheels turned by steam power; a foot was still needed to regulate the speed. Some ware was hand turned as late as 1917, but by that time most was molded or jiggered.

Jiggering, sometimes alternately called jollying, is an automated turning process done by a special lathe. The clay is placed in a plaster mold which contains the shape to be formed. A paddle or template hinged to the machine's framework is brought down onto the clay while the mold is revolving on the wheel head. The paddle forces the clay between it and the mold to take the shape desired. Identical pieces can be produced one after the other until the mold wears out from the effects of moisture and abrasion from the clay. The molds are cast from a master which is specially made. The original Red Wing Stoneware Company factory began with three jiggers or "jollys" for making milk pans; as time went by more and more varieties of ware were made this way, rather than hand turned. Records of business letters in the Minnesota Stoneware Company's first year show that they bought their molds from Ohio. This might explain why the shapes of the various companies' products were so much alike; they got their molds from

the same source, not by copying each other. Around 1883 Gottlieb Hehr was hired by Red Wing Stoneware Co. to make molds locally. His son George continued at this trade until 1946.

It is sometimes difficult to determine whether a finished item was hand thrown or jiggered. Finger ridges remaining in the clay can be a clue, but care must be exercised in this determination. Turners used "ribs," thin pieces of wood, to shape and smooth the outside of pieces, removing any ridges. At the same time, jiggering will often leave swirls inside the bottoms and sometimes on the inside walls that are much like finger ridges. Smooth, *straight* walls are persuasive evidence of jiggering; lettering on the bottom is more or less positive evidence. Mold parting lines or seams where tops or bottoms were assembled should clinch the case but there is a catch here as well. David Hallum's churn displayed by the Goodhue Co. Historical Society has a band around its middle which *could* represent a parting line. Hallum certainly was familiar with mold making, having worked for Philleo, but we believe the churn to be hand turned.

Another process using a mold is slip casting. Clay, reduced to a slip so that it will flow like cream, is poured into a plaster mold, much the way molten metal is cast. The plaster absorbs water from the slip and the clay congeals on the inside surface. After the deposit of clay

Another scene in the warehouse. This photo and the one on page 24 in the kilnshed were used on picture postcards, one of which has been discovered with a November 30, 1909 postmark. These and the one on page 25 were presumably taken at the same time. An exact date for the first use of the wing trademark is not known, but here is evidence that it was at least this early.

has reached the necessary thickness, the excess slip is poured out leaving a hollow form which is left in the mold to firm up. As it does, it shrinks away from the plaster making it easier to open the mold. The mold parting lines are smoothed with a damp sponge and the piece is dried, glazed and fired as usual. The souvenir pieces — the bulldog, cow and calf, pigs, etc. — were made this way in stoneware. Later this method produced many vases, figurines and some tableware pieces.

A third molding process uses upper and lower plaster dies which are forced together with a lump of relatively dry clay between them. The clay is squeezed into shape and removed when the press opens.

The most rudimentary process of all, hand forming, was used to make and apply handles to jugs and large jars. On jugs, a lump or coil of clay is pulled between moist fingers into the desired cross section and taper and worked on to the neck with the aid of some slip to promote adhesion. A loop is made and the tail attached likewise further down. Such handles are called "pulled handles" because their shape is pulled into the clay as if it were taffy.

Characteristics of Red Wing pieces that can aid in identifying an unsigned article are best learned through experience and direct, side-by-side comparison with

known examples. Since certain styles of ware were made over a span of as much as half a century with the same basic form, it is inevitable that some variations and exceptions will crop up. In fact, this is one of the joys of collecting Red Wing pottery; even the most casual collector has an excellent opportunity to own a previously undiscovered form.

The factory of the Red Wing Stoneware Company was represented in this lithograph done in 1885 when these buildings were just a year old. This is the most detailed and lifelike of any of the renderings done of the factories. RWSCo. used it in their letterhead stationery (see page 75) and it was reproduced in Red Wing Printing Company's 1891 *Souvenir of Red Wing* **booklet.**

Goodhue County Historical Society photo

This photograph was taken in the 1890's during the period when RWSCo. shared its office with the John H. Rich Sewer Pipe Works. The office building had been expanded to accommodate the additional workload. In 1896 the J.H. Rich Sewer Pipe Works joined with the Red Wing Sewer Pipe Co. in the Union Sewer Pipe Co.; a similar arrangement to the Union Stoneware Co. The companies formally merged into a single company called the Red Wing Sewer Pipe Co. in the fall of 1901.

Goodhue County Historical Society photo

Red Wing Potters and Their Wares
The Early Days

Red Wing Stoneware Company, pre-1900
Goodhue County Historical Society photo

Who were the potters of Red Wing and what manner of wares did they produce? In the early days, they were experienced craftsmen hired from the established pottery industry in the East, primarily Ohio. The 1876-77 Red Wing Directory listed but seven people connected as proprietors or potters in the fledgling local factories. By 1894 just over 200 were employed by the three large companies. Another sizable group worked at the two factories of the related sewer pipe industry. A letter to the *Daily Republican* in October of 1892 complained that "... the clay shops in the west end employ so many men now, that morning and night the sidewalks are alive with them."

Mabelle Miller started as stenographer for Minnesota Stoneware Company in the early 1890's as only the second in the city to use a typewriter. Women were never seen in the actual shops until long after the turn of the century. This was a place for only men and young boys.

We know the stories of only a small, small number of the early potters. They were neither noble nor even

Minnesota Stoneware Company employees outside the old, wooden factory; 1893.
Goodhue County Historical Society photo

heroic in the classic sense, yet they command a respect in our imagination because of the poignant honesty of their devotion to their craft. It was carried out not as an artistic expression, though the beauty and uniqueness of several items was certainly not accidental, but as a way to make a living.

The wares which they made were as common as the clay from which it was formed. Simple, sturdy implements to store, prepare or dispense the produce necessary for domestic existence. Perhaps it is easier to understand the need and importance of these items if one considers things that did not exist at those times. Neither mechanical refrigeration, supermarkets, convenience foods nor indoor plumbing were found in these newly settled western territories.

Employees of Red Wing Stoneware Company posing on benches of planks stretched across upturned stoneware. The work force included a number of young boys to fetch and prepare the clay for the potters and to smooth the finished pieces.
Goodhue County Historical Society photo

Meat was smoked or salted to protect from spoilage and stored in impervious stoneware jars. Butter made in stoneware churns was said to be sweeter than that from wooden ones. Wines and liquors to drive the chill from the bones during a winter blizzard on the prairie needed handy jugs. And the frothy beer to clear the dust from the throat on a hot summer's day in the wheat fields needed blue banded mugs to insure that the taste was pure.

We will try to present here a sampling of those wares. Because of the scarcity of examples of wares of Paul, Philleo and Hallum, the photos displayed earlier sum up the total of the known styles. Our presentation begins with the products of the major factories in the period 1877-1900. Since North Star's story is so unique and their life so short, we will present their items separately.

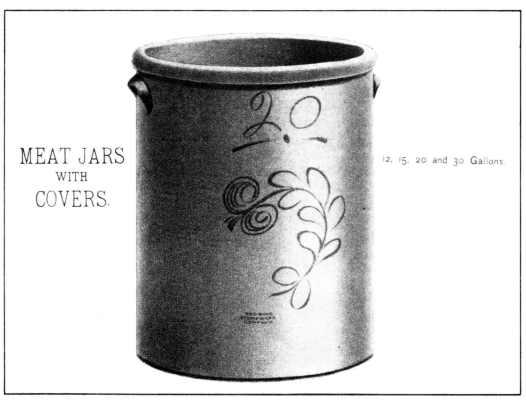

MEAT JARS
WITH
COVERS.

12, 15, 20 and 30 Gallons.

Above and following are illustrations from an 1894 Red Wing Stoneware Co. catalog. An expanded catalog with the RWSCo. identification removed from the lithographs was issued shortly thereafter for the Union Stoneware Co. (see pages 68-70). By the end of the salt-glaze era the size limit had grown to 40 gallons (see page 77), but still hand turned. This decoration has been nicknamed the "lily." Though shown in the catalog, it is an uncommon decoration.

And here is an actual example. The finger ridges in the outside walls reveal the method of manufacture; though the wheel may have been rotated by steam power, human hands still shaped the clay.

This piece is signed with the Red Wing Stoneware Company stamp as shown on pg. 23, but it also has a stenciled signature, a highly unusual feature.

29

The "butterfly" decoration is one of the most familiar on Red Wing hand decorated stoneware. This one is signed with the full side stamp signature of RWSCo.; the initials alone were also used. Minnesota Stoneware Co. made butterflies, but not as commonly.

This entirely uncommon decoration has been named the "boysenberry" by the owner of this piece. It is signed with MSCo.'s "split oval" side stamp.

Perhaps the most common decoration and certainly the most artistic is the "leaf." Both Minnesota and Red Wing signatures are noted; this one being Minnesota.

Red Wing Characteristics

There are certain characteristics that are typical of hand turned stoneware from the major companies. First, and perhaps most reliable is the heavy, rounded rim. The shape of the "ear" handles is also quite distinctive. A triangular, never round, strip of clay was applied at each side just below the rim. It was bent in a slight arch and then the tapered ends make an abrupt curve downward. They provide a much better hand-

hold when lifting or moving than does a handle of constant arc or one made from a round "rope" of clay.

The impressed signature marks were often omitted. Perhaps as few as 20% of the total production were ever so identified. The piece would have to dry a little before stamping because the clay would be too soft and sticky immediately after turning. Perhaps this was the reason; by the time the clay was right for marking it was too far back on the drying rack to be reached.

The uniformity of color and smoothness of salt-glaze was something in which the companies took understandable pride. Old business letters indicate more than one occasion where discolored ware was offered at a discount.

The color is most often a light tan; sometimes tending toward light brown or, less frequently, a metallic grey. Clay color is affected by kiln atmosphere as well as clay composition. A smoky, oxygen deficient fire as was common in the old, up-draft or "bottle" kilns robs oxygen from the iron oxide in the clay. This will result in a grey appearance from the free iron. An excess-oxygen or efficient, neutral flame does not reduce the iron oxide which yields the brown or tan. Red rust is, after all, iron oxide.

The cobalt blue decorations are most often translucent and glassy, less frequently are opaque and dull. The interior browns have an even greater range of color and gloss.

Because of the relatively small number of signed pieces it is important to be aware of these "Red Wing" characteristics when acquiring pieces for a collection. Equally important is to be aware that there were numerous other potteries producing stoneware sometimes with similar decorations. The value of a company signature cannot be overstated.

Leaves are not commonly found in fours like on this magnificent though unsigned example, but the style of leaf and all the other characteristics are distinctly Red Wing.

A graceful if unimaginative descending squiggle has been called the "quotation marks 8" or "dropped 8." This one is signed by RWSCo., we have not seen this decoration used by MSCo.

As we will show later, this decoration style is a derivation of one used on smaller jars. We call them "rib cages." This one is unsigned.

lower photos courtesy of Lyndon Viel

Here are some outstanding examples of Red Wing's rare "bird" decorations. The 20 gallon jar at left is one of the few signed examples, but all of those shown can be attributed by their other characteristics. Their scarcity suggests that they were produced only on special order. The intricacy of the designs was obviously more time consuming to apply than the popular leaf.

Occasionally simplified or "primitive" decorations are found. The popular butterfly was produced in many varieties, ranging from the classic and graceful one shown previously to the crude type above. The flower at right is less common and may be an interpretation of the lily.

The bird was also depicted in this style, suggesting a different decorator. Old-time slipper Emil Shotola is believed to be the creator of the decorations on opposite page, doodles in the margins of an early 1900's notebook he kept have similar style.

The 20 gallon was a popular size in the salt-glaze era judging by the number that have survived. Here the leaf decoration is shown in its primitive version.

Here is a complete collection of the salt-glazed, leaf decorated jars and representative examples of a hand turned jug, water cooler and churn. The 3, 4 and 12 through 30 gallon jars are signed by MSCo., the 5 and 6 gallon jars by RWSCo. and the rest are unsigned. The product of nearly 10 years of collecting.

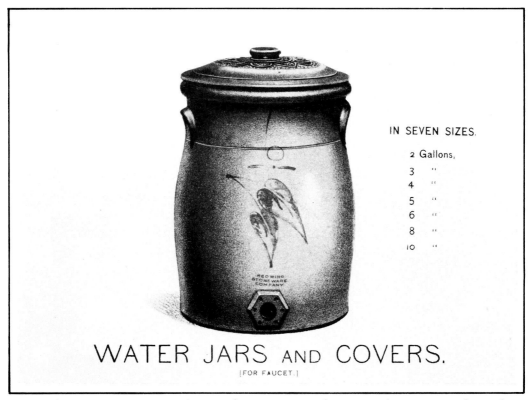

IN SEVEN SIZES.

2 Gallons,
3 "
4 "
5 "
6 "
8 "
10 "

WATER JARS AND COVERS.
[FOR FAUCET.]

Water·refrigerator jars were a staple item of stoneware manufacturers and were among the products mentioned as being in the product line of the Red Wing Stoneware Company from their first year. They are one of the most sought after and highly valued items. Salt-glazed examples are quite hard to come by.

Just like in the catalog. The lid shown here has a large star around the knob and may or may not be a Red Wing product. Lids from this era are perhaps harder to find than the jars themselves so mismatches are frequent.

The spigot hole was reinforced with a molded hexagonal slab with slotted screw heads simulated in the clay. Here is the classic Red Wing butterfly.

34

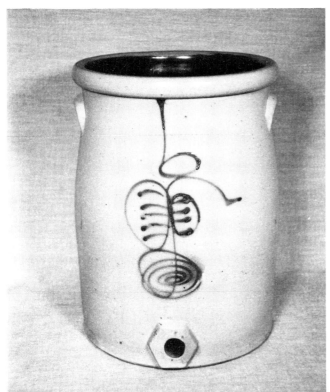

Here is an unsigned "double P" or "rib cage" decorated water cooler. While all of the signed examples shown here are RWSCo. and have hex shaped reinforcements, MSCo. also made identically decorated pieces, sometimes with round reinforcements as in the ad on page 57. Recent discoveries of hex reinforced, signed MSCo. pieces, however, belie company attribution by reinforcement shape.

This decoration style is nicknamed the "single P," though this one is more like a sideways figure 8 than the letter P. All of the signed water jars shown are RWSCo.'s but MSCo. made them as well.

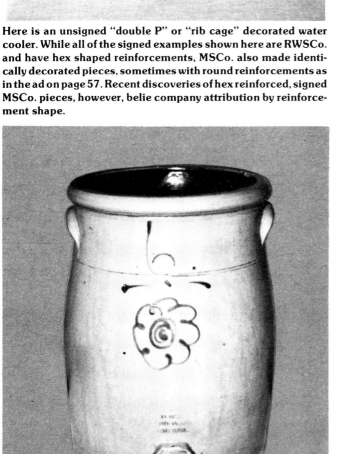

The decorator of this one wasn't too expressive. The capacity number and dash-dot-dash highlight are typically flowing but the "daisy" seems restrained.

There was no holding back on decorating this one. A spritely flower and "pussy willows," a highly untypical design. Also unusual on a salt-glazed piece is the "ice water" label.

35

The dropped 8 decoration on a signed water jar which must have had the hole stoppered and been used to store lard judging by the discoloration.

These are broken pieces retrieved from the dump where RWSCo threw their rejects. Many unusual pieces have been discovered by digging through the mounds of shards. The straight-sided water cooler, for instance, and signed butterfly cooler and lily jar.

The Pottery Dump

While on the subject of the pottery dump it is appropriate to take a look at what can be learned there. Mounds of broken and discarded stoneware are now the domain of muskrats, mosquitoes and serpents. This view is of shards from before the turn of the century, still exposed in abundance. Because of the incompactible nature of the piles, the dump provides a perfect habitat for snakes. Casual exploring is inadvised.

In the process of making pottery it is inevitable that some pieces be flawed. A tiny air bubble or a lump of some foreign matter can cause the clay walls to burst during firing. Too high of heat can make the red hot ware sag like wax. Too rapid of temperature rise or cooling can cause cracks. And of course, even the best ware is not safe from being dropped or banged together.

David Hallum merely tossed such rejects into a heap next to his back yard factory. Here they remained until the early 1950's when this lot was graded during rerouting of Highway 61.

The larger factories cast their scraps into the swampy area across the C.M. & St. P. railroad tracks. The Red Wing Potteries, Inc. carried on this tradition until production ceased in 1967. These later discards which were piled over the top of the Minnesota Stoneware Company's dumpings have now themselves been covered over with landfill. Intriguingly, beneath the building foundations of some of the attendant structures of the remaining pottery building can be found an indeterminate amount of MSCo. salt-glaze era shards. These are in the same location and are perhaps the same shards shown to the left of the windmill in the 1893 photo on page 14.

Red Wing and North Star shards are still accessible behind the present pottery salesroom. A couple of acres remain uncovered and inveterate diggers have found that the piles are more than 10 feet deep in spots. Whole pieces have been dug but the real value lies in identifying and discovering uncommon forms. The shards sometimes provide the only method of attributing the many unsigned pieces in untypical styles.

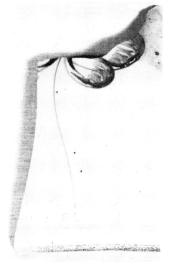

This shard of a butterfly decorated jar was found in the RWSCo. dump. It is signed: John H. Rich; Sewer Pipe Works; Red Wing, Minn. John Rich was the president of both companies. Why it was marked that way, we do not know; this stamp was used on sewer pipe from that sewer pipe factory.

One thing that can be learned from this piece is that the butterfly decoration was being produced in the 1890's because the sewer pipe company didn't start production until 1893.

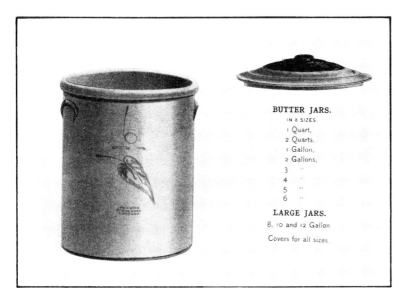

BUTTER JARS.

IN 8 SIZES.

1 Quart,
2 Quarts,
1 Gallon,
2 Gallons,
3 "
4 "
5 "
6 "

LARGE JARS.

8, 10 and 12 Gallon

Covers for all sizes.

Though we know them as crocks, they were termed "jars" when they were made. From 2 gallons on up they were decorated; almost never below that size. From 1 gallon up were most commonly brown slip inside and salt-glazed outside; the others were usually all brown.

Surprisingly, though salt-glaze was not used after the turn of the century, bottom signed MSCo. 1 gallon jars are rather common . . . not so for the other sizes.

LEFT: The most perfectly proportioned piece of salt-glazed stoneware ever produced in Red Wing is the 6 gallon leaf.

RIGHT: But other decorations were used as well; here is the "single P."

BELOW LEFT: This is an MSCo. 5 gallon salt-glaze and brown lid. The ring between the brown center portion and the salt-glazed rim was for stacking in the kiln, one lid upon another in a column.

BELOW RIGHT: The lid at the top of the stack would be exposed to the salt vapors over its entire upper surface so the brown was skipped. Because of its position at the top it usually got an extra heavy coating and often caught a few globs of glassy goo dripping from the ceiling. This is RWSCo.'s lid style with characteristic "daisy petals." Since lids weren't signed they are attributed by dump shards.

Bottom signed ware as large as 5 gallons has been reported but is uncommon in sizes larger than 3 gallons. Bottom signing is an indication of machine turning.

By this example it can be seen that "the single P" is related to the "lazy 8." It is not too common to find handles added to 3 gallon jars.

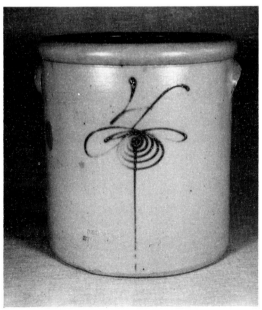

The "lazy 8" is the name given to this decoration which could be thought of as being related to the "double P" or "rib cage" displayed previously. The sideways figure 8 is sometimes less prominent than shown here, often overpowered by the "target" beneath it. This one is shown on a side stamped RWSCo. piece but it is commonly found on bottom signed MSCo. examples.

It would be difficult to classify whether this 6 gallon beauty is a "classic" or "primitive" butterfly. By either description it would not be prettier.

38

MSCo. and RWSCo. bottom signed "target" decorated 2 gallon jars.

A challenge that several collectors have taken up is to acquire as many different variations of 2 gallon jars as can be found. The most common decoration in the salt-glazed versions has been named the "target." Strangely, it is not found by itself on other than 2 gallon ware though it forms a part of other decorations. The bottom signed Minnesota ones are not too difficult to find because the signature was included in the mold of machine made pieces. MSCo.'s signature is in raised letters in a circle. RWSCo.'s is in three lines of indented letters but is much rarer than the Minnesota.

Side stamped RWSCo. "dropped 8" and RWSCo. bottom signature.

The "quotation marks" or "dropped 8" is not too common a decoration despite its simplicity. Based upon the fact that the "quotation marks" seem always and exclusively to accompany the "dropped 8" squiggle it might be presumed that they were all the product of a single decorator. This is the only decoration for which we make that presumption.

Unsigned "single P"   MSCo. bottom signed "double P"

The "double P" is the second most common decoration variety on 2 gallon jars. Again bottom signed MSCo. examples are not too difficult to acquire. This is a variation of the "lazy 8" or "rib cage" seen on larger ware. The "single P" is most often seen unsigned or sidestamped by RWSCo. though bottom signed MSCo. pieces have been reported.

39

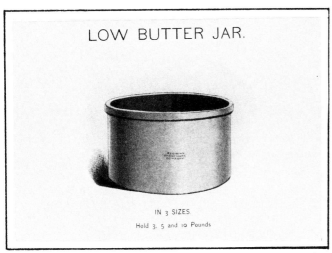

LOW BUTTER JAR.

IN 3 SIZES
Hold 3, 5 and 10 Pounds

Today we think only of small, squat jars like these as butter crocks; originally, tall jars up to 6 gallons as well as this low variety were called butter jars in the advertising and business correspondence.

Here are two identical appearing 3 lb. jars in brown Albany glaze; note the finger prints from dipping. Left is bottom signed RWSCo., right is MSCo. See below for bottom view.

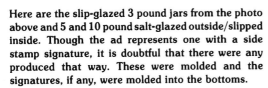

Here are the slip-glazed 3 pound jars from the photo above and 5 and 10 pound salt-glazed outside/slipped inside. Though the ad represents one with a side stamp signature, it is doubtful that there were any produced that way. These were molded and the signatures, if any, were molded into the bottoms.

This grouping shows that butter jars came in more than the 3 sizes indicated in the ad. And in more than one style. The small one would be right for one pound of butter. All of these are in brown and bottom signed by RWSCo. or MSCo.

40

At left is a collection of the standard or tall butter jars in the smaller sizes. These were classified by liquid volume.

Below is a bottom signature from one of the quart jars. This signature is also seen on jugs.

The one quart jar above has "Red Wing Stoneware Co" in small, indented letters in a partial circle. Both this and the upper one have a "foot ring" to make it easier to get the jar to stand steady.

Above is an unusual, indented script style Minnesota bottom signature on a 5 lb. low jar. The glaze was partly wiped away from the bottom before firing to keep from obliterating the markings.

Below is a 3 lb. brown, low butter jar by RWSCo.

The 5 lb. jar below also has a foot ring and had the glaze wiped clean with a damp sponge before firing. Unglazed bottoms and upper rims allowed stacking in the kiln without fusing to the shelves or other pieces of ware.

41

Business Letters of Minnesota Stoneware Co. 1883-1886

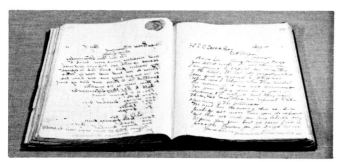

A volume of tissue copies of business letters. The original letter was placed under a tissue page; the tissue was dampened to transfer a copy onto the back of the tissue.

Among the holdings of the Goodhue County Historical Society Museum in Red Wing is a 500 page volume of business letter copies from the Minnesota Stoneware Company for June 1883 to January 1886. The earliest letters were written during the first months of the company's existence and concern the construction of the factory itself. Revealed here is that most of the machinery and equipment was purchased from Webster, Camp & Lane of Akron, Ohio which was a foundry and machine builder that supplied the Ohio pottery industry. Evidence suggests that this company also provided the plans for the plant layout.

The company's first molds also came from Ohio and it is not unlikely that the older firm obtained their molds from the same source. In fact, one letter refers to the mold maker as "Mr. Hahr of Akron." It is possible that this was Gottlieb Hehr who reportedly came to work at the Red Wing Stoneware Company from Canton, Ohio around that time to make molds.

May 28, 1884; M.V.B. Wagoner; Albany, N.Y.; Dear Sir, Send us another carload of dry slip clay in bulk in addition to the one ordered the 24th and ship this in care of C.M. & St. P. Ry. from Chicago. The two roads are cutting rates is why we wish to stock up and want to give each road 1 carload. Our slipper complains about the last car we had of you not being dry and also that it was dirty. Be careful and give us good, dry, clean clay and get off soon as possible and be sure to ship this % Chicago Milwaukee & St. Paul Ry.; Yours Truly; Minnesota Stoneware Co.; Mallory.

Most of the letters were written by E.T. Mallory, the superintendent, who coincidentally was a nephew of E.T. Howard who was the original superintendent for RWSCo. and was later associated with North Star. If nothing else the letters give a distinct impression of Mallory as a meticulous, serious minded businessman. He overlooked no opportunity to ask for the best possible price and promptest service. He demanded that commitments be kept and was no less quick to uphold his and his company's side of the bargain. When it came time to dig for the building foundations he reported with enthusiasm, "I can get it excavated cheap, for almost nothing as the brick men want the clay and will dig it. All they can use of it."

He was ever requesting suppliers to load items on the

Aug. 31, 1883; John Carins; Dear Sir; I am informed by several of the boys from Akron that you would like to come and take the pan jolly. I have fixed as well as money can do it to have everything handy and will run 1500 molds (pans) and will pay 35¢ per 100 for them. I have letters from several others but I am told you are a good workman and wish to come and that is what I want. Shall not get second kiln done so I can run both jollys for about 5 weeks that I want you or some one else. Please write me soon as you get this and tell us whether you will come or not. They all say we have the best arranged shop they ever saw. Hoping to hear soon I am – Yours Truly; E.T. Mallory; Supt.

42

same car with other shipments coming from another nearby firm and always specifying the railroads over which to ship. His orders included, ". . . crowd it out as soon as you can."

The spirit of cooperation and good will that existed between the Minnesota and Red Wing Stoneware companies as well as its limitations can be seen in the letters. Mallory frequently referred to RWSCo. as "the old company." There was apparently an agreement made not to speak bad of each other, but in letters to prospective customers he did not hesitate to point out the superior quality of his company's ware due to the modern design of their shop and kilns.

In December of 1883 RWSCo. had burned their first kilnload of ware in their new down-draft kiln and it was a failure. Mallory allowed his burner to tell them what to do to get proper results.

When MSCo. started turning out ware Mallory wrote to potters throughout Ohio offering employment. In one letter he stated that he had two turners from the old shop, the rest were from Ohio. He was paying 70¢ per "day's work" to turn jugs, 80¢ for 2 gal. pots and 90¢ for 3-4-5 & 6 gal. pots. Molding milk pans on the pan jolly paid 35¢ per 100 and $1.75 per day was offered for a sober, experienced kiln setter, $2.50 for a burner. The pay for turners was not as it seems because "day's work" was apparently related to some old standard. For

instance, 27 three gallon jugs made a "day's work" and 5 "day's work" per day were expected. 6 to 8 days work per day were expected of 3 to 20 gal. ware turners. Turners were assessed $1.50 per week for steam power.

At this same time ware was selling for around 5½¢ per gal. F.O.B. Red Wing in wholesale, carload lots. Freight would increase this by a penny or so depending upon distance. Rail rates posed an endless challenge. The railroads, indeed all of business and industry, were not regulated to anywhere near the degree that they are today. Business practices reacted to this laisez faire attitude by being freewheeling and volatile; not always fair by modern standards.

Because of the longer haul, certain rail lines gave better treatment to Ohio companies shipping stoneware into the surrounding territories than the Red Wing companies could get on the short trip. After a round of price competition the companies entered an agreement with the Ohio factories late in 1885 called the Western Stoneware Assoc. which fixed prices at 6¢ per gallon on ware through 6 gal., 8¢ per gallon on 8 through 12 gal. and 10¢ per gallon for 15 and 20 gallon ware (which was as large as was then made) F.O.B. Red Wing. This association was not long lived as the participants did not hold to their obligations to one another.

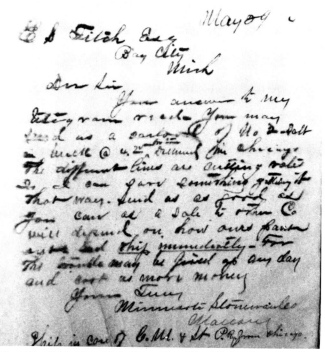

Aug. 3, 1883; Messrs Suman Bros.; Akron, Ohio; Dear Sirs, Yours of 31 with sample blueing enclosed recd. I do not pretend to be a good judge of blue until it is burned then I know a good article as well as any one. I will buy a keg of you on condition that it makes a good blue when properly used, at price quoted 30½¢ and want you to put it in car coming from Webster, Camp & Lane Machine Co. If it can come that way in safety. They may ship in open car, will not do it any good to get wet. Yours Truly; Minn. Stoneware Co.; E.T. Mallory; Supt.

May 29, 1884; E.S. Fitch, Esq.; Bay City, Mich.; Dear Sir, Your answer to my telegram recd. You may send us a carload of No. 2 salt in bulk @ 4.75 pr ton, delivered in Chicago. The different lines are cutting rates so I can save something getting it that way. Send us as good as you can as a sale to other Co. will depend on how ours pans out and ship immediately for the trouble may be fixed up any day and cost us more money.; Yours Truly; Minnesota Stoneware Co.; Mallory; Ship in care of C. M. & St. P. Ry from Chicago.

The graceful, bottle shape of the hand turned butter churn accounts for its popularity with persons using them as decorating accessories as well as with collectors. Ready identification of its original function adds to its appeal as a classic antique. It can be understood from these photos why ware up to 6 gallons was termed butter jars; how else would you store the product of so large of churns?

It is very difficult to find intact churn lids; they were broken entirely too regularly. For this reason it is not uncommon to find a non Red Wing or even wooden lid touted as "original." Attributable lids were molded, brown and dish shaped with a cup in the center.

Salt-glaze era churn lid shard.

Right Above and Below are unsigned leaf decorated pieces; we have previously stated our affection for this decoration.

Right Center is a 4 gallon single P with Red Wing Stoneware Company signature on the back.

Below is a rare prize, a signed specimen with the butterfly decoration. The butterfly is not commonly seen on churns.

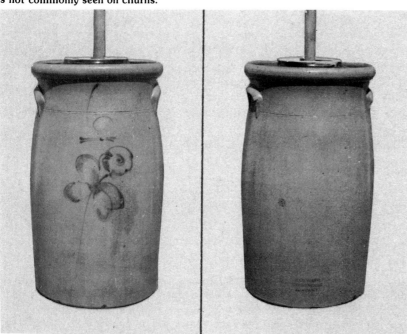

44

Because of their beauty and scarcity, the spectacular bird decorated pieces are the envy of stoneware collectors and consequently are highly valued. Only a few of them are signed, one being this 3 gallon, molded churn at right. Examples of this style of churn are also found in early white-glaze. Date estimate would be mid to late 1890's.

LEFT: A side stamped Minnesota single P hand turned churn.

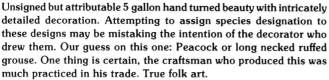

Unsigned but attributable 5 gallon hand turned beauty with intricately detailed decoration. Attempting to assign species designation to these designs may be mistaking the intention of the decorator who drew them. Our guess on this one: Peacock or long necked ruffed grouse. One thing is certain, the craftsman who produced this was much practiced in his trade. True folk art.

When you talk about utilitarian pottery the image immediately evoked is of bulbous brown jugs like these. They are called "beehive" jugs by collectors and are not uncommon in the smaller, unsigned variety. Since every pottery in the country made jugs with little variation, attribution to a particular maker is risky. Neither of the above pair is signed, but they were found in or around Red Wing and their owner believes that they are local. Hand turned and in a dull, rough Albany slip finish they have the aura of age.

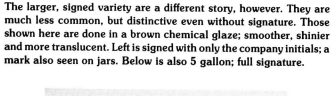

The larger, signed variety are a different story, however. They are much less common, but distinctive even without signature. Those shown here are done in a brown chemical glaze; smoother, shinier and more translucent. Left is signed with only the company initials; a mark also seen on jars. Below is also 5 gallon; full signature.

46

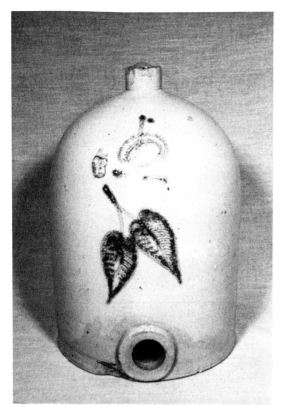

Perhaps this jug should be classified along with the refrigerator jars, but its shape requires that it be placed here. Probably intended for field use where a separate lid would be cumbersome we call these "threshing jugs." They are not mentioned as being part of the "standard" product line in any of the literature.

The eternal leaf on a salt-glazed beehive jug. Neither this nor the threshing jug is signed.

Above are early 1/2, 1 and 2 gallon molded jugs. The mold parting line was at the band in the center. The 1 and 2 gallon have a style mark which resembles a headlong view of a bird in flight setting off the lines of lettering; hence the nickname, "bird jugs." There were "bird" 1/2 gals., too, but not available for this group photo. Also see the "bird" butter jar on page 41.

The catalog from which these ads were taken was printed in color by lithography. The ink on the brown images "offset" onto the facing page over the years and tore away from the paper when the catalog was opened. All of the catalogs we have seen from this era suffered this fate.

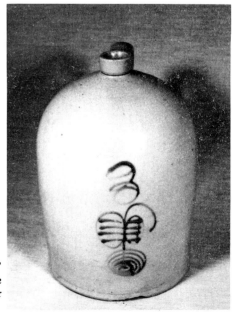

An unsigned 3 gallon "rib cage" beehive jug. Four gallon jugs were always an odd size and are scarcer in all styles than the 3's or 5's.

47

TOMATO or FRUIT JUG.

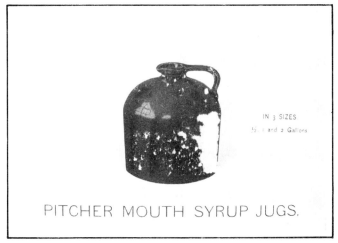

PITCHER MOUTH SYRUP JUGS.

IN 3 SIZES
½, 1 and 2 Gallons

Here is a comparative view of the tomato jugs vs. the common jugs. These two pair of 1/2 and 1 gals. are all bottom signed by Minnesota Stoneware Co. A wide variety of shades of brown and height of gloss are seen in jugs of this style. Some were done in slip and others, presumably latter, were done in chemical brown mixes.

The best photo we had available of an attributable syrup jug was this dump shard. The jugs at left were all molded, this shard was hand turned so signature, if any, would have had to have been added later; it is questionable whether these small ones were ever signed.

This little souvenir jug is shown approximately full size; it is the same size as the dated one on page 9. It was hand turned and glazed in Albany slip with the signature scratched through the slip before firing. Identical sized jugs by MSCo. have been found with paper labels similar in design to the ad at right pasted to their bottoms.

T. B. SHELDON, President. G. H. CRARY, Treasurer. E. T. MALLORY, Sec. and Supt.

MINNESOTA STONEWARE CO.,

MANUFACTURERS AND JOBBERS IN ALL KINDS

STONEWARE AND FLOWER POTS,

RED WING, MINN.

New Buildings and Machinery throughout and with experienced workmen in every department we have built up a reputation for making a quality of ware second to none in the United States.

WRITE FOR PRICES.

September 1884 newspaper advertisement

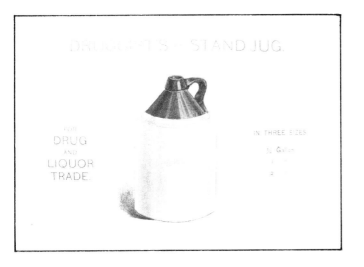

The standard or shouldered jugs. Top right are one-half, one and two gallon Red Wing Stoneware Company cone top style; signed in a circle on the bottom. Above and center right are Minnesota dome top counterparts with two slightly different treatments at the neck. One has the opening setting abruptly atop the bulging hemisphere, the other is more swoopy yet maintains the dome shape. The signatures of these are shown at bottom right.

The Shoulder Jugs

The shouldered jugs, called simply "shoulder jugs" in the industry, represent a technical advance over the older styles. They were much better suited for mass production than the traditional, hand turned jugs. And, because the molded common jugs mimicked the turned jugs' shape they shared their greatest disadvantage; they could not be stacked closely in the kiln. In order to make economy of kiln space a jug was covered by a larger, upside down jar. Another jug was set on top of the upturned jar with another jar placed over the top of that. The jugs had to be slip-glazed since they were covered and the salt vapors could not reach them. If they were to be salt-glazed they had to be set alone or set at the top of a stack of jars.

The shoulder jugs, however, could be packed more

densely in the kiln since a matching diameter jar could stack upturned directly on the shoulder. A much greater number could be put into a single kiln load.

The two-toned effect caught on rapidly and was well accepted. So well in fact that even after chemical glazes eliminated salt-glazing the tops of jugs continued to be done in brown even though the whole jug could have been done in one color for less trouble.

49

The classic Red Wing Stoneware Company cone top salt-glaze and slip jug at far left above contrasts with the more modern styled jug next to it. But, as the above photo shows, both are early RWSCo. products. The darker, shinier glaze on the right hand jug is a concoction of oxides, clay and glassy chemicals and are nicknamed manganese or iron glazes because of their coloring oxides. Albany slip alone will produce a good gloss if fired high enough, but the advantage of the chemical glaze is that it is more uniform batch to batch and its properties can be adjusted to suit the needs of the potter.

No, the jugs at left are not identical. A slightly different curve can be seen to the domes. The one on the left is signed Minnesota Stoneware Company and the one on the right Red Wing. A signed Minnesota salt-glazed and brown jug with a cone top has also been reported; we will show white glazed examples later. These "mistaken identity" examples are rare.

T. B. SHELDON, President.   F. BUSCH, Treasurer.   E. T. MALLORY, Secretary and Manager.

MINNESOTA STONEWARE COMPANY,
MANUFACTURERS OF THE
CELEBRATED RED - WING - STONEWARE.
THE FINEST OF ITS KIND IN THE COUNTRY.

ALL SIZES.   ALL PATTERNS.   GOOD WORK.   LOW PRICES.

WRITE FOR OUR ILLUSTRATED CATALOGUE.

MINNESOTA STONEWARE CO.
RED WING, - MINNESOTA.

All of the catalog pages we have shown thus far have been from an 1894 Red Wing Stoneware Company booklet; it is the earliest illustrated catalog that has been displayed. However, the above 1890 newspaper ad reveals that Minnesota Stoneware Company offered a catalog as well.

The first indication of this catalog was in the October 30, 1889 *Advance Sun* which said, "The Minnesota Stoneware Company is

preparing a handsomely gotten up catalogue of their ware to be issued to their patrons soon." Before that date the companies had only price lists and order books to describe their product offerings.

The engraving of the factory layout appeared in the same newspaper as the advertisement. Such engravings were quite popular in the late 1800's and MSCO. appears to have been particularly fond of them. They had at least four different ones done over the years before 1900.

BEER MUGS.

If you ever knocked one over, you'd know the importance of that claim.

How much Remmler's or Jacob Christ's Red Wing Brewery beer did these two see? Solid and substantial it is certain that beer would taste better and stay cold longer in one of these. Molded, with detail added by "coggle wheel" and blue band decoration. These are unsigned.

The hole in the side was for emptying. These were molded in two pieces, the drain hole cut out, the top and bottom joined and smoothed and the fancy decoration rolled on with a "coggle wheel." The basin and interior were done in brown and cobalt blue bands drawn around. Finally, stacked and salt-glazed outside.

Classic hand turned cuspidors were also offered. This style was also produced later by molding. Though we have found shards of the turned variety we don't have a photo of the actual article. Some people consider spitoons to be vulgar and wouldn't want one in their possession. Fragility of this style also accounts for its scarcity.

Two signed spittoons; upper salt-glazed, side stamped; lower brown, bottom marked by Minnesota.

These jars were intended for longer term storage of perishable fruits and jellies. A tinned lid was set into the ring at the top and sealed by pouring melted wax around. Mallory wrote several letters asking for the covers to be made to his specifications. On February 23, 1885, he ordered 10,000 from Chicago Stamping Co.

Here are a pair of one gallon preserve or storage jars with slip-glazed lids which may or may not be original. The one on the left jar corresponds with the shape verifiable by dump shards. Its jar is bottom signed by RWSCo. while the other has Minnesota's circle of raised letters.

The one quart size "wax sealers" (as they are called) are the most popular with collectors. They are cute, a handy size and offer a tantalizing variety while being basically "the same." Here are the known major RWSCo. types. Left is rarest, straight sided with highly atypical raised letter signature. Center and right show more "usual" style and signatures; one in a circle, the other straight across.

Here are two smaller jars; the left one additionally has a bail which pivots in indentations at the sides of the rim. These are both signed on the bottom by MSCo. It can be seen that there were a number of variations to these. All of them make excellent cookie jars.

Minnesota Stoneware's jar looked the same in side view but had the MSCo. circle of raised letters on the base.

This bean pot is a slightly later style as indicated by the bail handle. The deep signature highlighted by the partially wiped away slip on the bottom makes it a real prize.

The owner of the one quart item below believes it to be a cream pitcher; but it has no spout. Who's to say; we think it's a bean pot. It is signed by MSCo.

The shoulder bowls; these were the "pans" for which Mallory offered 35¢ per hundred to the mold jolly operator in 1883. These larger sizes usually have salt-glazed cuffs and are only brown on the insides and bottom. The rim and portion under the shoulder were unglazed for kiln stacking. Minnesota Stoneware Company bowls are actually quite rare.

Water quality could not always be counted on from shallow, hand dug wells so filters were a popular item of trade. This four gallon household size filter top has stenciled lettering; something not often seen on Red Wing ware.

The lower portion of this stencil, "MADE BY THE RED WING STONEWARE CO.; RED WING, MINNESOTA" was used on the lily jar on page 29. The stencil may then date that jar to after July 2, 1889.

There were two patents issued on that date for water filters; one to Lewis W. Mozingo of Kansas City, Mo. for combining a filter with a cooler is most likely the basis for the Success design.

The Perfection filter was a later water filter/water cooler combination patented by Thomas T. Luscombe of Carthage, Mo. on January 30, 1894. The names Perfection and Success may have been local terminology for filters based upon particular patents. This one is complete with lid and a fancy base ring to raise it up so a cup can fit beneath the spigot. Stencil reads: "PERFECTION FILTER, LUS-

COMBE PATENT, PAT. JAN. 30, 1894." It is signed by Minnesota Stoneware Co.

The lid from the Perfection filter is of a unique design; the petal points are the same as on MSCo. flower pots. Compare with lid styles on page 37.

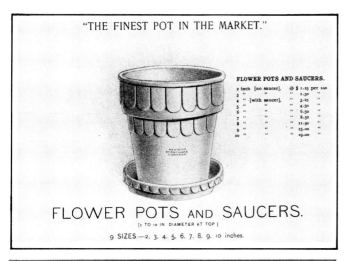

"THE FINEST POT IN THE MARKET."

FLOWER POTS AND SAUCERS.

2 inch	[no saucer],		@ $ 1.25	per 100	
3	"	"		1.50	"
4	"	[with saucer],		3.25	"
5	"	"		4.50	"
6	"	"		6.50	"
7	"	"		8.50	"
8	"	"		11.50	"
9	"	"		15.00	"
10	"	"		19.00	"

FLOWER POTS AND SAUCERS.
[2 TO 10 IN DIAMETER AT TOP]
9 SIZES—2, 3, 4, 5, 6, 7, 8, 9, 10 inches.

Red Wing Stoneware Company set the design pace with the bands of petals around the rims. The other companies modified this theme slightly and adopted it. These "daisy petal" scallops were a lasting style theme which carried over onto other lines of articles for over half a century.

A set of Red Wing Stoneware Co. saucers, four through ten inch, all signed. These are cleaned up and look like new; soaking in bleach and lime remover does the trick.

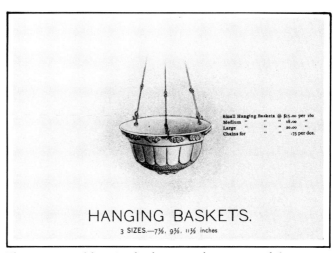

HANGING BASKETS.

Small Hanging Baskets	@ $15.00	per 100	
Medium	"	"	18.00	"
Large	"	"	20.00	"
Chains for	"	"	.75 per doz.	

HANGING BASKETS.
3 SIZES.—7½, 9½, 11½ inches

Flower pots and hanging baskets were long a part of the pottery tradition and Red Wing potters were no exception. Among the first articles ever made here were F. F. Philleo's vases and hanging baskets in 1868.

Minnesota Stoneware Company, however, did not make their own flower pots until mid 1885. Earlier, Mallory contracted with Jonas Swahn's Pottery in St. Anthony, near St. Paul, to supply pots and baskets which MSCo. sold in carloads of stoneware until they tooled up enough to make their own.

Their design has "tipped" petals on the pots and saucers.

Unusual brown-glazed MSCo. pot.

55

STORK UMBRELLA STAND. RUSTIC STUMP.

These Umbrella Stands are also furnished without raised designs. Furnished in plain Terra Cotta. These articles are specially designed with a view to decorate them as taste may indicate.

CHAMBERS

WITH OR WITHOUT COVERS.

Nothing can adhere to these vessels, owing to its peculiar glazing and thorough finish. Only made by The Red Wing Stoneware Co.

This page sums up the stoneware product line offered by the 1894 Red Wing Stoneware Co. catalog. The catalog additionally lists and describes the products of the John H. Rich Sewer Pipe Works, but it is not necessary to display them in this book.

It is known that other items were regularly produced by this and the other companies at this date, but in choosing the items to put in their catalog RWSCo. apparently felt that the examples and descriptions displayed satisfactorily represented their range and capability to potential customers.

Some of the items shown on this page, the stork umbrella stand for instance, we have only seen in dump shards. Others, like the flower urns have been photographed still in use in cemeteries. Many of the items presented thus far were carried on after the turn of the century in white-glaze. There were also other specialty items that were produced and we will show some of them in a special grouping.

STONEWARE.

1-4 Gal. Butter Jars,	1-2 Gal. Preserve Jars and Covers,	1 Gal. Fruit Jugs,
1-2 " " "	1 " " " "	2 " " "
1 " " "	2 " " " "	Fruit Jug Corks, @
2 " " "	1-4 " Bean Pots and Covers,	1-2 Gal. Syrup Jugs,
3 " " "	1-2 " " " "	1 " " "
4 " " "	1 " " " "	2 " " "
5 " " "	1-2 " Covers for Butter Jars,	Total Gallons Jugs, @
6 " " "	1 " " " "	8 " Butter Jars,
3 " Churns and Covers,	2 " " " "	10 " " "
4 " " " "	3 " " " "	12 " " "
5 " " " "	4 " " " "	8 " Churns and Covers,
6 " " " "	5 " " " "	8 " Water Jars and Covers,
Churn Dashers @	6 " " " "	10 " " " "
1-2 Gal. Pans,	Total Gallons @	8 " Covers for Butter Jars,
1 " "	1-4 " Jugs,	10 " " " "
1 1-2 " "	1-2 " "	12 " " " "
1-2 " French Pots,	1 " "	Total Gallons @
1 " " "	2 " "	15 " Meat Tubs
2 " Water Jars and Covers,	3 " "	20 " " "
3 " " " "	4 " "	30 " " "
4 " " " "	5 " "	15 " Covers for Meat Tubs,
5 " " " "	1-4 " Fruit Jugs,	20 " " " "
6 " " " "	1-2 " " "	30 " " " "

JUGS 1 CENT PER GALLON ADVANCE.

All Jar Covers 1 to 6 count 1 gallon each.	All 1/4 gallon ware counts 1/4 gall.	Preserve and Fruit Jar Covers count 1/3 gallon.
" " 8 " 20 " 2 " "	" 1/2 " " " 1/2 "	8, 10 and 12 gallon ware, 2 cents per gall. advance.
Churn Covers, up to 6 gallons, count 1 gallon each.	Bean Pot Covers " 1/3 "	15 to 30 " " " 4 " "

Low Butter Drums.
1, 2, 3, 5 and 10 lbs.

Churn.
2 to 10 gallon.

Water Jars.
2 to 10 gallon.

Minnesota Stoneware Company

MANUFACTURERS:

Red Wing. Minn.

LARGEST STONEWARE FACTORY IN AMERICA.

The ware made by this Company is superior to any other in strength, finish, and large and uniform size. This superiority has been attained by adopting the latest improved machinery and methods in the manufacture of stoneware, bringing these to bear on the CELEBRATED RED WING CLAY.

See that our stamp is on the bottom of all your ware.

Carload prices quoted on application, either f. o. b. factory or delivered at your station. We are frequently making up cars for delivery in your vicinity, and can save you money.

Jars (Pots), Churns, Pans, Preserve Jars and Bean Pots....per gal.	$ .7½
Jugs, Russian Pots and Water Jars........ .... "	.09
Low 3 lb. Butter Drums...per 100	4.00
" 5 " " " .... "	5.00
" 10 " " " .... "	7.50
Stoneware Cuspidores, dark glaze, strongest earthenware	
cuspidore made...per doz.	1.75
Pint Pans..	.40
Quart Pans..	.45
Wood Churn Covers..	1.00
" " Dashers.. "	1.50
Stoneware Chambers, large size, covered, brown glaze....... "	3.00

8, 10 and 12 gallon ware, 2 cents net per gallon advance.
15 and 20 gallon ware, 4 cents net per gallon advance.
30 gallon ware, 5 cents net per gallon advance.
All 1¼ gallon ware counts 1½ gallon.
All ⅝ gallon ware counts ⅔ gallon.
All ¾ gallon ware counts 4-5 gallon.
Preserve and Fruit Jar Covers count ⅓ gallon.
Bean Pot Covers count ⅓ gallon.
Butter Jar Covers, 1 to 6, count 1 gallon.
Butter Jar Covers, 8 to 20, count 2 gallons.
Churn Covers count 1 gallon.

PRICES ON THIS PAGE ARE NET.

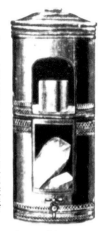

Perfection Gravity Filter.
Family Size, capacity 4 gallons per day.........$3.50
Hotel   "   "   10   "   " 7.50

Russian Pot.
½ and 1 gallon.

Bean Pots.
½ and 1 gallon.

Pans.
Pint, quart, ½, 1 and 1½ gallons.

Jars, Pots .... 12 gallon
Meat Tubs. 15 and 20 gallon
"   30 gallons

Common Jug.
¼ to 5 gallon

Syrup Jug.
1 and 2 gallon

Fruit Jug.
2½ inch mouth ½ to 2 gallon

Druggist Jug.
½, 1 and 2 gallon

Preserve Jar
½, 1 and 2 gallon

1895 MSCo. advertisement

THE NORTH STAR STONEWARE CO.

MANUFACTURERS OF THE

Celebrated Red Wing Stoneware.

WEST MAIN STREET.

E.T. HOWARD, Sec'y & Gen'l Mang'r.

Red Wing, Minn. _____ 189_

Letterhead stationery of the North Star Stoneware Company. This letterhead was probably printed after the death of first North Star President F.W. Hoyt in August of 1892 but before A.J. Meacham was appointed to fill that position in November of the following year. E.T. Howard resigned as Secretary and General Manager in 1894.

Goodhue County Historical Society collection

North Star 1892-1896

The story of the North Star Stoneware Company is unique enough to rate separate handling. Unlike the two earlier giants, its history is compressed into a span of only four years. In 1887, the Red Wing Stoneware Company was recognized as being the largest single producer of stoneware in the nation. Minnesota Stoneware Company surged ahead about two years later. By 1892 Red Wing's clay industry was really flexing its muscles and had expanded into the lucrative sewer pipe business.

North Star was born in this boom period with $100,000 of stock subscribed and twice that amount authorized. It was intended to be larger than either of the former plants. Assessments against the capital pledges for the building amounted to $55,000. That same year, however, the Minnesota and Red Wing Stoneware Companies spent $25,000 and $100,000 respectively in increasing their stoneware capacity and building the John H. Rich Sewer Pipe Works. As the dust settled, North Star had a capacity of six kilns with plans for a seventh and MSCo. had nine.

Just as it had taken Minnesota Stoneware Company several years to establish its prominence despite their more efficient shop, North Star did not immediately take over large shares of the market already held by its two neighbors. An economic down turn in 1893 wounded all three companies, but to North Star the injury was mortal. The following year the companies agreed to sell through a joint venture, the Union Stoneware Company. One of the bylaws of the co-operative was that orders would be divided according to shares of the market at the time of the formation of the agreement. Minnesota held 42 percent, Red Wing

34 percent which left 24 percent for North Star.

While 24 percent of a healthy market could certainly have sustained an established company, the market had been decimated. All of the manufactories in town were closed for extended periods of time. North Star never recovered from the weakening effects of this short but acute depression.

Perhaps the investors behind the organization lost faith, their hopes being dashed by the realization that their market share was frozen by the agreement with the Union. A share which could only be increased by consent of two-thirds of the Union directors.

In September of 1896 the leadership of the other two firms bought out seven-eighths of North Star's stock. The Union agreement was rewritten giving MSCo. 55 percent and RWSCo. 45 percent of the shares and hence, the market.

Because the story has been misreported for half a century, North Star and its wares have taken on a mysterious aura. Since they were so short lived all of their wares can be termed rare. The basic styles and types of products offered were essentially the same as from the two older firms, but there is enough uniqueness to fuel the flames in the hearts of eager collectors.

Unfortunately, five-pointed stars are not the most unique geometric figures and there were several other potteries who used stars in their trademark or took Star as their name. This company chose that name because Minnesota is the North Star State; there were, and continue to be other firms in Minnesota and Red Wing with that name.

But, to pottery collectors there was only one North Star.

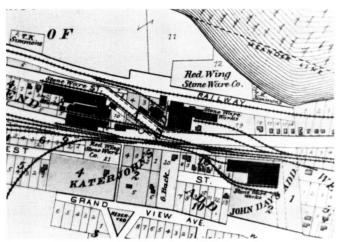

A plat map of the City of Red Wing from 1894 shows the arrangement of the stoneware factories in the west end at that time.

Red Wing Stoneware Co. had its cone top jug, Minnesota its dome; North Star's was a stylish pear shape. Salt-glazed cylinder with semi-gloss slip-glazed top. The shoulder jug is the best recognized North Star piece.

These are the signatures of the two, one, and one-half gallon jugs above; on these the letters N-O-R-T-H are all arranged counter-clockwise. This was not always the case; clockwise lettering has been seen on some two gallon jugs.

This two gallon is inexplicably done all over in glossy brown, even the bottom. Bottom lettering is clockwise

On the north wall of the building, in place of a window on the third floor, was put a large, brickwork star. In the center of this star was a recess into which a brown, beehive jug was set. In the early 1950's long after North Star had been forgotten, during the process of repainting the red brick exterior, workmen became curious as to the possible contents of the jug. Since it was mortared in place it could not be shaken, so it was smashed with a hammer . . . it was empty.

The smaller stars are iron castings acting as washers on rods running through the building to keep the walls from buckling. Their shape has nothing to do with North Star, in fact the MSCo. building has similar star washers.

The wide mouthed style "tomato" shoulder jugs were also offered.

The molded, brown, common jugs were part of the North Star product line, too. It would be safe to say that all three company's product offerings were basically the same. These are one, one-half and one-fourth gallon.

The signature on these has caused much anguish among collectors and adds to the North Star mystique. Since there were other companies with "Star" in their name or marking, how do we know these are North Star?

Here is how. This one gallon jug is stenciled in an impure cream colored compound, possibly white glaze adulterated by the brown beneath. It was probably a display piece for the 1894 State Fair.

The star on the bottom has no letters; the plain, one gal. brown jug at top is identical except for the stencil.

The shape of this bailed "vinegar" jug seems unique to North Star. However, Red Wing Stoneware Co. made jugs in this shape with pulled handles in white-glaze.

This signature style is not known to exist on any other North Star piece and is possibly the fanciest signature on any piece of Red Wing ware.

Photo of the interior of North Star Stoneware Company, 1896. Potter is applying the handle to a jug which will shrink to one gallon size when dried and fired. Positions for nine hand turners are seen in this photo; there may have been three of four more out of frame to the left, behind the camera position, and perhaps more on other floors of the three story building. Whether any of the hand turned ware at the right is signed or not is unknown; none has ever been reported.

This photo exhibits a method of operation used by all of the companies. A plank was pulled out from the drying rack, right up to the turner's bench. As he completed each piece it was set on the plank until the plank was full. The full plank was shoved back in and an empty one was pulled out.

Minnesota Historical Society photo

After North Star folded, the machinery and equipment were removed and the building converted by adding the grain elevator at right and adding height to the brick portion at left end. A conveyor system was built on top adding several stories and doubling the height of the entire structure. In 1900 Minnesota Malting Company began making barley malt in the plant.

Red Wing Yearbook, 1902

This picture was taken in the fall of 1980 from the opposite side of the building. The Red Wing Malting Co. took over the plant in 1940, two years after the Froedert Grain & Malting Co., which had purchased the building in 1924, had closed. Malting continued into the '80's, but after sitting idle for several years, the building was razed in 1994 to make room for a new motel.

61

The tall butter jars. Acquiring this series is quite an accomplishment for the collector. These are 1/2 gallon, quart, pint and 1/2 pint. Wall thickness is less than other company's jars.

Bottom signatures are stars with no lettering. Size of star and diameter of 1/2 gallon jar is the same as 1/2 gallon shoulder jug.

Three pound low butter jar with another "leaves no doubt" signature. In its short life North Star used a variety of signatures.

All of the characteristics of this salt-glazed two gallon jar are "right" for Red Wing; but is it North Star? A similarly decorated shard was unearthed in 1994 from the North Star dumpsite.

This pairing has been called a cream and sugar set; though it could serve that purpose in the proud possession of a collector it is actually the one-half pint tall jar with a matching size pitcher.

The pitcher possibly was for cream so the theory isn't too far fetched. The pitcher is signed with a plain, raised star like the jar; some have unglazed bottoms.

North Star bean pots one-half and one gallon. These have no foot ring so the star is indented since bottom is flat across. Dark brown slip-glaze. All of the articles with stars on the bottom were molded.

A one gallon wax sealer fruit jar. It would be assumed that North Star also made these in the cute one quart size and shape though none have been reported.

Here are the preserve jars; much like the MSCo. and RWSCo. ones on page 52. Shown are one-half and one gallon; two gallon has been seen but was not available for photo.

Another shape of one gallon preserve or storage jar made for a stoneware cover.

The bottom signatures on these also have indented stars but include raised letters in the star points. An inattentive mold maker got the N backwards on the one gallon; things got straightened out on the one-half gallon though.

Both of the jars above have a plain, raised star with no letters. Note the sand fused to the glaze where it was setting; this was to keep pieces from sticking together without necessitating the separate step of cleaning the glaze from the bottom before firing.

An individual bean pot; see ad on page 68

Photo courtesy Wayne Hunter

Bowls are undoubtedly the most available North Star products, but not often with this signature; the same as the butter jar on page 62.

A bailed handled stew pan with three foot-lugs and a raised star signature. Such a product was shown in a Union Stoneware Co. catalog, see page 68.

Nor with this signature; indented letters in the star points. Most of the bowls found have a plain, raised star.

Here are the two smallest of the set, a 6 inch and 7 inch diameter. These were supposedly graduated by volume, but the small one holds 1½ pints.

And here is the top end of the set; 9, 10, 11 and 12 inch bowls. All of these have the simple, unlettered stars but are attributable by shards.

The North Star Dump

In the spring of 1994, the North Star building was demolished and the lot excavated. Underground, at the east end of the building, was a 75 x 200 ft. layer of shards, 4 ft. thick.

Although many examples of decorated ware were noted, no side-stamp nor previously unknown bottom signatures were discovered. There were "lazy eight" decorations indistinguishable from those on RWSCo. or MSCo. products; "targets," however, seemed always to be missing the "tail." The "leaves" were found only in their primitive form, even a dated example, similar to the one on pg. 82. There were flowers, like the example on pg. 32, but no butterflies.

Verification was made for many of the forms signed with only a plain star, either by shards, or the large number of plaster molds also present.

North Star's flower pot and saucer style borrowed from each of its neighbors for the design of the scallops around the rims. The bottoms were signed with an unlettered star and size number.

This hanging basket can now be confirmed as North Star by the discovery of the discarded plaster molds in the dumpsite.

A one gallon, salt-glaze and brown North Star lid. The larger sizes were similar, but included the capacity number in the center of the star on the button.

Here is a white-glazed lid and shard in a different style. The shard is from the RWSCo. dump, but from a different area than the North Star shards. A salt-glaze and brown example and one in white with three blue bands, like those used on water cooler lids, has also been displayed. Since all of the lids seen in this style have been four gallon size, and since no shards of this style were found in the North Star dump, it is believed that they are RWSCo.'s Success Filter lids.

There have also been other lid styles bearing stars displayed, but none can be verified by dump shards as being Red Wing or North Star.

This 12 gallon lid was found "in the wild," but the shards came from the same dump that RWSCo. used; other North Star shards are found there as well. It is speculated that stock leftover after North Star closed was "inherited" by RWSCo. and later dumped to free up warehouse space.

———— 0 ————

Collectors Beware!

The value of a piece in a collection depends upon several issues; the age, the scarcity, the condition, the origin, the beauty to name a few. Since the North Star company was in business for only a few years in the 1890's all of their pieces have age, scarcity and origin that increases the interest in them. Unfortunately, attribution of a piece signed only with a star can be troublesome.

There are many pieces which have been mistakenly attributed to North Star based solely on the presence of a star in the trademark or elsewhere on the piece. Notable among them are white-glazed jars, churns and jugs with a rubber stamped star circumscribed by and enclosing a pair of circles. Some of these jars have bail handles attached to clay lugs at the rim. Red Wing Union Stoneware Company was granted a patent on such handles in 1915; no patent could have been granted if North Star had used such handles prior to 1915.

Another mistaken attribution has been to bail handled, covered casseroles with a large star and the words "The German" on the bottom. There are several similar varieties, including some bearing "The 20th Century German" and simply the word "Star" for Star Stoneware Co. of Crooksville, Ohio.

One of the better known misidentified pieces are milk pitchers in "Grape and Trellis" motif in various sizes and colors with either raised or indented stars on the bottom. These appear in the 1928 Brush McCoy Pottery catalog.

As noted with the 4 gallon lids above, even pieces which can be attributed by shards to having been made in Red Wing can be uncertain. The items we have displayed and represented as authentic North Star products are the sum of the known forms. But just as surely there were others, salt-glazed large jars for instance which are yet unreported. Caution and discretion is advised.

White-Glazed Ware

Toward the end of the nineteenth century stoneware potteries throughout the country were beginning to experiment with white-glaze as a replacement for the brown and tan of the slip and salt-glaze tradition. These new glazes were chemical mixes of flint and feldspar, kaolin, calcium carbonate and zinc oxide. No longer could they simply be dug from the ground and used, they now had to be skillfully formulated.

The benefits were that since they were a combination of ingredients they could be adjusted by experimenting with the proportions of the components. Once the proper "recipe" was determined each batch could be made as perfect as the next, the amount of spoiled ware decreased. Also, the creamy white finish looked new and clean and its popular acceptance was immediate.

The solid white background provided a perfect billboard for decorating with slogans and logos of companies using the ware to contain their products and of the potteries themselves.

The first hint of the use of white glaze is in a price list dated November 15, 1895 among the records of the Union Stoneware Company held in the State Archives by the Minnesota Historical Society. One through five pound jars, pint and quart bowls, cuspidors, one-half

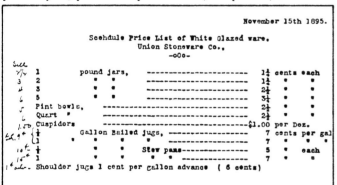

November 15, 1895 Union Stoneware Co. white-glaze price list

and one gallon bailed jugs and stew pans and shoulder jugs were offered in white glaze.

On June 16, 1897 the *Red Wing Daily Republican* contained an article headed: "WHITE WARE, Manufactured at the Stoneware Works Here the Equal of any Produced in the Country." The reporter wrote of his surprise upon making a casual visit to the Minnesota Stoneware Company's plant and finding that a kiln of, " . . . white ware had just been opened after having been burned. Two years ago had you told the managers of these works that white ware would be made here they would have looked at you with the eye of a skeptic. Yet here was presented a kiln of ware of the purest creamy white glaze, uniform in color throughout, firm in body, perfect in form; in short fulfilling in every particular all that could be desired by anyone in stoneware manufacture." " . . . so rapidly is it growing in favor that at the limited number of points, comparatively speaking, where it has been introduced, it is supplanting to a considerable extent the salt glazed ware of the rich chocolate brown and kindred shades."

In the first years the items offered in white-glaze were limited to small articles which would fit inside larger jars or into saggers, protective fire clay containers used to keep the ware out of the direct draft of the kiln fire. While the salt-glazed pieces were little affected by the soot and ash of the wood and coal fuels that stoked the kilns, the white-glaze would be spoiled by these impurities. By mid 1895, the companies had converted to oil firing. The perfection of this fuel allowed firing without saggers.

By 1900 the switch over had become total as it was reported in the 1902 *Red Wing Year Book.* "Their most radical change in wares was about three years ago when they discarded the dark glaze in favor of the white glaze which is the highest stoneware product to be made. After that comes the art of making wares from mixed bodies in every degree of intricacy."

Many of the classic styles that had been offered in salt-glaze continued to be offered in white-glaze before being replaced by more modern or standardized designs. Here are, left to right, a one gallon, wide mouthed North Star jug; a RWSCo. cone top and a 1/2, 1 and 2 gallon set of MSCo. dome tops. (Both varieties of MSCo. dome tops have been seen in white-glaze.)

Combined Capital paid in $410,000#

Union Stoneware Co.
Red Wing, Minn.

E. H. Blodgett, President
D. M. Baldwin, Vice Prest.
H. S. Rich, Secretary.
E. S. Hoyt, Treasurer.

Yearly Capacity
9,000,000 Gallons
or
2000 Carloads

Circa 1895 Union Catalog

The Union Stoneware Company was formed in September of 1894 as a sales outlet for the three member firms. Sometime shortly thereafter they issued a product catalog printed by the same firm and done up in the same manner as the 1894 Red Wing Stoneware Co. catalog. Most of the illustrations were identical to the earlier catalog except that the Red Wing Stoneware Co. name was taken off the ware and pages.

There were some notable additions, however, Shown here are some of the pages offering new items. Perhaps most significant is not the new products, but the new glaze offering. The factories were just beginning to offer articles in white-glaze.

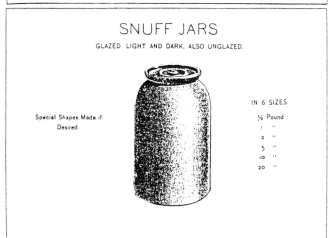

FRENCH POTS.

IN TWO SIZES
½ Gallon and 1 Gallon

BAILED COOKING CROCKS
OR STEW PANS.
BOTH IN LIGHT AND DARK GLAZE.

IN TWO SIZES
½ Gallon and 1 Gallon

PLAIN AND BAILED
"BOSTON" BEAN POTS.

IN 4 SIZES
Quarts, Half, One and Two Galls.

INDIVIDUAL BEAN POTS
OR JELLY CUPS.

SNUFF JARS
GLAZED LIGHT AND DARK, ALSO UNGLAZED.

Special Shapes Made if Desired.

IN 6 SIZES.
½ Pound
1 "
2 "
5 "
10 "
20 "

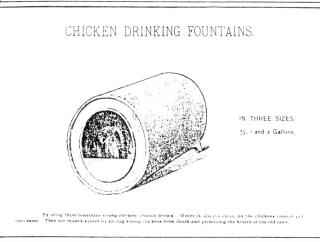

CHICKEN DRINKING FOUNTAINS.

IN THREE SIZES
½, 1 and 2 Gallons.

By using these fountains young chickens cannot drown. Water is always clean, as the chickens cannot get into same. They are money savers by saving young chickens from death and preserving the health of the old ones.

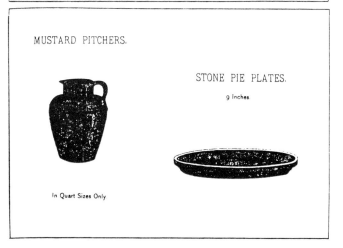

MUSTARD PITCHERS.

STONE PIE PLATES.
9 Inches.

In Quart Sizes Only

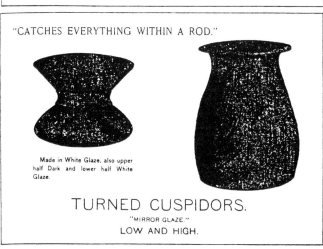

"CATCHES EVERYTHING WITHIN A ROD."

Made in White Glaze, also upper half Dark and lower half White Glaze.

TURNED CUSPIDORS.
"MIRROR GLAZE."
LOW AND HIGH.

BAILED JUGS.
BOTH IN DARK AND WHITE GLAZE

IN TWO SIZES
½ Gallon and 1 Gallon

PIPKINS OR SMALL PITCHERS.

RUSSIAN MILK PITCHERS.
WITH AND WITHOUT NOSES.

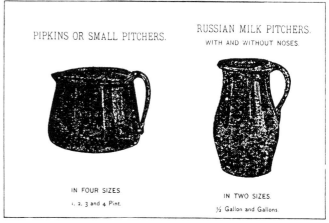

IN FOUR SIZES
1, 2, 3 and 4 Pint.

IN TWO SIZES
½ Gallon and Gallons.

They have become known as vinegar jugs and are a popularly collected item. In brown glaze like these are quite hard to find because they were some of the first pieces to be offered in white-glaze. As with most of the early pieces, signed RWSCo. pieces are scarcer than MSCo.

The item we called a beanpot on page 53 may actually be a pipkin as in the ad above, but pipkins have spouts. Russian pitchers were so named because of their popularity with the Mennonite settlers in the Dakotas who used them by the thousands.

The Russian pitchers or "flip-jars" held a peculiar prominence in the product line. Even when they were being made it was understood that they were an antiquity. Supposedly, a skilled wrist could flip the cream accumulated in the neck to another container with a single turn. To broaden the appeal some where offered with lips for more convenient pouring. Because they were hand turned it is doubtful they were ever signed. In his 1946 book *Art in Red Wing*, L.E. Schmeckebier displayed an unfired example made years earlier by C.L. McGrew. The fate of that fragile specimen is unknown.

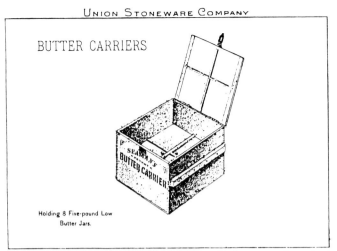

UNION STONEWARE COMPANY

BUTTER CARRIERS

Holding 8 Five-pound Low
Butter Jars.

A must for taking your butter to market was this butter carrier patented by Sherman C. Seaman of Clinton, Iowa on August 13, 1889. The sturdy, machine mortised box was probably made in one of the furniture factories, if manufactured locally at all. This rare, surviving example has been converted to practical modern use as an end table by the addition of a set of legs.

White-glazed Russian pitchers are not extremely rare, but the one with "MOTHER" stenciled on and the two-toned one are unique. Later, during the period when the first glazed art ware was being made Russian pitchers were made in green.

Small jars, bailed jugs, chambers, turned cuspidors and stew pans were among the first items offered in white-glaze. All of these were small and all were items which could not be stacked efficiently in the kiln so they had to be set inside large jars or in saggers.

The four bailed jugs shown here present a striking variety of signatures. From left is MSCo. with indented letters and unglazed bottom; MSCo. in raised letters and rubber stamped emblem (!), glazed bottom; RWSCo. with "Red Wing" in an arch over "Stoneware Co." and the classic straight line, indented letters RWSCo. signature, unglazed bottom.

Below is a close-up of rubber stamped emblem.

Above are salt-glaze and brown and white-glazed versions of pie plates by RWSCo. and MSCo. Either type is rare; probably due to attrition through use rather than lack of popularity. Pies were a customary part of hearty, farm meals.

Center and Bottom Left is a molded cuspidor in the traditional hand turned shape.

Below. Individual bean pots or jelly cups have been found from all three companies. RWSCo. signed theirs "RED WING Co.", a signature style they also occasionally used on small bowls. MSCo. signed theirs with initials around the inside of the foot ring and North Star used a plain raised star. The RWSCo. ones are by far the most numerous.

71

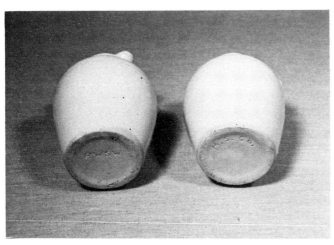

To save a midnight trip in times not modern enough for indoor plumbing, a chamber pot was kept beneath the bed.

Mustard sauce thin enough to be poured from a pitcher was a standard condiment at the turn of the century. The nearly matching pair above represent the Red Wing and Minnesota versions. All of these are one quart size as the ad on page 68 states (3 cups actual measure); we would otherwise identify the ½ pint North Star piece on page 62 as a mustard pitcher as well.

The signatures in initials show additional variation; RWSW suggests a two word spelling of stoneware. Such spelling was occasionally used.

The white pitcher at bottom is signed MSCo., the two-toned one is unsigned but photo was included because it bears the remnants of a Gedney's Mustard paper label. An identical, two-toned pitcher with RWSCo. signature has been seen.

Molded beehive jugs were made in three distinctive shapes by MSCo.; these two in addition to the one shown on page 48. While that one is most often brown these two types are most often white; suggesting a sequence of origin.

The Duluth, Red Wing & Southern ran for 25 miles between Red Wing and Zumbrota carrying freight and passengers. Its roundhouse was just behind the Minnesota Stoneware Company whose building can be seen in the background. Building is three story and frame so photo dates 1892-1900. Goodhue County Historical Society photo

The main line ran within two miles of the clay pits and the clay was carried here by cart to be loaded until 1892 when a spur was built into MSCo. and RWSCo.'s fields. The following year North Star secured a direct link as well. Goodhue County Historical Society photo

The Importance of the Railroads

That the railroads played an important role in the history of the pottery industry can perhaps best be learned from this article from the October 24, 1893 *Red Wing Daily Republican:*

"Hon. J.C. Pierce says that the railroads have done much for Red Wing, notwithstanding the belief of many that what has been given in bonuses has been a waste of money . . . In the early '80's, when our potteries were comparatively infant industries, the Akron people and other pottery ware manufacturers were just awakening to the fact that this territory was slipping out of their hands. They formed a compact with the C.M. & St. P. railroad to ship all their ware into Minnesota over that line, and thus secure greatly reduced rates. It cost our potteries more to ship a carload to the Twin Cities than it cost the Akron people, and as a result they were in a position to undersell our products. This, says Mr. Pierce, would have forced our potteries to close down, and when once closed it would have been a matter of uncertainty whether they would have been able to resume. The M. & St. L. came in, and thus our stoneware works got fair rates and an equal chance to work up the northwestern territory for their goods."

Red Wing had its share of local railroad activity; the most notable being the Duluth, Red Wing and Southern founded in 1886. This line proposed to run from Duluth, through Red Wing to Sioux City, Iowa. The only section of track actually laid was from Red Wing to Zumbrota with a spur line run directly into the clay fields at Claybank in 1892. Understandably, the potteries accounted for a major share of the road's business. In 1895 clay accounted for 32,185 of the total of 88,290 tons of freight carried. The line was absorbed by the Chicago Great Western in 1901.

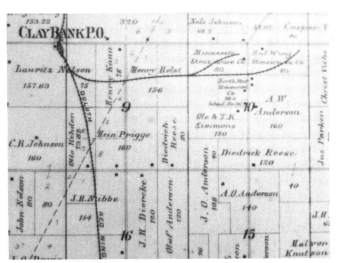

1894 plat map shows the location of the clay fields and the railroad spur.

Special clay cars brought the broken-out lumps of clay directly to the factories. Here the cars are sided in front of the Red Wing Stoneware Company in 1906. The cars now bear the initials of the Chicago Great Western.

Goodhue County Historical Society photo

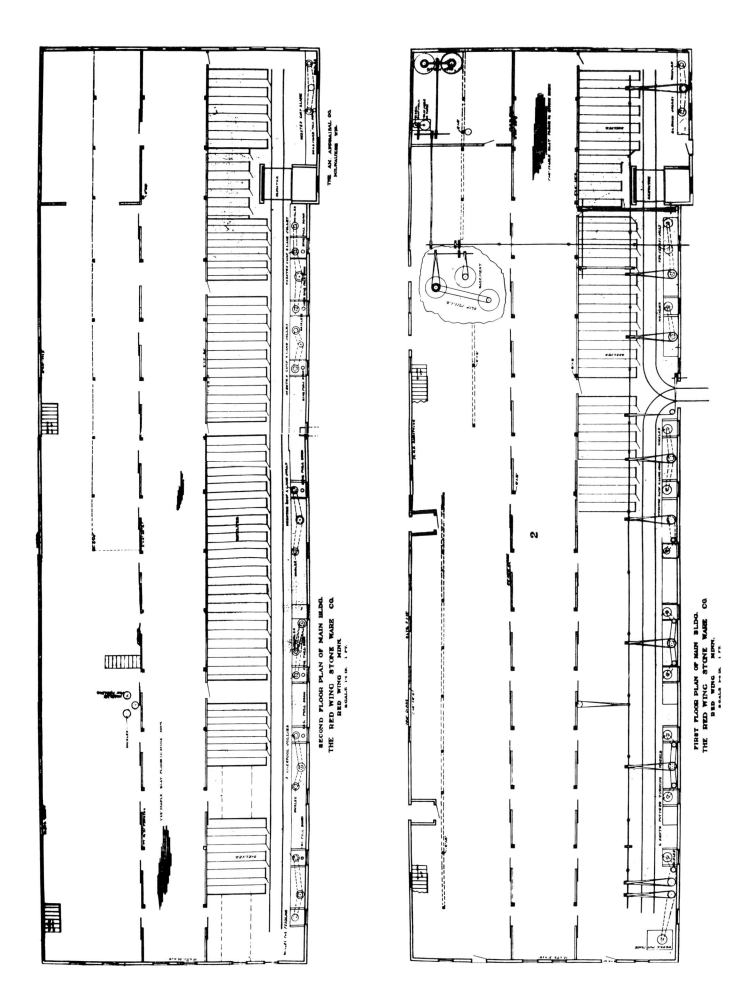

SECOND FLOOR PLAN OF MAIN BLDG.
THE RED WING STONE WARE CO.
RED WING MINN.
SCALE 1-8 IN. 1 FT.

THE AM. APPRAISAL CO.
MILWAUKEE WIS.

FIRST FLOOR PLAN OF MAIN BLDG.
THE RED WING STONE WARE CO.
RED WING MINN.
SCALE 1-8 IN. 1 FT.

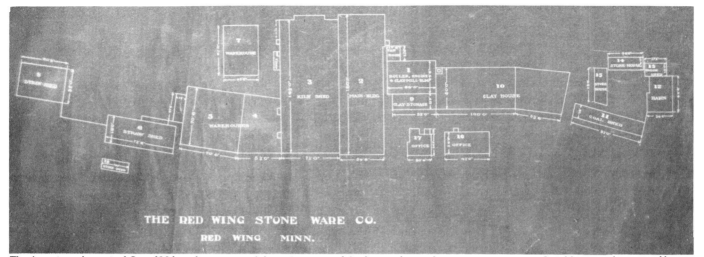

The American Appraisal Co. of Milwaukee prepared these drawings of the factory layout for insurance purposes. In addition to the general layout above, detailed floor plans and cross sections of each building were made. On opposite page are the floor plans of the main building.

Division of Archives and Manuscripts; Minnesota Historical Society

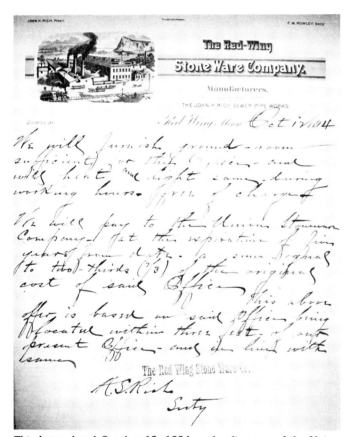

This letter dated October 12, 1894 to the directors of the Union Stoneware Co. offered ground room and operating services for an office building to be built on RWSCo.'s property. Similar offers were submitted by the other member firms of the Union, but this one was accepted and on October 25 the *Red Wing Argus* reported that construction had begun. This office building can be seen in the post-1900 photo on page 17. The plans thus date 1894-1900.

Division of Archives and Manuscripts;
Minnesota Historical Society

RWSCo.'s down draft kilns were round, NSSCo.'s and MSCo.'s at this time were rectangular. In either case the fire boxes were around the periphery. The heat was deflected upward by a "bag wall" inside and swirled down through openings in the floor leading to tunnels going to the chimney. Heat was also ducted to the drying room in the center of the main building.

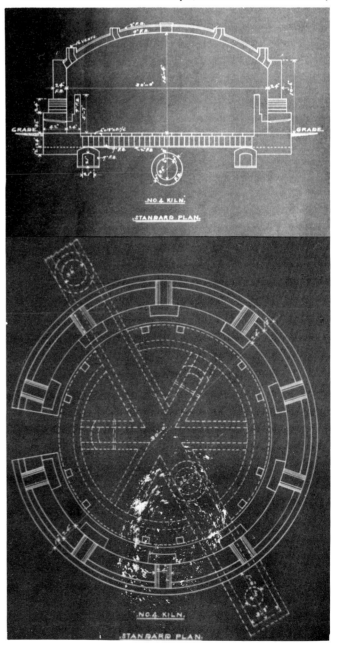

SCHEDULED PRICE LIST
of the
UNION STONEWARE COMPANY.

All open ware up to and including 6 gallon -------- .04 per gal.
8, 10 and 12 gallon ---------------------------------- .05 " "
15 and 20 gallon ware--------------------------------- .06 " "
30 gallon ware -- .07 " "
Jugs, --- .05 " "
Chains for hanging baskets ------------------------- .50 " Doz
¼ Gal. Fruit jars and tin caps ---------------------- .40 " "
½ " " " " " " -- .50 " "
1 " " " " " " -- .65 " "
Stone cuspidores ------------------------------------ .75 " "
Plain spittoons ------------------------------------- 1.75 " "
Fancy " -- 2.50 " "
Chambers with covers -------------------------------- 1.75 " " 1.60
7" Beer mugs --- 90 ~~1.00~~ " "
Pie plates -- .35 " "
½ Gal. Chicken founts ------------------------------- 1.20 ~~.75~~ " "
1 " " " --- 1.85 ~~1.25~~ " "
2 " " " " " --- 2.20 ~~1.65~~ " "
Fruit jug corks, ------------------------------------ .10 " "
Flower pots, and saucers & H. Baskets -------------- 60.% from list
Lawn vases --- 40% ~~30%~~ from list
1 and 2 pound low butter pots ----------------------- .01½ Each
3 pound --- .02 "
5 pound --- .02½ "
10 pound -- .04 "
Pint and quart pans --------------------------------- .02 "
Perfumery jugs -------------------------------------- .02 "
4 Gal. Filters complete ----------------------------- 2.00 ~~2.25~~ "
Hotel " " --- 5.00 ~~5.25~~ "
Sheepshead vase and base ---------------------------- 2.00 "
Rustic stumps --------------------------------------- .50 "
Seaman's Patent Butter carriers -------------------- .90 "
Plain umbrella Stands ------------------------------- .70 ~~1.00~~ "
Stork " " --- 1.00 ~~1.50~~ "
Churn dashers --------------------------------------- .05 "
Mustard pitchers ------------------------------------ .03 "
Russian milk pitchers jug price
½ gal jar covers count 1-3rd al. each
1 and 2 " " ½ gal. each
All jar covers, 3 to 6's count 1 gallon each
Seconds in stoneware 1 cent per gallon less than firsts.
Crates empty each ~~30~~ 7¢ cents
3 pound butter pots seconds ------------------------ .01½ Each
5 pound butter pots seconds ------------------------ .02 "
10 pound butter pots seconds ----------------------- .03 "
Barrels - each - 15¢ "
Chambers - only - no covers - 1.40 doz.
Covers - for Chambers - 35¢ "
¼# Jars - for Butter Pkgs sample - 2¼¢ each
7" Chambers - with covers - per doz. 1.60.
7" Covers - only - " " .35¢
High Cuspidores " " 4.00

Changes and additions to Schedule price list under
date of August 21st 1895.
-oOo-

8 to 20 gallon Jar covers, count 2 gal.
30 " " " " 3 "
Churn covers up to 6 gal. " 1 "
Churn covers over 6 Gal. " 2 "
All ¼ Gal. ware " ½ "
All ½ Gal. ware " 2-3rd Gal
Bean pot covers " 1-3rd gal.
Preserve jar covers, " 1-3rd gal.
8, 10 and 12 gal. ware 1 cent per gal. Advance
15 and 20 gallon ware 2 " " " "
30 gallon ware 3 " " " "
Lawn vases 40% off list
Flower pots and saucers, count 1-3rd list.
Pint and ½ pans and bowls 2 cents each.
Bailed jugs, 6 cents per gallon
Bailed beans and covers, 5 cents per gallon
Bread bowls, 20 cents each
½ Gallon stew pans, 4½ ~~5~~ cents each
1 Gallon stew pans, 6 ~~8~~ cents each
1 pint pipkins, 3 cents each
2 pint pipkins, 3¼ cents each
3 pint pipkins 3½ cents each
4 pint pipkins, 4 cents each.
Pigs, 12½ cents each
Cow and Calf, 40 cents each
Dogs, 18 cents each
Shoes 4 cents each
Jelly nests, 1.05 per dozen sets
Match Safes, 4 cents each
Dasher sticks, 3 cents each
Dasher bottoms, 2 cents each
Filter covers, 10 cents each
Upper filter jars 4 gal. 40 cents each
Lower filter jars 4 gal. 40 cents each
Filter Blocks, 75 ~~1.00~~ " "
Filter tubes 15 cents each
Filter faucets, 30 cents each
Ice jars and covers, 4 gal. 15 cents each
Ice jar covers only, 4 cents each
Upper jar Hotel filter, 1.00 "
Lower jar Hotel filter, 1.00 "
Cover for hotel filters, 10 cents each.
Water jar covers count the same as churns.
Hogsheads, 40 cents each
Casks, 25 cents each
Crating jars 15 cents each
Individual Bean pots, 25 cents per doz.
Tin caps for fruit jars 50 cents per gross.
Jardineers, 10 cents each
Coffee Coolers, 60 cents each.
½# Snuff Jars - each 2½ " "
1# " " " 3 " "
1# " " " with Cov. 4 " "
5# " " " " " 6 " "
10# " " " " " 10½ " "
20# " " " " "

Preserved along with the minutes of meetings and other records of the Union Stoneware Co. at the Minnesota Historical Society Archives and Manuscripts Division are carbon copies of price lists from the mid 1890's. All of the prices are wholesale, carload prices; retail prices would be nearly twice these but still a pittance compared to today's collector price.

Above is undated but may be the August 21, 1895 list referred to by the sheet of additions above right.

Scheduled Price List of White Glazed Ware.
Union Stoneware Co.
-oOo-

1 Pound Jars ------------------------------------- 1 3/4¢ each
2 " " --- 1 3/4¢ "
3 " " --- 2 1/2¢ "
5 " " --- 3 1/4¢ "
Pint Bowls --------------------------------------- 2 1/2¢ "
Quart Bowls -------------------------------------- 2 1/2¢ "
1/2 Gallon Bailed Stew pans ---------------------- 5¢ "
1 " " " " -- 7¢ "
1/2 " Jugs --------------------------------------- 7¢ per gal.
1 " " -- 7¢ " "
Cuspidors -- $1.00 per doz
All shoulder jugs 1 cent per gallon advance (6cents)
Perfumery jugs ----------------------------------- 2 1/2¢ each
1 gallon [illegible] bailed jars ----------------- 8¢ per gal.
Olive jugs --------------------------------------- 7¢ " "
1/2 gallon white glazed pickle jars with covers --- 6¢ [illegible]
1 gallon white glazed pickle jars with covers ----- 7¢ [illegible]
White glazed chambers and covers --- 9" ----------- 30¢ per doz. advance
" " " no " 9" ------------------------------------- 20¢ " " "
" " " and " 7" ------------------------------------ 25¢ " " "
" " " no " 7" ------------------------------------- 15¢ " " "
1/2¢ per piece for stencilling up to and including 2 gallon ware.
1/2¢ per gallon for stencilling above 2 gallon ware.
1# & 2# white Glazed ~~Bailed~~ Jars - with Covers - 3¢ each
3# Bailed white Glazed " " 3½¢ "
5# " " " " " 5¢ "
10# " " " " " 7¢ "
20# " " " " " 14¢ "

The schedule of white-glazed ware prices at right accompanied the October 1, 1896 lists on opposite page. It contains several items in addition to those on the November 15, 1895 white-glaze price sheet on page 67. It can be seen that white-glazed items were carried at a slight premium over the standard brown or salt-glazed finish for the same item.

Some of the items found on these lists do not appear in any of the illustrated catalogs and a few are complete mysteries having never been identified by an attributable example.

SCHEDULED PRICE LIST
of the
UNION STONEWARE COMPANY.

Oct. 1-1896

All open ware up to and including 6 gallons,	4¢ per gallon
8, 10 and 12 gallon ware,	5¢
15 and 20	6¢
25 and 30	5¢
Jugs,	5¢
Imperial Jugs,	5 1/4¢
Bailed Jugs,	5¢
Bailed Bean Pots,	10¢
40 Gal. Jars.	
Seconds,	1¢ less first
1/2 gallon covers count,	1/3 gallon
1 and 2 gallon covers count,	1/2
3 to 6 gallon covers count,	1
8 to 20 gallon covers count,	2
25 and 30 gallon covers count,	3
Churn covers up to 6 gallons count	1
Churn covers over 6 gallons count	2
Water jar covers up to 6 gallons count	1
Water jar covers over 6 gallons count	2
All 1/4 gallon ware counts	1/2
All 1/2 gallon ware counts	2/3
Bean Pot covers count	1/3
Preserve and fruit jar covers count	1/3
8, 10 and 12 gallon ware per gallon advance,	1¢
15 to 20 gallon ware, per gallon advance,	2¢
25 and 30 gallon ware, per gallon advance,	3¢
1/4 gallon Fruit Jars and Tin Caps,	40¢ per doz.
1/2	50¢
1	65¢
1 and 2 pound low butter pots,	1 1/2¢ each.
3	2¢
5	2 3/4¢
10	4¢
1/8 and 1/4 Pans or Bowls,	
2" Flower pots, no saucers,	$1.25 per 100
3"	1.50
4" & saucers	3.25
5"	4.50
6"	6.50
7"	8.50
8"	11.50
9"	15.00
10"	19.00
Small Hanging Baskets,	10.00
Medium	12.00
Large	15.00

60% discount from above list.

No. 1 Lawn Vases, 29 inches high,	5.00 each.
2	34	7.50
3	43	9.00
4	50	12.50

40% discount from above list.

Flower pot saucers count	1/3 of list.
Chains for Hanging Baskets,	50¢ per doz.

Sheepshead Vase and Base,	$2.00 each
Rustic Stumps,	50¢
Stone Cuspidors,	75¢ per doz.
Plain Spittoons,	1.75
Fancy	2.50
Perfumery Jugs,	2¢ each.
4 gal. Filters complete,	2.00 each
Filter cover,	
Upper Jar,	10¢
Lower Jar,	
Block,	50¢
Tube,	
Faucet,	
Electric Blocks,	10¢
4 gallon ice jar and cover,	15¢
Ice Jar cover only,	4¢
Hotel Filter complete,	5.00
Hotel Filter, three blocks,	
Upper jar,	60¢
Lower jar,	60¢
Cover,	10¢
Faucet,	30¢
Tube,	
ice jar and cover for 10 gallon filter,	20¢
Ice jar cover only,	5¢
9" Chambers with covers,	1.75 per doz.
9" Chambers without covers,	1.40
7" Chambers with covers,	1.60
7" Chambers without covers,	1.25
Chamber covers only,	35¢
Beer Mugs,	90¢
1/2 gal. Stew Pans,	4 1/2¢ each.
Toy Spittoons,	10¢
Seaman's Patent Butter Carriers,	90¢
Pie Plates,	35¢ per doz.
1 gallon chicken founts,	1.20
	1.85
	2.20
Plain Umbrella Stands,	70¢ each.
Stone Umbrella stands,	1.00
Mission Milk Pitchers,	5¢ per gal
Mustard Pitchers,	3¢ each.
Churn Dashers,	5¢ each.
Dasher handles,	3¢
Dasher bottoms,	2¢
Fruit Jug Corks,	10¢ per doz.
Bread Bowls,	20¢ each.
3 pound pots, seconds,	1 1/2¢ each
5"	2¢
10"	3¢
1 Pint Pipkins,	each
2	1 7/8¢ each
3	
Blind Pigs,	1 1/2¢
Cow and Calf,	10¢
Dogs,	10¢
Shoes,	4¢

Jelly Pails,	1.05 per doz.
Match Safes,	4¢ each.
Hog Medicine jugs,	7¢ per gal.
Large Crates,	75¢ each.
Small Crates,	25¢
Hogsheads,	50¢
Barrels,	15¢
Casks,	25¢
Crating Jars,	15¢
Tin Caps,	50¢ per gross.
1/2 pound Snuff jars,	2 1/2¢ each
1	3¢
3	with covers	4¢
5	6¢
10	10 1/2¢
20	20¢
Individual Bean Pots,	13¢ per doz.
Jardinieres,	10¢ each.
Coffee Coolers,	65¢
High Cuspidors,	1.00 per doz.
10 Gallon Jar,	10¢ per gal.
High Curacoa jugs,	8¢ each
3 gal. Bbl shaped water jars,	per gal.
15 gal.	
10 gal.	
1/4 Sample butter jar,	2 1/4¢ each.
Druggist's Acid jars, with clay corks,	6 1/2¢ per gal
Candy jars with covers, per sample,	60¢ each.
Slop jars, no covers,	40¢ each
Slop jars, with covers,	60¢ each.
20 gallon jug, Salt glazed, Stenciled,	2.50

Clark's Coffee Jars: 1 gal.	14¢
2	23¢
3	32¢
4	41¢
5	50¢
6	59¢
8	92¢
Clark's Pitchers, 1/2 Gal.	5¢
1	8¢
2	11¢
1 Gal. Jelly jars, heavy,	4¢
1/2 Gal.	2 2/3¢ each.
1 Gal. with covers	5 1/3¢
1/2 Gal.	4¢
Modeling clay, per 100#	50¢
Sidewalk Tiling,	
Large Blocks,	3¢ each
Small	
Half	
End	
Curbing,	3¢ per foot.

Pottery Plaster - pr bbl - 2.00#   2.75
8" Nappies pr dz - 35¢
9"   "   "   40¢
10"   "   "   50¢

The third sheet was cut apart here to fit page.

Out of the Ordinary

Most of the ware we have displayed thus far while not necessarily common today was hardly unusual when new. Certainly there were variations that set individual styles apart but the differences were mostly esoteric.

There were, however, some truly unusual pieces; different because they were made to be different. These fall into several categories. The first of which is souvenir pieces; items outside the utilitarian line. Some were charms or miniatures of the common stoneware items, but the most striking were statues and figures of dogs, pigs, cows and so forth. These were regular production items and are listed on the price lists on the preceding pages.

The second consists of glorified or customized regular stoneware; a special decoration, a date or a name was added to an otherwise standard item to personalize it or commemorate an event.

Thirdly was the completely individual expression. Starting from a shapeless lump of clay a one-of-a-kind piece was produced and fired among the production run. These have been named "lunch-hour pieces" because they were "unofficial," made at the potter's own whim and on his own time.

Shown here actually larger than life, the charm jug is barely seven-eighths of an inch tall. According to the *Red Wing Advance* of March 26, 1879; "The Railroad boys on the river road all carry a little brown jug; not the dangerous sort, however, but the little charm jugs that have been turned out in such great quantities from the Red Wing pottery."

Mallory wrote to Peter Kunn of Faribault, Minn. on August 28, 1885 in reply to an inquiry; "Dear Sir; We can sell you the large size jugs, hold about an ounce for $4.00 per 100, they retail for 10¢ and the charm jugs for $2.50 per 100, sell for 5¢ each . . . Minnesota Stoneware Co.; E.T. Mallory, Supt."

Below are some of the "large size," one ounce jugs approximately full size. We have shown these previously, they have additional personalization which adds to their uniqueness.

In the category of regular production items were slip cast pig statues like these. Usually found in translucent, glossy brown; the semi-gloss, solid brown and spotted one here provide pleasant variety.

Among the Minnesota Stoneware Co. business letters was one to, "Messrs. McLaughlin, Sheldon & Co., Owatonna (Minn.); Gentlemen; We have taken out of kiln this morning 19 pigs that we intended to send you but the marking is a total failure. The slip runs and fills it up. We send one of the best by mail today so you can see how it is. We are satisfied that we can not make them that way so they would be satisfactory to you or ourselves. And think the only way we could would be to make them plain and you put on stickers.; Respectfully Yours; Minnesota Stoneware Co.; S" (presumably written by T.B. Sheldon, president) This was dated December 24, 1885.

Of the several varieties of pigs which have been displayed here none are signed by the Red Wing companies. However, Monmouth Pottery of Monmouth, Illinois produced signed ones, apparently overcoming MSCo.'s earlier difficulty.

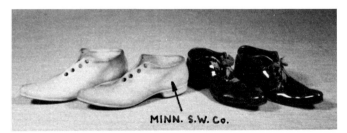

Little shoes, four and one quarter inches long in a variety of finishes have been found. The earliest of these are signed along the arc of the heel stitching "Minn. S.W. Co." At left is bisque (glazeless), right is glossy brown. They have also been seen in light brown, green and dark blue. The mold for these was around for a long time as we have a pair in a much later art glaze of ivory with brown accents.

The bulldogs are most often seen in glossy brown; the black one with the white chest and paws is a rarity, so is one other one seen in grey. Monmouth also made these; Red Wing's weren't signed. Six inches tall.

One of the rarer of the statuary pieces is the regal lion doorstop. Production after the turn of the century is guessed at because it does not appear on the 1895-96 price lists; but, it could have been earlier as well. These reportedly came in two sizes.

Cows and calves were a fragile and beautiful item for the what-not shelf. The base was either a simple clay slab as above or a fancy, molded pedestal. The one below is the only signed example known, unfortunately it was mishandled long ago. Varieties have been seen with the calf and cow standing in the same direction and the cow is looking straight ahead. Another is reported with two pair on one base.

This mother and offspring are done in white and grey on a molded base. The length of the horns varies from piece to piece because they had to be added separately after the main part of the body was removed from the mold. The base measures five by three and three quarters inches.

Spotted brown, little charm piglets with a looped tail. The "adult" pigs are seven inches long; these are about one and one-quarter inches.

Here the pigs are white-glazed with brown spots, except for the all brown one in the trough.

On the underside of the base of the piece at right is the signature, "H. Darling; Red Wing, Minnesota; April 1, 1893." Inside the rim, partly obliterated by a chip, are the initials "MSCo." This is one of the only "artist signed" and dated pieces known.

Whether the companies produced set pieces like this for sale or if they were created by some ingenious individual employees for their own use is unknown. It is our feeling, because of the occasionally crude finish, that they were not commercially available. Two of the "regular" pigs and several charm piglets were arranged on an oval base around a feed trough. This one is bisque except for spots of brown slip.

The base of this piece is simply the bottom cut off a molded jar. (See below left.)

80

Identical to the yellow ware dog on page 13 which C.L. McGrew presented to his girlfriend's mother in the 1890's is this Rockingham glazed "Staffordshire" dog. This one was purchased in Michigan a few years ago by a collector who admired it purely for its beauty, never imagining that it might be a rare Red Wing product. Though it is documented that the Red Wing Stoneware Co. made Rockingham ware and yellow ware these dog doorstops are the only attributable product.

Measuring four inches long by three and one-quarter tall are a ram and ewe. This ram is in salt-glaze and the ewe in white. Unsigned and not found on the price lists. Moldmaker George Hehr of Red Wing Stoneware Co. made a 78 piece nativity scene for display in the center of the city at Christmas time in 1896 according to the December 25 *Red Wing Journal.* The whole piece measured 8 x 12 feet and included, "... Mary and Joseph, the manger, the three wise men, Jesus the babe, a shepard and his flock of sheep, his dog, the 12 disciples, the 10 virgins, five wise and five foolish, and a number of other figures ..." "... All of the figures are of stoneware or plaster of Paris. Mr. Hehr first modelled them in clay, the molds were made of plaster and in these the figures was cast ..." It is speculated that the molds for these sheep were originated for that nativity scene.

The hen-on-a-nest has also been seen in salt-glaze. The tiny dog, as the other pieces, is in stoneware rather than yellow ware as the large one. Attribution of these is by presumption; they were found in the Red Wing area.

81

Personalized common stoneware is not at all plentiful. Englishman Robert Jeffrey scribed his name and the date into the hand turned, half gallon jug above. Jeffrey was listed in the 1893 directory as a kiln builder.

Above is a 20 gallon salt-glazed jar with a slightly crude leaf decoration and the date 3/3/94.

Left is a one quart North Star jar with "D.H." scratched into the glaze before firing.

Below is a real gem; an individual bean pot with a pulled handle added to make a coffee cup. Crude, backwards initials make one wonder whether the maker was confused by the fact that letters have to be backwards in a mold in order to come out right on a molded piece (see preserve jar on page 63) and hadn't figured out that when scribed directly on the piece that they needn't be reversed, or if he was simply semiliterate. This is certainly a lunch hour piece; or would it be better called a coffee break piece?

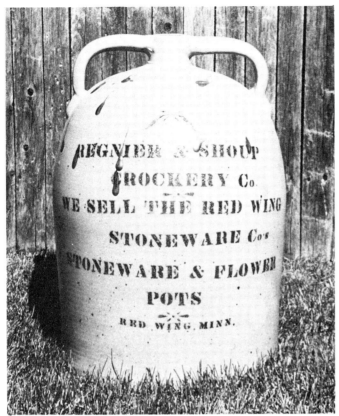

This 15 gallon hand-turned jug was an advertising display item for the Regnier & Shoup Co. of St. Joseph, Missouri which dealt in china, glass and stoneware (1882-1938). It has an RWSCo. side stamp on the back.

This unsigned, salt-glazed water cooler embellished with oak branches was handed along from the family of George Thompson. George was listed in the 1893 and '94 directories as an employee and foreman for North Star Stoneware Co. The oak leaf and acorn decor was used on early artware, also the charm on page 81.

Goodhue County Historical Society collection

Two handmade mailboxes. These were made at the sewer pipe factories, which accounts for the heavier, darker salt-glaze. The sewer pipe clay was of a lower grade, higher in iron oxides. Salt-glazing remained the standard finish on sewer tile long after the stoneware companies had switched to white.

Above is simple, rustic and functional. Right is a splendid example of lunch hour art with careful attention to texture and detail.

This little bird house was made in 1925 as a school project by Orville Olson, now curator of the Goodhue County Historical Society Museum. The clay and firing were provided by his father who worked at the sewer pipe factory.

A tree stump bank with grape and vine decoration. Note that the bird house also sported grapes, another popular motif.

Though there are several varieties of the smaller, Red Wing Sewer Pipe Co. souvenir pieces, the John H. Rich and Union Sewer Pipe miniatures are very early and rare (see page 27). The later, smaller pieces had an insert disk with a small hole in the center to snuff cigarettes.

Here is a handmade match holder/ash tray in tan salt-glaze. The mug at right goes to show that not all lunch hour work was skillful nor artistic.

84

C.L. "Lou" McGrew, shown here in 1936, was one of the best known "old timers" in Red Wing. He began in the pottery trade at age 12 in Louisville, Nebraska. There he learned hand turning in 1885. He came to Red Wing from Sioux City, Iowa in 1892 to be a turner at the brand new North Star Stoneware Co. After North Star closed he went over to Minnesota Stoneware Co. and later became foreman under Red Wing Union Stoneware Co. in 1918 when hand turning went out of use. He didn't retire until 1947, the same year that Red Wing ceased making stoneware.

His skill at the potter's wheel was often exhibited at fairs and other occasions. The *Daily Republican* of April 18, 1912 announced that McGrew would be going to Winona on Saturday to give a demonstration to the manual training students at the Normal School. One of his last demonstrations was at the Red Wing Art Association open house in February of 1952 at the age of 82. We have a 16mm color film record of that demonstration.

Here are two of his early lunch hour pieces. Both are classical shapes with very little adornment; insides are glossy brown and outsides are bisque. Goodhue County Historical Society collection

These two pieces of later work have square cross section handles and a more modernistic feel. True artistry. In faithful McGrew style, the exterior is in the natural bare clay; insides are glossy brown. One of these is even artist signed with a scribed "C.L. Mc." on the bottom, a rare gem.

A Minnesota Stoneware Co. two inch flowerpot was made into a match or toothpick holder by the addition of tree branch feet. Attribution of frog is by guess.

A hooded bust formed an "official," commercially produced toothpick holder. These have been seen in green, white, brown and bisque.

This reclining dog is handmade; fully qualified to be termed a lunch hour piece. The molded bulldogs were not "lunch hour" made.

Goodhue County Historical Society collection

Here is a slightly later, handmade toothpick holder; dated.

William McKinley, 25th President of the United States, was assassinated in 1901. In tribute to the fallen leader, Minnesota Stoneware Co. produced these white-glazed busts. Some enterprising individual cast a mold from the finished piece and turned out unsigned copies in brown; smaller because of the double shrinkage.

Whether the "little boy" statues were produced commercially or not is questionable. The amount of handwork on each piece and dissimilarities portend individual, lunch hour efforts. Somebody went to a lot of trouble to make a mold just for fun. The results seem well worth it though.

One of these was attributed to John Nelson by Sarah Schouweiler in her November, 1946 *Golfer and Sportsman* article, "Red Wing, Haven of Beautiful Pottery." It is our theory that the mold was purchased or copied from the chalkware (plaster) figure shown below. Chalkware figures were a popular Victorian decoration and the "little boy" was one of the favorite subjects. We have seen three, slightly different versions in chalkware.

This one is individualized in a way that attributes its origin; a case of Red Wing Brewing Co. beer. Each statue is somehow different from the next.

87

"Imnaha" was modeled in stoneware clay and fired without glaze. Other artists, notably Susan Frackelton of Milwaukee, sent their greenware here for firing, but this creation is entirely local. This and the pieces below and opposite were made by Albert H. Olson who worked in the factories in the 1890's and then studied art and sculpture in St. Louis, Chicago and New York beginning in 1903.

Eddie Swanson Memorial Collection
Goodhue County Historical Society

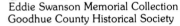

The October 30, 1907 *Red Wing Republican* carried the news of a likeness of Red Wing's Civil War hero Col. William Colvill in the form of a bust in burnt clay displayed in the window of Lidberg's art studio. The leader of the 1st Minnesota Regiment in their courageous and historic action in the battle of Gettysburg was sculpted in clay by A.H. Olson while at home during the summer.

A November 27th article told of Albert's studies under French artist George Julian Zollnay at the art institute in St. Louis and announced an exhibit at the Red Wing Public Library of several busts, four or five reliefs, two figures and numerous smaller specimens.

It was also reported that among several bas reliefs offered his was one of two accepted for exhibit at the St. Louis World's Exposition. Goodhue County Historical Society collection

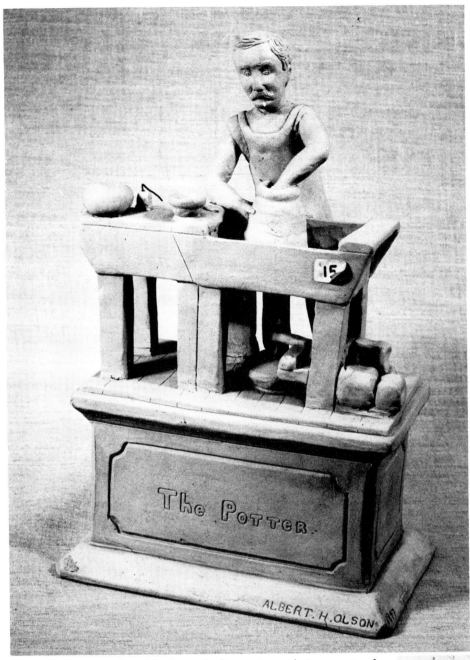

Albert H. Olson was listed in the early directories as being a potter for Minnesota Stoneware Company. His signed and dated "The Potter" can be regarded, therefore, as a knowledgeably accurate representation of its subject. The attention to detail is evident, but not carried to such a degree as to remove all evidence that the figure was made by hand. The piece retains a simplicity that perfectly suits the craftsman it depicts.

Albert changed his name to Albert O. Stenwick and entered the building trade in Red Wing as a carpenter. He continued his artistic pursuits as a woodcarver. Some of his woodcarvings earned mention in L.E. Schmecke- bier's 1946 *Art in Red Wing.*

Eddie Swanson Memorial Collection
Goodhue County Historical Society

Masterpieces

Two gallon jar with applied oak leaves
and acorns decoration.

89a

Goodhue County Historical Society collection

Top Left is the lovely, multi-color lithographed cover of the 1894 Red Wing Stoneware Company catalog.

Top Right is a toy spittoon in salt-glaze and brown with blue bands.

Balance of page shows the beauty of the hand decorated, salt-glazed utilitarian wares.

90

Marriage Jugs

Marriage jugs were supposedly a special "inside" item bestowed upon a pottery worker on the occasion of his marriage. The specially molded and decorated 1/2 gallon jug was made up, glazed with the honored couple's names and filled with wine to be consumed on the honeymoon. It's a good story anyway.

Of these known examples only one seems appropriate to a wedding. That is the bisque example below on opposite page. It is decorated with borders and outlined hearts formed of impressions made with a "daisy flower" stamp. The initials G.G.N. were applied above the cherub on the front in Old English letters. Was this a gift to a sweetheart rather than a wedding present? The single set of initials casts the wedding notion into question.

Though the history of the jug at top on opposite page is lost, it obviously celebrates Christmas rather than nuptials. The similar jug below, however, is still in the family for whom it was made. It has an interesting story to go with it that is at least partly verifiable. It was reportedly made for the uncle of the present owner's mother. His name was Hattimer. The design on the back of the jug shows two figures, a man and a woman like on the other glazed jug. But these figures look down, as if mournfully into the waters below a large boat. One of the greatest disasters in Red Wing history was the capsizing of the excursion boat *Sea Wing* on Lake Pepin, just downstream of Red Wing during a windstorm on July 13, 1890. Aboard or on an attached barge were 200 passengers from Red Wing and surrounding area. Ninety-eight were drowned. Among them were young Fred Hattimer and, so the family legend goes, his fiancee.

What is mysterious about the jug is that it is in white-glaze with blue and black decoration. This should date it to after 1895. Were the Hattimers still mourning their lost son so long passed or was white-glaze somehow used earlier in a very limited way?

Also unknown is who were Rex, Mary Etta or G.G.N.

91

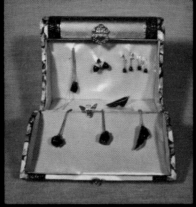

At Center Top is an antique jewelry box filled with stoneware trinkets and charms; tiny jug earrings and necklaces, little slippers, acorns and a bumble bee pin.

The salt-glazed pig and the bird in the grouping of animals in the center of the second row are probably not Red Wing, but doesn't it make a fine picture? Bird has a whistle in its tail.

The turkey and squirrel in the bottom row are signed lunch hour pieces made at the sewer pipe factory.

Miniature urn at bottom right is decorated with the same impressed "daisy" stamp as the bisque marriage jug on page 90.

91a

Advertising and Memorabilia

PRESIDENT AND MRS. CLEVELAND

They Pass Through Red Wing on their way to the Twin Cities.

The announcement that the presidential party would pass through this city on its way to St. Paul and Minneapolis, Monday afternoon, had the effect of congregating, at the depot, an assemblage, numbering several thousand people, all intent on catching a glimpse of the ruler of this great republic, and his charming young wife.

MRS. GROVER CLEVELAND.

The crowd commenced gathering at 3 o'clock and an hour later, the platform, box cars and all places which could be utilized to secure a view of the party as it passed, were filled to overflowing. The down passenger, arriving at 3:40, was side tracked here and the passengers utilized every available window in the coaches, every one intent on seeing the president. It was just 4 o'clock when a sharp whistle caused the assemblage to turn their eyes toward the lower yard. Soon afterwards an engine richly decorated, hove in sight and some one yelled, "Here they come!" The engine came, but alone, and proved to be only a wild engine running ahead to clear the track. Slowly it glided past the depot and then onwards on its journey. Ten minutes more of waiting in the cold and another whistle announced the approach of the train. The crowd went nearly wild, and for a time a panic seemed imminent. The train slackened its speed and soon approached the depot. No stop was made, but the train moved very slowly.

President Cleveland appeared on the rear platform, standing on one side of the doorway. Soon afterwards Mrs. Cleveland appeared in the door and remained standing there until the train had passed through the city. The assemblage cheered and yelled while the president bowed and his wife smiled.

PRESIDENT CLEVELAND.

As the train slowly passed the upper end of depot platform a neat and costly case, covered with rich gold silk plush, with solid silver mountings, was placed by the side of Mrs. Cleveland. It was a present from the employes of the Red Wing Stoneware company to Mrs. Cleveland. It contained a very richly modeled vase made at the Red Wing Stoneware company's works, and the whole was a product of this county and city. The clay was dug in the town of Goodhue, hauled to this city, fashioned into a thing of beauty by the hands of a skillful Red Wing potter, burned in one of the wonderfully perfect up-draught kilns of the Red Wing Stoneware company's works. The case was made at A. W. Pratt's bookstore by G. D. Ashelman, covered with gold silk plush and lined with plush and richest blue silk. The trimmings were made of solid silver by Hauenstein Brothers. It was a handsome tribute to the first lady of the land.

Red Wing Daily Republican; **October 11, 1887**

Red Wing Argus, **December 2, 1887**

Acknowledgment from Mrs. Cleveland.

It will be remembered that when the Presidential train passed through this city on the 10th of last October the employees of the Red Wing Stoneware Company presented Mrs. Cleveland with a handsome vase, as a specimen of their work, and which was enclosed in an elegant casket also the work of our citizens. Last Thursday the following letter was received from Mrs. Cleveland, acknowledging the receipt of the gift:

Executive Mansion, Washington,
Nov. 21, 1887.
Geo. D. Williston,
Red Wing, Minn :

Dear Sir : I beg leave to acknowledge the receipt and to express the pleasure which the kind attention of the employees of the Red Wing Stoneware Company during my presence in their vicinity afforded me. The vase of which they have reason to be proud as a result of their skill and handiwork will be treasured not only as a pretty souvenir of a pleasant visit, but will be more highly prized as a token of the regard and esteem of those whose good will is ever grateful to me. Be good enough to convey to your associates my appreciation of their courtesy, and assure them that it added much to the interest of the journey. Very Respectfully,
FRANCIS F. CLEVELAND.

The Cleveland Vase

An artware vase with oak leaves and acorns motif and lions' heads with rings in their mouths was presented to the wife of President Grover Cleveland on October 10, 1887 during a trip through the city. Copies of the vase were later mass produced and were known as the Cleveland Vase.

Photo courtesy of Beverly Radkey

Grover Cleveland was a popular President, serving two nonconsecutive terms, the first beginning in 1885. In addition to his own popularity was the adoration of his young wife. It was natural, therefore, that when they made a transnational railroad tour in 1887 that huge crowds turned out to greet them wherever they appeared.

As their train passed through Red Wing a box containing a gift to Mrs. Cleveland presented on behalf of the workers of the Red Wing Stoneware Company was hoisted on board. It was with considerable pride that the letter acknowledging its receipt was displayed.

Later, in the November 2, 1901 *Minneapolis Journal* Helen Gregory Flesher reported on the potteries of Red Wing and found, "One of the prettiest pieces is a vase made by the Red Wing Stoneware Company, a copy of the one presented to Mrs. Cleveland, President Cleveland's wife, when she visited the potteries several years ago. This pattern has ever been called the Cleveland vase."

The example pictured above is one of those copies. It is marked faintly on the bottom "SAXON; RED WING, MINN." in embossed letters as were other pieces of early art pottery. The fate of the original is lost as no records were kept; the legislation dealing with gifts to Presidents and their families being relatively recent.

In addition to the copies which were complete with the inscription to Mrs. Cleveland, vases in this style were made without the lettering. Derivatives without the lions' heads were later produced in matte green brushed stain and even glazed in bright yellow and green. (See pgs. 166-167) The originals were in bisque (the pictured vase has been painted).

The Cleveland vase is an example of Red Wing's very earliest art pottery.

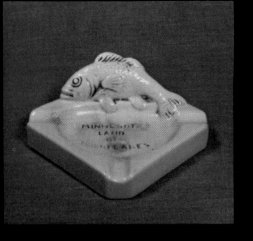

Above are an Albert Stenwick designed fish ash tray, similar to one of the plaster models on page 176 and a painted plaster Stenwick wing ash tray.

At Left are stoneware flowerpots from each of the three major companies. These are from the authors' collection and now are complete with matching five inch saucers.

Below is a green glazed Christmas tree stand; unlike the white ones it is unsigned.

At Bottom Left is a 50 gallon birch leaves jar in the "as found" setting.

Bottom Right are wax sealers with a package of the original wax.

This page, perhaps better than any other, demonstrates the effective use of color and texture responsible for making Red Wing pottery such a popular collectible.

This series of photos demonstrates the method of making molded ware. The photo at left above was taken on the fourth floor of "Factory M." Judging by the hand turned jug on the floor, the date should be 1900-1918. Henry Tiedeman operates the jigger, filling each plaster mold in succession by throwing in a glob of clay from the mound on the bench and forcing it into shape with the template attached to the "pull down" lever. In the above right view, at an earlier date, Tiedeman is shown at far left demonstrating how two filled molds, one containing the top of a jug, the other its base, are put together. Moving to the right, the other workers hold a mold for the bottom, an assembled top and bottom which would be set on a drying rack to firm-up the clay and a formed jug needing only "fettling" to smooth it and the addition of a handle before being slipped and fired.

Photos this page courtesy of Phil Revoir

Henry Tiedeman

Henry G. Tiedeman was a local boy, born February 15, 1871, in Hay Creek Township. He took an active part in both community and potters' union affairs. He served as a Red Wing alderman and president of the city council for a total of 24 years. He was president of the potters' union for an equal period.

He was listed in the 1893 and 1894 city directories as a potter for Minnesota Stoneware Company and remained at the pottery for a total of 51 years.

In the lower two photos, an older Henry Tiedeman is shown, still at work at the same job, operating the jigger at left, and applying handles below. In the lower photo, the jug is sitting on a "fettling wheel." Stringy scraps of clay, which were trimmed from mold parting lines, are heaped on the bench. Note the sticks of clay partly covered with a cloth to keep them moist; these were for making handles.

Barnett F. (Barney) Seiz was born at Brantford, Ontario, Canada to American parents on April 1, 1857. He grew up in Akron, Ohio where he learned the pottery trade. When E.T. Mallory began looking for workers for the brand new Minnesota Stoneware Company in 1883, Barney was one of his key contacts; he acted as a conduit for information and recommendations between superintendent Mallory and the Ohio workers. When Barney arrived and the shop started up, he held the honor of turning the first piece of ware for the new plant.

In 1899, he left Red Wing for a job at the Fort Dodge Stoneware Co. of Fort Dodge, Iowa. In a letter to that company, MSCo. general manager E.S. Hoyt called Seiz, "... one of the best large ware turners in the country. He is sober, steady, industrious, and think he will render you good service."

He returned to town shortly and managed the St. James Hotel for two years and, thereafter, became deputy game warden for the Minnesota Game and Fish Department. He served as chairman of the Goodhue County Republican Committee and two terms as sergeant-at-arms of the Minnesota House. Although he was most remembered at his death on July 1, 1925 for his 35 years service as a conservation officer, we will think of him as a potter.

Barney Seiz

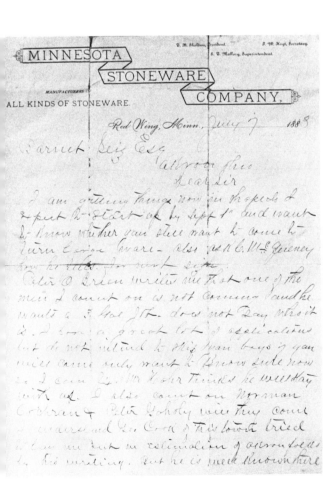

July 7, 1883; Barnet Seiz, Esq.; Akron, Ohio; Dear Sir, I am getting things now in shape so I expect to start up by Sept. 1 and want to know whether you still want to come to turn large ware — Also ask C. McQueney how he feels for next sizes.

Peter O Brien writes me that one of the men I count on is not coming and he wants a 3 gal job. Does not say who it is. I have a great lot of applications but do not intend to skip you boys if you will come only want to know sure now so I can fix. Mr. Hahr [sic] thinks he will stay with us. I also count on Norman Cochran & Peter Gaholy will they come I understand Geo Cook of this town tried to lay me out in estimation of Akron folks by his writing. But he is well known there and it did no harm. He is now foreman in my old shop and is having lots of trouble with his men. They perfectly despise him. They tried to hire Hahr [sic] to stay with them but he says he would not for anything. I have written Chas Rhodenbaugh about burning and hope to hear from both of you as soon as mail will go and return write and tell me all and much oblige; Yours Truly; E.T. Mallory; Supt.

This reply was written at the end of the letter:

Akron, Ohio; July 19, 1883; We received this letter and I now send it to you. Norman Cochran and Cornelius Mc'Queny are not going and from Gaholy we dont know nothing. Charley Rodenbagh is going but he corresponds with the Boss himself. John Crisp and two others started for Red Wing, the 15 of July. Peter O Brien is going also.; From Mr. Seiz

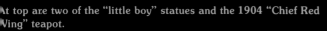

At top are two of the "little boy" statues and the 1904 "Chief Red Wing" teapot.

Above and Right are views of a hand made jewelry chest ornately decorated with a lion and a bear. A modeled figure of another animal originally served as a handle for the lid, but has been broken and lost.

Below is the "Mary Etta" Christmas marriage jug and Albert Olson's cupid.

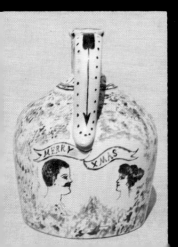

The planter at left is marked, "Annie W.; Daughter of B & C Peterson; Born Oct. 31, 1887; Died June 29, 1899." Charles Peterson was listed as a Red Wing Sewer Pipe Company employee. The dark salt-glaze and cylindrical shapes verify its origin.

Below is a sewer pipe "tree stump" planter set with geraniums.

In addition to the commercially produced lawn vases, the cemeteries in and around Red Wing hold other remembrances of the clay industry, these immeasurably more personal and touching. Here are found handmade, stoneware gravestones and plant stands marking the resting place of loved ones. The markers are mostly for children who passed away during the years that their fathers were employed. Infant mortality was much greater in those days and the loss of a young one was marked simply though no less sadly. The potters held no sentimental kindredship to the clay, no more than a carpenter to wood nor a blacksmith to iron. When a potter died his grave was marked with a marble or granite headstone. These memorials to lost children, however, show a labor of love and a personal statement of faith.

Above is a planter bearing the name Carl Lindberg, near this planter is a regular headstone inscribed Carl J. Lindberg; June 2, 1889; Sept. 1, 1892.

Left is for Mrs. C.M. Nelson; Born May 14, 1858; Died August 13, 1902; "to thee I lift my soul Oh Lord, My God I trust in thee," a sewer pipe worker's wife.

Above marks Lillian Marie, Daughter of Mr. and Mrs. Loken; Born Feb. 1898; Died Sept. 1898. This marker is set into a common sewer pipe conduit beneath it which is buried into the ground. The planter below is near the Loken marker.

At right is the most colorful and detailed of any of the markers seen. The Morley family had a long history in the pottery industry in Red Wing, going back to the Philleo Terra Cotta factory days. Louise died of peritonitis.

See the color section for more detail of this remarkable memorial.

Some of the most remarkable and news filled documents remaining from the early pottery industry are the above letters from E.T. Howard to the widow of E.T. Mallory. Howard had been the first superintendent of Red Wing Stoneware Co. before leaving for health reasons and returning to B.F. Sheldon & Co. Dry Goods store; his position was filled by E.T. Mallory, his nephew. He opened his own fur business in Red Wing which he ran until the North Star Stoneware Co. was formed in 1892. He resigned from North Star shortly after the Union Stoneware Company was formed. Mallory, meanwhile, had joined Minnesota Stoneware Company when it formed and helped push it into the number one position in production. Mallory died of perityphlitis (intestinal inflammation) in September of 1891.

The two-page letter dated July 11, 1892: "Mrs. E.T. Mallory; Sharron, Wisconsin,—Dear Friend; Your letter of about two weeks ago came promptly. Please excuse me for not writing sooner. — I called at the Printing office and had you booked for the Paper. Which I presume you are receiving regular. Nothing new in this city but a Sewer Pipe Factory which the Red Wing Stoneware Co. are going to build. The Minnesota Stoneware Co. are now putting in a new engine, building a new engine room and raising this end of shop to three stories. — The railroad is building out to the clay pits. Each company will have a track to the pit. So you see we will be saved the trouble of hauling on wagons which will be quite an item in both labor and money. — Mrs. H. [came] home about three weeks ago. She is feeling much better than when she went. We are all at the St. James and rather like it. Still may go back to the house for a short time this summer. Tell Helen I have been looking for some children to send down. When I find the right kind will ship a carload. — The Minnesota Co. have their annual meeting tomorrow to find out how much money they made. I will attend and write you the result. I think they have made good money and will pay a dividend. — Yours Respectfully, E.T. Howard"

The second letter was written the following day, "Mrs. Leo [Lenore] Mallory; Sharron, Wis, — Dear Friend, We had the meeting this afternoon and by some figuring will get a [dividend] of fifteen (15%) percent. Which will net you $885.00. This will be paid on the full amount. You know the stock was doubled last season. If left as it was the dividend would of been 30 percent. This will be paid in about 30 days. What shall I do with it? Put in Bank and send you the certificate or send you a draft for the amount. So you see it will not trouble you to buy bread and potatoes for another year. — Allow me to congratulate you and hoping the profits continue as large in the future. — I am yours, E.T. Howard."

Goodhue County Historical Society collection

————————— 0 —————————

E. T. Mallory,

RED WING,

SUPERINTENDENT
MINN. STONEWARE CO.   MINN.

E.T. Mallory business card
Goodhue County Historical Society collection

The Minneapolis Tribune, November 16, 1887

MINNESOTA STONEWARE COMPANY

MANUFACTURERS

B. SHELDON, President.
G.H. CRARY, Treasurer.
E.T. MALLORY, Secy. & Supt.

Red Wing Minn 6/28 188 9

Sold to Mr *Geo Warren & Co*
Warren Mills Wis

TERMS: *60 days –*

7 2	1 *Gal Jars*	*72*	
4 6	2 *"* *"*	*42*	
2 3	3 *"* *"*	*60*	
			JUL 5 1889
1 *Crate*		*224* 5½	*12 32*
	F.O.B. Red Wing		*1 25*
			$ 13.57

Rate in crate 4th class
" Loose Once + a half 1st class –

We have previously shown letterhead stationery from the Red Wing and North Star Stoneware companies. Here is a bill from the Minnesota Stoneware Co. for ware shipped to George Warren & Company of Warren Mills, Wisconsin on June 28, 1889. Seventy-two one gallon jars, forty-six two gallon and twenty three gallon jars at five and one-half cents per gallon came to $12.32; another $1.25 was charged for one packing crate. The crated ware was shipped at fourth class rate. The uncrated ware went at one and one-half times the first class rate.

HENRY LOHMAN,
SUCCESSOR TO J. A. KEMPE & CO.

Wholesale and Retail Dealer in

PURE, IMPORTED AND DOMESTIC

Wines and Liquors
OF THE HIGHEST QUALITY.

No. 321 Main Street, = = RED WING, MINN.

We were puzzled about the possibility of this item being Red Wing until we found the ad for Henry Lohmann's liquor outlet. Barrel shaped water jars were listed on the 1896 price list, facts we learned too late to purchase this fine specimen.

After the turn of the century, mechanization began to aid muscle power in the whole of the pottery industry. At the clay pits this was a welcome relief. This photo was loaned to geologist Heinrich Reis by the Red Wing Stoneware Company and used in his book *Clays-Occurance, Properties and Uses,* 1906.

A MIRACULOUS ESCAPE

Edward Johnson Buried Alive In A Sand Pit At Claybank.

One of the most marvelous escapes ever recorded occured during a part of Saturday and all of Sunday at Claybank, of this county. Edward Johnson is an employe of the Red Wing Stoneware company at their claypits. A new pit had just been opened and Johnson had descended into an old abandoned pit for the purpose of transferring the curbing of the old pit to the new one. While in this old pit one end, which was sand, caved in and though in a standing position, covered him completely. The chains attached to the bucket was worked from side to side allowing a little air to reach the imprisoned man. Nearly a car load of sand was bearing down upon him. By desperate work Johnson's head and shoulders were freed from the sand about 10 o'clock in the evening. One of the men had procured a length of garden hose from a neighboring house thinking it might be found useful and one end of it had been taken down into the pit. John-

son's rescue seemed just about accomplished when a second cave-in was foreseen. The other man in the pit who had been clearing away the sand quickly passed Johnson the end of the hose and just escaped the second avalanche of sand -- in fact it just grazed his feet as he was hoisted to safety and the unfortunate man below was again buried from sight. Steps to rescue him were immediately taken. Meanwhile Johnson, buried beneath ten feet of sand, breathed through the hose for over twenty hours. The Claybank residents worked continuously

from the time of the accident. A telephone message was sent to this city from Claybank Sunday morning stating the case and asking that a doctor be sent out. A special train left soon after, conveying Dr. Dimmitt and a number of citizens. John Landeck, of this city, descended into the pit immediately on the arrival of the train at the pits and began to remove the sand. The work was very slow the pit being fifty-two feet deep and it was necessary to draw the sand up in small buckets. It was about five o'clock in the afternoon that Mr. Landeck called up that the man's head and shoulders were clear. Water and stimulants were hurried down, the first which the man had tasted in twenty-six hours. In two hours more an attempt was made to get him clear but he was pinned in by a plank to the bucket. Mr. Johnson at this juncture showed his wonderful endurance and pluck. He cleared away the sand on the plank and then sawed it in two with a saw that was handed to him. At eight o'clock he was landed safely on the surface of the earth. He was at once taken to a house near by and examined by Dr. Dimmitt. No injury of any kind was found although he was naturally very weak owing to the length of time since he had taken any food or water. Mr. Johnson is said to have experienced another accident of this same kind in Sweden in a pit two hundred feet deep. Mr. Johnson is about thirty-five years old, of medium weight. He is a married man and has five children.

Red Wing Argus **January 28, 1899**

Analyses of buff to white burning Cretaceous shales.

	1	2	3	4	5	6	7	8
Silica	69.92	69.84	68.298	69.050	59.72	70.10	87.70	68.70
Alumina	17.39	23.07	18.266	18.830	30.00	16.99	7.24	18.04
Ferric oxide	1.68	.48	2.867	2.607		Trace.	Trace.	1.53
Ferrous oxide								
Lime	.60	.11	.719	.296	.82		.67	1.24
Magnesia	1.11	.14	.802	.622	.51		.07	.56
Sodium oxide	.07	Trace.	.81	1.066			3.17	.24
Potassium oxide	2.25		.60	1.461		10.69	.49	5.28
Phosphorus oxide								.09
Sulphur trioxide						.23		
Titanium	.63							
Moisture	1.10	6.35	1.29	.898	10.34	1.98	Trace.	1.40
Ignition	5.45		6.155	4.912			Trace.	
	100.20	99.99	99.807	99.742	101.39	99.99	99.34	97.08

1. Red Wing, Goodhue County. Clay sampled at stoneware plant. F. F. Grout, analyst.
2. Red Wing, Goodhue County. Analysis reported by J. H. Rich to Heinrich Ries.
3. Red Wing clay. Sample from Minnesota Stoneware Co., Red Wing, Apr. 22, 1902. C. P. Berkey, analyst.
4. Red Wing stoneware clay, air dried. C. P. Berkey, analyst.
5. Ottawa. Ottawa Brick Co. Ries, Heinrich, Clays; their occurrence, properties, and uses, 1906.
6, 7, and 8. Minnesota Geol. and Nat. Hist. Survey Final Rept., vol. 1, p. 438, 1884.
6. Near Mankato. Clay filling hollows in Shakopee dolomite.
7. Near Mankato (sec. 20). White clayey bed of considerable extent.
8. Near Mankato. Clay or shale between Shakopee dolomite and Jordan sandstone in L'Huillier Mound.

Clays and Shales of Minnesota **Frank F. Grout, 1919**

Emil Shotola

Emmanuel G. (Emil) Shotola immigrated to Kenosha, Wisconsin with his parents six months after his birth in Bohemia, on December 13, 1865. He came to Red Wing in 1883 and went to work as a slipper at Minnesota Stoneware Co.

He worked for 52 years before retiring November 10, 1936 at age 71. When his wife died in 1943, he moved to California to live with two of his daughters. One of them relates that he became homesick and longed to return to Red Wing. One day he asked them to drive him to the Haldeman Pottery in Burbank so that he might look it over. Upon returning to the car, a smile lit his entire being. The sisters turned to each other and exclaimed, "Oh, he's taken a job!" He worked for Haldeman for about six months before returning to Red Wing, where he again took work at the pot shops where the younger men had been called away for the war effort.

Applying the hand drawn decorations was part of Emil's job in the salt-glaze era. In 1894 he created the personalized pot shown here. This piece was part of a large collection of old crocks, jugs and souvenir stoneware animals kept in the cellar of his home until sold in an estate auction in 1984. It is now owned by a great grandchild.

Emil died May 2, 1955 in Red Wing, at 89 years of age.

This photo is reproduced from a frame of a 16 mm color film taken during the 1952 Red Wing Art Association Open House, which featured Red Wing pottery and several of the old time potters. Emil was a "slipper," one who applied the glazing slip to ware and did the hand drawn decorating in the salt-glaze era.

And what manner of decorations did he draw? Here is a pencil doodle from a notebook he kept in 1903 to record the quantity of ware he slipped. Although with the adoption of white-glaze the hand decorating had been supplanted, the old art was still alive in his heart.

Here is Emil's signature piece which he showed off in the Art Association movie. It would probably be described as a cream pot, although it is not known that Red Wing produced such an item as a regular part of the product line. The handwriting is a perfect match for his signature as it appeared in the notebooks where he recorded his work output.

101

Red Wing Potters and Their Wares
The 1900's

By the turn of the century the potters of Red Wing had established their identity and their wares had gained widespread acceptance. Major changes had taken place in the industry and in the product line, changes that accelerated as time went by. The changes had come because the territory had grown up. It was no longer sufficient to cater only to the crude needs of a predominantly agricultural, frontierlike society. The population was now centered in cities and the needs had burgeoned.

In addition, competition had grown. Where they had previously been the only modern factories in the west they now had able, organized competition. In diversity was growth and survival.

In order to gain an understanding of the operation of the plants and life within them we will quote from writings of the day.

"Long flat cars loaded high with great lumps of hardened clay, run up under open sheds on the side of the factories, and deposit their contents through square openings in the millrooms.

"All this clay comes from one place, a station most appropriately called Claybank, on the Red Wing, Duluth & Southern, about fourteen miles out.

"This clay, which is of a light blue color, is delivered in the sheds in the great shapeless lumps and is there put in the huge mills or clay crushers, where four large iron wheels under tremendous pressure turn round and round until the clay is reduced to a sufficiently fine state to be easily handled. A factory averages from two to four carloads of clay a day.

"Small truck cars, running on narrow rails, carry it from the mill room to the factories where the potters stand at work. Here moist, shining, and about the consistency of gum, it is piled up at intervals on low tables or shelves running all along the factory sides, where the potters can easily reach it."[1]

"Each workman has a boy as his helper. This boy stands between the clay bin and the clay worker. Taking the clay from the bin, he weighs enough for one jar or jug and prepares it by repeatedly cutting it on the cord stretched above his table. Slap goes the lump of clay across the cord, and slap the two sections go together, only to be cut again and again. The motion is regular and the boys gain a splendid development of chest and arm.

"Three processes of manufacture are now in use — hand turning, machine turning and plaster molds. The first requires time and greater skill than the second, for work can be turned by machine three or four times as rapidly as by hand. Machine turning is almost indispensible for the largest pieces, such as thirty to fifty-gallon jars. Plaster-paris molds are used chiefly for small pieces, which can be made very rapidly in this way, but occasionally the molds are used for four or five-gallon ware."[2]

"Older potters think the grain is smoother and the texture more even under their shaping than by mechanical process. It is marvelous to see one of these skilled men take a lump of clay, set it on his spinning wheel, differing only from Bible times by the introduction of a power shaft, and, judging by the eye and the touch, bid its walls climb in uniform thickness to a jug or jar perhaps half as big as its maker.

"But most of the ware is made in molds to fit the exterior, while a bit of wood shaped to one half the cross section of the inside is pressed into the center of the spinning lump of clay so that the walls are firmly and truly thrust against the mold at the same time that the correct form is given to the inner surface. Small mouthed jugs are made in two pieces, one in a mold that comes up to the shoulder of the jug and the other from the shoulder to the neck. Then they are clapped together and baked into one piece. Ears are made by hand and stuck on and jug handles are pulled from a lump like pulling candy, pulled from the lip to the right length, deftly bent into shape and patted to the right place on the shoulder. Making the plaster of paris molds is a job that keeps two men constantly busy.

"After the jugs and pots have stood in a hot room a day or two they are pretty well set, though they will still take the impression of a thumb nail, and are ready for glazing."[3]

"In the glazing or 'slip' rooms stand deep wooden tanks on wheels, filled with a liquid which looks like water but which contains a composition that gives the baked clay a glassy finish."[1]

"The glaze is manufactured by grinding in big tubs and is applied inwardly by a small force pump and outwardly by simple dipping."[3]

"The grey glaze is a mysterious compound, containing eight or nine ingredients. Among them are feldspar, flint, and oxide of zinc."[2]

"Much of the ware is stamped under the glaze with a design or even a long printed statement of the intended contents. That is done with a rubber stamp padded with

102

an air cushion so that slight irregularities of the surface may not make it incoherent.

"The only remaining process is the baking. The kilns are bricked up, fires are built all around in pockets in the wall and the heat by a strong draft is drawn in at the top and out through the bottom, the down-draft which is the chief difference of the modern kiln from the obsolete pattern is the secret of getting even heat and even baking throughout."[3]

"One of the most picturesque sights of the potteries (are these kiln rooms) where red and glowing square openings into the mouth of the furnaces lighten the dark, wooden sheds with a lovely, rich glow that on a wet or cold day is most agreeable, but on a hot one, awful in its intensity. But it is a scene for a painter, the dark figures of the men as they fill the furnaces, the deep, blood-red crimson of the glowing fires, or the leaping flames of the newly kindled furnaces. Each set of furnaces is lighted in turn. Then the first is allowed to die out, and the next lot is lighted, and the stoneware in all the kilns baked in succession. All this makes brilliant patches of light and sharp contrast. About ten carloads of stoneware are shipped weekly from Red Wing at a very conservative estimate.

"In each factory there are about twenty skilled potters who work incessantly, molding and shaping all the time. They wear apparently as little clothing as possible, in warm weather a thin shirt, short sleeved, a pair of overalls and a pair of loosely-laced boots being considered enough. And it certainly is for they are daubed with the clay from head to foot. It was the greatest wonder to me how they ever dare go into the kilns at all, lest they might begin to dry in those molds of clothes, and be of no use save as statues or cigar-store figures. How any of those clay-coated boys get in or out of their clothing is an unsolved mystery.

"The potteries and the diggings give employment to some 400 to 500 men, but, strange to say, there are no women employed in the factories, though in the east, and in England, one finds them in the molding and glazing-rooms."[1]

———————— 0 ————————

[1]"The Clay Potteries of Red Wing" by Helen Gregory Flesher, *The Minneapolis Journal*, November 2, 1901.

[2]"The Clay Industry" by Frances Densmore, *The American Thresherman*, Volume VIII No. 4, August 1905.

[3]*Red Wing, the Desirable City*, Argus Press, 1903.

This is the signature found stamped on the side of most jars, churns and large jugs of this period. Collectors call it simply the "Union oval"; it is two and one-half inches wide.

A rare Minnesota oval, two and one-half inches wide.

An even rarer Minnesota oval, slightly wider.

103

The Transition to Modern Times

During the change-over years between 1895 and 1900 pieces were occasionally turned out using a combination of the old and new techniques. Shown here are three pieces in white-glaze with hand drawn decorations. The 15 gallon jar strangely has both hand and rubber stamp applied markings. Another jar has been seen with a rubber stamp applied leaf decoration but, an impressed Red Wing Stoneware Co. side stamp in the clay. A number of salt-glazed pieces have been displayed with rubber stamp applied leaves and Union Stoneware Co. trademark. Occasionally a jar and more frequently a jug will be found white-glazed outside and brown inside.

This 20 pound butter jar has part of a Union oval on the back. Hand labeled, white-glazed jars like this with molded bottom signatures are also known.

The line on the inside wall of this churn is not a crack, it is a lap mark made by the template in the jigger molding process.

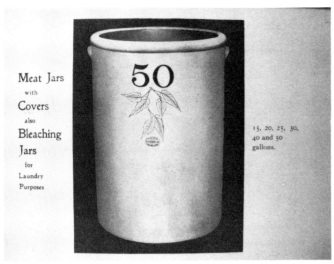

Meat Jars
with
Covers
also
Bleaching
Jars
for
Laundry
Purposes

15, 20, 25, 30, 40 and 50 gallons.

Machine turning had now expanded the size capacity to 50 gallons. This and the following ads with photo illustrations are from a Union Stoneware Co. catalog from right around the turn of the century; part of the Goodhue County Historical Society collection. The smaller jars were also pictured but we would rather show the actual article. Covers continued to be offered for all sizes of jars but, the variation in styles between the companies was shortly eliminated and the same daisy petal version used by RWSCo. in the salt-glaze era became exclusive.

This monster has a drain hole to facilitate emptying. The leaves, capacity and trademark oval were applied by rubber stamp.

The large, outturned "elephant ear" leaves were used interchangeably with the tapered "birch leaves" in the early days of the era, but their use died out before long. Both types of leaf have been seen on salt-glazed "transition period" pieces, so it is difficult to say which one pre-dates the other. The birch leaves remained in use until displaced by the red wing in 1909.

The leaves were either black or blue; the black ones are generally felt to be from early years though the two colors were used concurrently. We have seen a couple of short, squat 20 gallon jars, larger in diameter, like a tub.

Some pieces have no ovals. It is speculated that these were sold through Sears-Roebuck or Montgomery Ward whose catalogs carried them shown that way. Or perhaps it was just a carryover from the haphazard practice of signing ware during the salt-glaze period.

The outturned leaves on 2 gallon jars were always in miniature. These two sport highly unusual Minnesota Stoneware Co. signatures. Each of them is additionally bottom signed. It is a mystery why these stamps were used. But then, it is also unknown exactly when or why the determination was made to use the "Union" oval; the member companies were still separate corporations. Bottom markings remained in some molds even after the formal merger in 1906. The "Minnesota" oval has been seen on jars, jugs and churns of various sizes; all presumably relatively early.

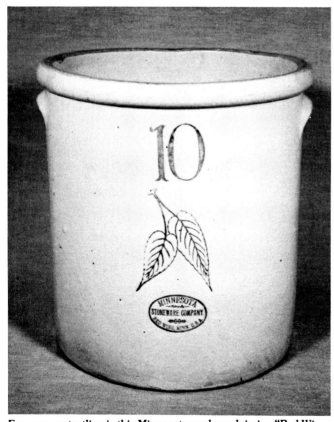

Even more startling is this Minnesota oval proclaiming "Red Wing, Minn. U.S.A." Somebody was thinking big!

Here are a rare pair of hand turned elephant ear, beehive jugs with Minnesota ovals. Note the differing treatments at the necks.

106

Stoneware Water Coolers

White Glaze, Nickel Faucets, Handsome,
Cheap, Clean.

Sizes like cut, 2, 3, 4, 5, 6, 8 and 10 gallons. Jar shape, straight sides, sizes 12, 15, 20, 25, 30, 40 and 50 gallons.

The "Success" Stoneware Water Filter

Made in two sizes. The family size has two 4-gallon jars, the upper one holding the filtering block and lower one being the water cooler. The hotel size has two 10-gallon jars, with three filtering blocks in the bottom of the upper jar, and the lower jar holding 10 gallons of filtered water.

The filtering blocks are four inches in diameter and height, hollowed out on the inside, and are turned out of natural tripoli stone, the best filtering material known. These blocks fit on metal tubes running through and fastened to the bottom of top jar, and can be lifted off the drip tube, cleaned and replaced in two minutes, and with no trouble. The water passes from the upper jar through the walls of the filtering block into the inside chamber of the filtering block, and thus through the drip tube into the lower jar. This is by far the best and cheapest water filter ever manufactured, and a complete success. Thousands in use.

Water coolers from this period are perhaps the prettiest of all; the leaves against the white background, the sharp "Ice Water" banner with its fussy detail. They're really quite breathtaking. They were available with smaller diameter holes for the nickel plated faucet or with the traditional, large, hexagon reinforced bung for a wooden spigot.

Though the 1890's Union catalog listed both RWSCo.'s "Success" and MSCo.'s "Perfection" filters this catalog lists only the former; it was a success after all.

Very rare and unusual is the 2 gallon jar style cooler at left. Just the thing to make a 2 gallon collection complete.

The traditional, hand turned jugs continued to be offered in the 3, 4 and 5 gallon sizes; the smaller common jugs were now always molded except occasionally, for 2 gallons. These smaller jugs did not

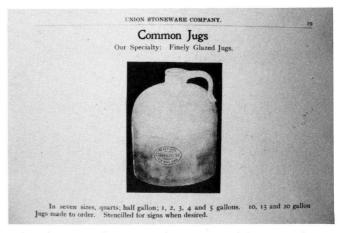

ordinarily receive the capacity, leaves nor oval decoration despite the photo in the catalog. It is curious that the large, molded shoulder jugs did not displace the hand turned style.

The shoulder jugs of this era are frequently found with bottom signatures; the four gallon jug here is bottom signed. MSCo. signatures are the only ones reported but both companies likely

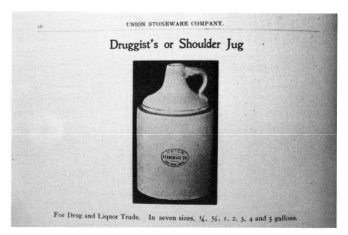

made them. We cannot confirm whether the outturned leaves were ever used on this style jug.

Occasionally a jug is found with double handles, a real blessing when you try to lift it when it's full. The leaves on the center jug are shorter than the others on this page and with the right leaf overlapping the left. These shorter leaves were used on smaller pieces and where the shape of the piece or an advertising banner reduced the space available.

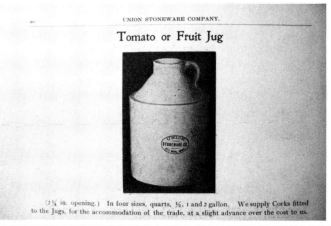

Tomato or Fruit Jug

(2¼ in. opening.) In four sizes, quarts, ½, 1 and 2 gallon. We supply Corks fitted to the Jugs, for the accommodation of the trade, at a slight advance over the cost to us.

By far the main product of a stoneware factory is jugs. They were made in an amazing variety of shapes and sizes; when you figure in the differing styles of company signatures the selection becomes even greater. Here is by no means a complete sampling.

Notable among the styles are the MSCo. cone top and the squat and tall varieties of one pint jugs. Far Left at Bottom compares MSCo. and RWSCo. tall styles; included in Top Right and Bottom Center are the squat. The RWSCo. squat style has the same shape except for the handle as the North Star bailed jug on page 60. Wide mouth fruit jugs were made in both shouldered and common jug styles. Both of the syrup jugs Bottom Right are MSCo.

109

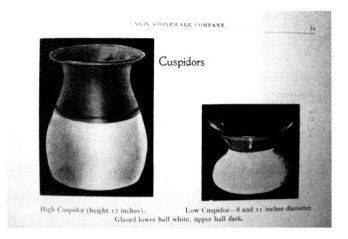

Cuspidors

High Cuspidor (height 12 inches).   Low Cuspidor—8 and 11 inches diameter.
Glazed lower half white, upper half dark.

German Spittoons

(10 inches in diameter.)

Plain and Fancy.   Especially designed for Bar Rooms, Lodge Halls
and other public places.

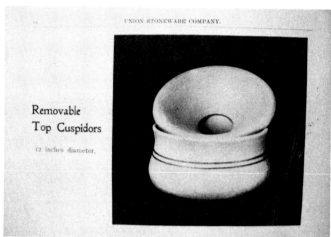

Removable
Top Cuspidors

12 inches diameter.

A new, two piece cuspidor was introduced to the line to complement the four existing styles.

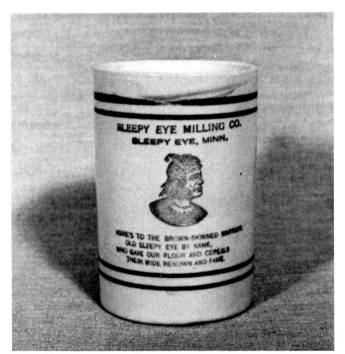

Beer
Mugs

The milling company in Sleepy Eye, Minnesota made a practice of including premiums in their flour sacks. Around 1902, MSCo. produced a small number of these in the form of stoneware mugs with the Indian, the verse and the uncommon bottom signature.

Bailed packing jars with covers were first pictured in this catalog though they were listed on the circa 1896 white-glazed ware price list. A patent was issued to Sylvester Hunter and John Sherwood of New Brighton, Penn. in February of 1896 claiming this to be a new and original design. Union Stoneware Co. advertised them in four sizes; 3, 5, 10 and 20 pounds and 1 and 2 pound sizes without bails. Above are 3, 5 and 10 pound.

Safety Valve Jar, Self-Sealing — For the preserving and pickling trade. Five sizes, 3, 5, 10 and 20 lbs.; also 5 gal. containers or storage jars.

The safety valve sealing device was patented in 1895 by Henry Dilworth of East Orange, N.J. A stamped metal cam lever hinged to a yoke which hooked into a ridge around the neck exerted pressure on the cover, holding it down on a rubber gasket. It was called a safety valve lid because it could vent internal pressure during cooking.

The trademark of the Hamilton Glass Company, by whom the potteries were licensed to sell the patented sealing device, appeared on many of the jars. The jar at left is bottom signed by MSCo.

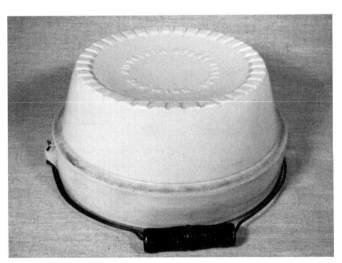

These were called nappies or pudding pans and were offered in 8, 9 and 10 inch sizes. They were a new product, appearing for the first time. The common shoulder bowls or milk pans, French pans and pie plates all continued to be offered as well.

A bread bowl, 17 inches in diameter, was listed on the 1896 price list. This one is evidently an early one as evidenced by the glassy drippings which fused to it during firing. It must have been made during the period of transition to white-glaze, the kiln ceiling was still coated from salt-glazing.

Here is a white-glazed, bailed cooking crock or stew pan. The bail hooked into the top loop of a cotter pin which was placed through a hole in the thick lug of clay and secured by bending the legs back.

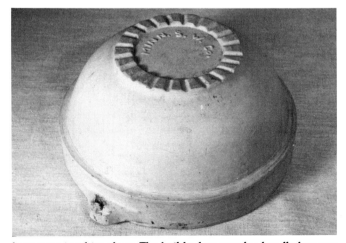

Bailed, covered meat roasters were advertised in 11 and 13 inch sizes. This one is unglazed outside and brown inside; they have also

been seen in white-glaze. The bail had no wooden handle because this item was intended for oven use.

Small Fancy Jugs

In four sizes, ⅛, ¼, ½ and 1 pint.

Many people refer to the one-eighth pint version of the fancy jug as a miniature or salesman's sample. It's just not so; they were a regular part of the line. It is true that they were often decorated with slogans and sold as souvenirs.

Center and Bottom Left are the smallest sizes from each company. MSCo. used a raised bead to help hide the mold parting line.

Center and Bottom Below is a more complete set of fancy jugs than was offered at the time of this catalog. Eight sizes were ultimately advertised; one quart through two gallons appearing in a slightly later catalog in addition to the one-eighth through one pint. This set lacks pint and two gallon sizes.

UNION STONEWARE COMPANY.

Pipkins or Small Pitchers

In four sizes, 1, 2, 3 and 4 pint.

UNION STONEWARE COMPANY.

Stone Mason Fruit Jars

Three sizes, ¼, ½ and 1 gallon.

These have become a popular collectible in fruit jar as well as stoneware circles. That competition, coupled with a relative scarceness has driven up the prices remarkably. The markings are seen in both blue and black. The round shouldered shape at right below became standard about the time that the companies merged into the Red Wing Union Stoneware Co. in 1906.

Though they were offered in four sizes we could not find a complete set to photograph. All of those that have been reported are signed, "Minn. S. Co. Red Wing, Minn." in a circle of raised letters around the bottom. These are slightly different in style from the pipkins advertised in the earlier Union catalog on page 69; almost a bean pot shape.

The Stone Mason Fruit Jar was called, " . . . a new item this year . . . " by the 1903 yearbook, *Red Wing, The Desirable City;* " . . . to be used instead of the familiar glass preserve jar for peaches, quinces and all that." In Julian Harrison Toulouse's *Fruit Jars,* 1969 the author states, " . . . Union Stoneware is now Red Wing Potteries, who tell me

that the jar was discontinued about 1910."
These have "Pat'd Jan 24, 1899" molded into their base, which related to a patent issued to Chas. Kettron and F.V. Maxwell of Macomb, Illinois for a method of manufacturing molds for fruit jars. Macomb Pottery Co. also made these jars.

UNION STONEWARE COMPANY

Bailed Fruit Jug

In three sizes, ¼, ½ and 1 gallon. (2¼ inch opening.)

On pages 69 and 70 we showed bailed jugs in brown and in white-glaze. We also showed them in three sizes which were not actually presented until this catalog. Also new at this time was the bailed,

wide mouth, fruit jug. Both the bailed and the regular fruit jug in this photo are in the one-quarter gallon size and are signed by MSCo. in a circle. (See bottom left)

These are one-half and one-quarter gallon fruit jugs. One with indented MSCo. full signature and the other with RWSW initials.

Here is a cute bailed jug with an advertising banner and an unusual, script-like "Red Wing Co." signature.

Slop Jars—With or without bails. (No cover.)

Chamber pots and toiletry basins were emptied into a slop jar to save separate trips. We have seen no signed examples; the unsigned ones we have seen have had handhold notches in the bottoms. A convenient touch.

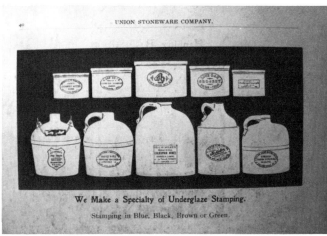

Though stenciled advertising under salt-glaze has been seen it is quite rare; due no doubt to the lack of detail possible because of blurring. White-glazing opened a whole new marketing potential. This ad boasts of blue, black, brown or green lettering. Anything but blue and black is almost unknown.

In addition to those old items carried over from earlier times which we have already mentioned, this catalog offered Russian pitchers, mustard pitchers, Boston bean pots and the little individual bean pots or cups. Hanging baskets and flower pots were still offered and, as was the case with jar lids, the style was RWSCo.'s daisy petal design.

Both snuff and preserve jars with stone covers were shown; the first sold by pounds capacity, the second by gallons, one-quarter through two. The only noticeable difference being that the preserve jars had more rounded shoulders than the snuff. Chambers and low butter jars remained as staple parts of the product line.

Notable by its absence was the wax sealer preserve jar, a victim of the twentieth century, displaced by the Safety Valve and Stone Mason jars.

This period had no shortage of odd and unusual pieces; here is a jar with no leaves. Such oddities make collecting fun.

A German wine bottle. Who would ever believe that this was a Red Wing product. Yet molded distinctly into the bottom is a Minn. S. Co. signature.

116

Otto Hartnagel gave this teapot to his mother for Christmas in 1904. Otto began working at Red Wing Stoneware Company in 1894 at the age of 17 and continued at the potteries for 60 years, retiring in 1954.

The motif of the teapot is identical to the "Old Sleepy Eye" steins made between 1903 and 1906 for the Sleepy Eye Milling Company by Weir Pottery Co. of Monmouth, Illinois. The teapot was made by adding a spout and fancy top to a stein.

Though there was a listing in the 1894 Red Wing Directory giving the occupation of George Hartnagel, Jr. as potter for RWSCo. Otto's older brother George was not known to have worked at the potteries at all according to his son. Their father, George J. Hartnagel, was a carpenter for Red Wing Manufacturing Co.'s furniture factory.

Who then was G.H.? The most likely person was master mold maker George Hehr. Just how the mold came to be used in the Red Wing potteries is an item of much tantalizing speculation.

In addition to this piece, two steins have been noted and there are unconfirmed reports of another teapot. One of those steins is emblazoned, "Earl, Xmas 1904" and has the mark "G.H. 54" on the bottom which leads to the conclusion that a special, numbered series was created for this occasion only.

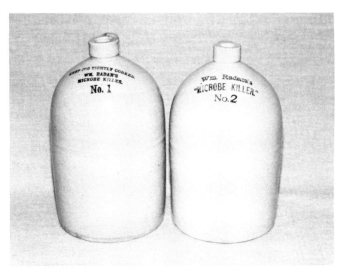

Patent medicines, elixirs and cure-alls were boastfully advertised and eagerly consumed by a public seeking remedy for any manner of ills. Analysis of William Radam's "Microbe Killer" gives a clue to its popularity; it was nothing more than adulterated wine. Although the pictured jugs are unsigned, dump shards and signed examples have been found.

This little shoulder bowl is shown approximately life size. A surprising number of regular size, signed, white bowls are still found. A large variety of Red Wing Stoneware Co.'s bottom marks are the most seen. This miniature is, alas, unsigned.

The tiny, one-eighth pint jugs became more popular as souvenirs than as containers. The one on the left is early enough that it contains MSCo.'s bottom signature.

Their popularity as souvenirs was not limited to Red Wing either. This one was made up for Excelsior Springs, Missouri.

The Great Northern Railroad commissioned stoneware potatoes for display in their dining cars to draw attention to their baked Idaho potatoes. Ben Amondson, who labored at the pot shops for 60 years, fashioned this one into a bottle.

Three more unsigned miniatures. Attributable by their clay, glazes and shape. (Except for the pitcher, no full size pitchers are known in this shape.)

Company G of the National Guard of the State of Minnesota served proudly in the Philippines during the Spanish-American War. Among the casualties was Lt. Frank Morley who had been a RWSCo. potter. (Frank was an uncle of Louise Morley, see page 97.) The miniature canteen was made to commemorate the completion of the Armory building on December 13, 1901. Some of these are signed with a rare MSCo. circle signature.

———— 0 ————

This is the earliest known example of Red Wing dinnerware; at least 30 years older than any of the popularly recognized forms. Equally fascinating is the fact that it is not stoneware but a higher grade of pottery, whiteware.

The 1902 *Red Wing Yearbook* told, "It is the history of the pottery industry that where the coarser forms of manufacture are established the finer forms are afterwards developed." "Already creditable specimens of white ware are shown." The following year it was written of the Minnesota Stoneware Company, "It is a part of the company's policy to appropriate a sum every year to experiment in new lines and it is only a question of time, and apparently a short time, when the manufacture of higher forms of pottery will be taken up. Making tableware, for instance, has advanced beyond the experimental stage but the management, as careful as it is energetic, will not consider manufacture for the market until the wares have stood the test of months of actual use."

There were earlier, more cryptic references to whiteware, but the "Minnesota circle signature" leads us to date this piece between 1901 and 1903. The other pieces using this signature, the canteen and the Sleepy Eye mug, both date from this span. The diameter of the signature circle is slightly smaller, though made from the same stamp. The greater shrinkage in firing the porcelainlike whiteware body with its more thorough vitrification is the reason.

Here is an interesting little mug; the rim deviation opposite the handle may be a lip, perhaps it was intended to be a pitcher. It doesn't look like anything else that the companies are known to have made at this time. The glaze is a deep cobalt blue. On the bottom, looking for all the world like it had been applied with one of those embossed plastic tape label makers is "MINN. S.W. Co." A pitcher in this style will be shown later in a two-tone glaze with Red Wing Union Stoneware Co.'s signature.

———————— 0 ————

These elegant cone top jugs were introduced sometime in this period though they weren't in earlier catalogs. They were obviously intended to be fancier than the common shoulder or druggist's jug. The handle does not attach to the neck, but makes a large loop so that it can be grasped with more than a single finger. Other companies made jugs in this style so, as always, a signature is necessary to prove origin. Happily these are both bottom signed by MSCo. RWSCo. signatures have also been reported.

Of the several Red Wing liquor jugs this is easily the prettiest. It is bottom marked by MSCo. and is one of the rarest local advertising pieces.

This was a store window advertising display piece made for the L.M. Pierron Company, the last of the old line of Milwaukee potters, relegated to selling pottery made by other companies after their own production ceased.

The Ladner Bros. one-half gallon jug is bottom signed by RWSCo.; the others unsigned. (As it turns out, the Ladners and the Seuferts were distant uncles of the authors.) The tops of white-glaze era jugs were not done in brown until near the 1906 merger; the two-tone style then became standard on jugs below 3 gallons.

The Red Wing Union Stoneware Company

In March of 1906 the Red Wing, the Minnesota and the Union Stoneware Companies formally merged into a single company called the Red Wing Union Stoneware Company. The individual plants became known as "factory R" and "factory M" and each continued to turn out the full line of ware.

There was no immediate change in the product offering except that new signature ovals were made up to proclaim the new company title. Old molds that were still in use continued to turn out ware with the previous, individual company trademarks in the bottom. The product line was beginning to expand at an ever quickening rate and early catalogs offer a number of new products as well as the old standards.

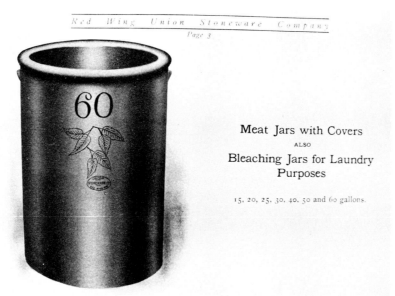

Red Wing Union Stoneware Company
Page 3

Meat Jars with Covers
ALSO
Bleaching Jars for Laundry
Purposes

15, 20, 25, 30, 40, 50 and 60 gallons.

The illustrations for this catalog were not updated to show the new Red Wing Union Stoneware Co. oval. The top of the jar line had now reached 60 gallons. The elephant ear leaves had disappeared, but the birch leaves continued until replaced by the red wing, around 1909. A slightly later catalog, presumably from shortly after the switch to the red wing trademark, still used these illustrations, though the cover was changed to show a jar with a wing.

The first RWUSCo. oval was slightly larger (two and seven-eighths) than the Union or Minnesota ovals. The 2 gallon jar at right carries MSCo.'s molded bottom signature.

122

Mottled Cuspidors

Blue or brown

Three sizes: 6, 8, and 11 inches

The first new product to appear in either of the early RWUSCo. catalogs is a set of mottled cuspidors in the old, turned shape. This decoration was applied over the white-glaze background by a sponge

dipped in blue or reddish brown glaze. The effect is quite lovely and was used on a number of items. The pair above are not signed.

Spongeware

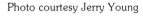

Here is another of the strange, straight sided water coolers as seen on page 107. This one has a RWUSCo. oval.

Photo courtesy Jerry Young

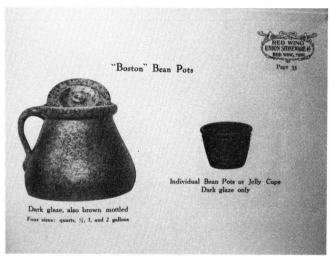

"Boston" Bean Pots

Page 33

Individual Bean Pots or Jelly Cups
Dark glaze only

Dark glaze, also brown mottled
Four sizes: quarts, ½, 1, and 2 gallons

Oh, how they brightened up the bean pot! These were warm and homey in the old dark brown, would be almost decorative in mottled brown.(My grandfather, Otis Tefft, lived on West 3rd St. around WWI and worked at the potteries for a short time as steam engineer and later as night watchman. My grandmother ran a boarding house and sold lunches to the potters. My father recalls grandpa taking a bean pot along to work where he would bury it in the hot ashes and coals of the firebox to bake overnight.)

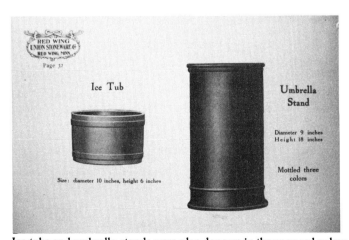

Page 32

Ice Tub

Umbrella
Stand

Diameter 9 inches
Height 18 inches

Mottled three
colors

Size: diameter 10 inches, height 6 inches

Ice tubs and umbrella stands were also done up in the sponged colors. Though the ad promises three colors, we know of only blue and reddish brown. The three examples at right above are each done in blue and red, the blue uniformly daubed and the red in patterns: stripes on the center one and spots on the left and right. These have also been seen in mottled blue alone and with the two colors evenly dispersed. The ice tubs have been seen in mottled blue and in mottled red alone.

Hall Boy Pitchers

For hotel or house use
Size: ¼ gallon

Mottled Pitchers

Blue or Brown
Size: ½ gallon

For the first time a pitcher was offered that looked like a pitcher. The old fashioned Russian pitchers, the one quart mustard pitchers and the squat pipkins were all still offered. These Hall Boy and tall milk pitchers have been seen in single color mottled blue or mottled red.

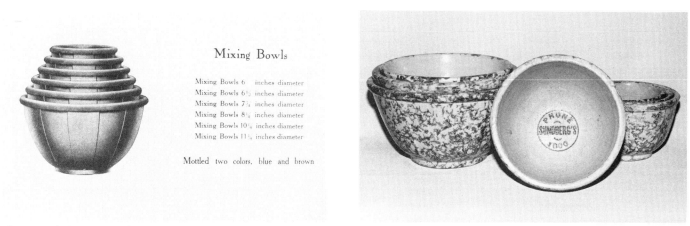

Mixing Bowls

Mixing Bowls 6 inches diameter
Mixing Bowls 6½ inches diameter
Mixing Bowls 7¾ inches diameter
Mixing Bowls 8¼ inches diameter
Mixing Bowls 10¼ inches diameter
Mixing Bowls 11¾ inches diameter

Mottled two colors, blue and brown

These paneled mixing bowls joined the shoulder bowls in the line-up and became one of Red Wing's most widely treasured products. They are one of a number of Red Wing products that have been widely collected for years with no notion of their origin as the bowls in this shape were not signed though often bore advertising banners. They were offered in 6-11 inch sizes initially with a 5 inch size available later on. Consequently the 5 inch bowl is rare.

The 8 inch bowl pictured in the collection above advertises Sundberg Bros. grocery store which was in Red Wing.

Chambers   Combinette

9s Covered Chamber (large)
12s Covered Chamber (small)

Finished in white, also blue or brown mottled.

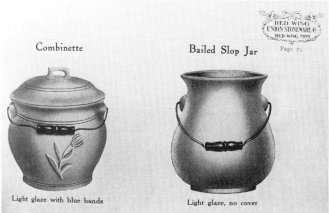

Combinette   Bailed Slop Jar

Light glaze with blue bands   Light glaze, no cover

The old chamber pot also got the mottled treatment as did a new item, the bailed "Combinette," a combination chamber and slop jar. The combinette in the right photo was another new item. It was later called the "Lily Combinette" and had a different flower.

Acid Proof Measure Set

Quart and one-half gallon, with funnel

The tough, impervious, non-reactive nature of stoneware made it perfect for use in handling corrosives. Later on a good market was found for large jars in laboratories. By the Union Stoneware Co. trademark it is obvious that these were available before the merger. The one quart measure in the photo at right is additionally bottom signed by RWSCo.

Chicken Drinking Fountains

Style Sanitary   Style Eureka

Three sizes: ½, 1, and 2 gallons.

By using these fountains young chickens cannot drown. Water is always clean, as the chickens cannot get into same. They are money savers by saving young chickens from death and preserving the health of the old ones.

The "Eureka" poultry drinking fountains go back into the salt-glaze times. The earlier ones have "Pat'd April 7, 1885" molded into their fronts. (It was not a Red Wing invention.) Many had company signatures on their rear like the one sporting the unusual Union Stoneware Co. molded signature despite a Red Wing Union oval. RWSCo. and MSCo. signatures are also seen, again often on the same piece with a Union or Red Wing Union oval.

125

B. L. Style Self-Sealing Packing Jars

For preserving fruits and vegetables

Four sizes: ½, 1, 3, and 5 gallons. (Opening 3¼ inches)
½, and 1 gallon without bailed handles

William Weir of Monmouth, Illinois and head of Weir Pottery patented a lever lock to seal glass and pottery packing jars in 1901. In 1903 he patented the feature of adding grooves on the sealing surface of the lid to improve the seal on the rubber gasket. Red Wing was soon to put his invention to use by coming out with self-sealing packing jars in one-half to 5 gallon sizes. Weir's patent covered a lever with a "T" bar to keep the lever from tipping. A further improvement resulted in a ball lever which rested in a rounded depression in the lid. The 5 gallon "applesauce" jar, as they are known, is bottom signed by RWSCo. Strangely, though they were later decorated with wings, none of these have been reported with leaves.

Except for the name in the oval there was little noticeable change in the product offering of the company to go along with the merger. As we have shown, many pieces still bore the molded signatures of the previous, individual companies. As time went by there was less and less use of molded signatures but more reliable inclusion of the rubber stamped marks. It is rare to find a jar without an oval, except for butter jars which lost all maker identification and consequently have no collector value unless they bear an advertising banner.

Though this catalog pictured the old style Union Stoneware Co. Stone Mason Jar as on page 114, the Red Wing Union Stoneware Co. produced jars with this shape and banner before they were discontinued around 1910. Below is view of the instructions on the back.

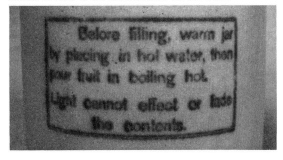

Around 1910 factory M was roughly doubled in size by the addition of the four story addition at left.

Goodhue County Historical Society photo

The Red Wing Trademark

The company had been using reddish brown glaze in the mottled brown umbrella stands, bean pots, and so forth, for a number of years. It seemed like only a matter of time before someone thought of putting a red wing on the product. Around 1909 it occurred. A May 25th article of the following year in the *Red Wing Republican* spoke of a display of stoneware in the show window of Boxrud & Hjermstad's bearing the *new* Red Wing trademark. This had to be one of the commercial art masterpieces of all time; it gave the product an indelible recognition. No other stoneware manufacturer decorated their product with any color but blue or black and none could muster such a captivating visual connection between the trademark and the company name.

The earliest ones, like this, can be identified by the large ovals, the size and clarity of the wing (a full 6 inches here on this 5 gallon jar) and that they have no handles. (Beginning in 1915 the 4 through 30 gallon jars were available with handles; they were still offered without handles but it is rare to find them that way.)

The hand turned, beehive jugs continued to be made in 3, 4 and 5 gallon size until 1917-18. The smaller beehives were molded. These three have matching, large ovals and the wings are located down on the front of the jug. Later ones had the wing mounted up on the domed portion.

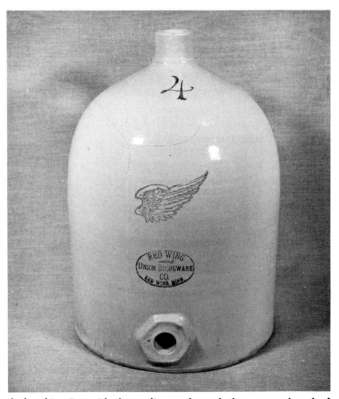

A threshing jug with the earliest style oval, the one used on leaf decorated RWUSCo. items.

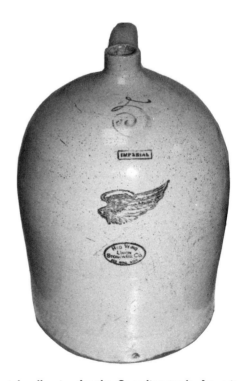

A 5 Imperial gallon jug for the Canadian trade. Imperial gallons equal one and one fourth of our U.S. gallons.

128

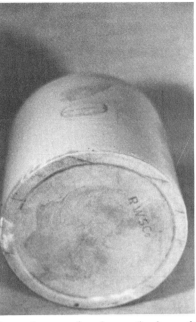

As a holdover from the birch leaves days the capacity number was placed up on the dome of the early "wing" shoulder jugs. These are frequently seen without ovals, but, not so frequently bottom signed by one of the pre-merger companies. Another indication of relative age is that early jug interiors were sometimes glazed in brown. Later large shoulder jugs, mostly 3 gallons, are sometimes bottom signed Red Wing Union Stoneware Co.

At right is the shoulder version of the Imperial measure jug. The capacity number was moved to the side, like this, only a few years after the start of wing production.

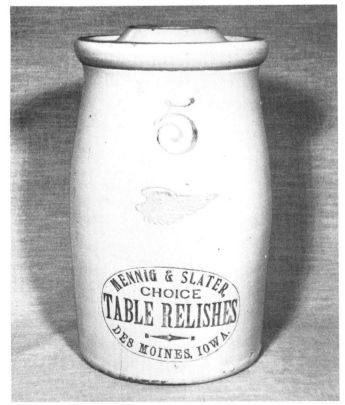

You won't find too many churns with advertising; the connection between butter and table relishes escapes us. The lids no longer had the pronounced cup which required hand trimming, they were simply molded . . . old literature shows them installed either side up; we prefer this way.

The hand turned shape coolers are sometimes found with the older "Ice Water" banner; this one became standard before too long. It is difficult to determine if these or the churns were actually hand turned or not; we believe them to be molded. The capacity number is on the inside bottom.

The pot belly water cooler became the standard in the mid to late teens. These were definitely molded, a vertical parting line can be discerned by careful observation. The little two gallon size is most sought after; the fives and threes, in that order, are the most plentiful. The lids for water coolers were of different diameters than for jars and have a "W" after the capacity number. These coolers were available with drinking fountains in place of the spigot and were very popular in country school houses.

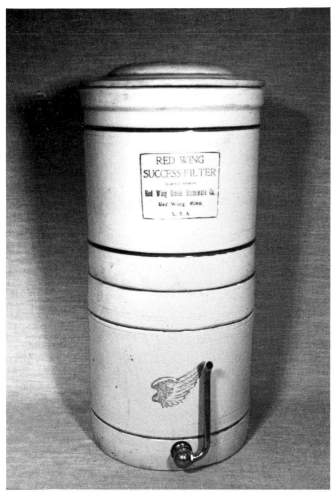

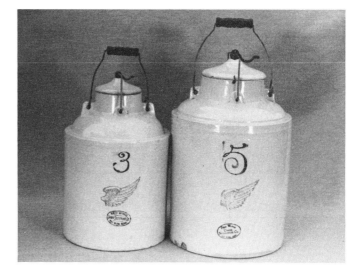

The old faithful Success Filter was peddled into the 1930's. This one has an interesting, swiveling dispensing tube which works like the pipe on a railroad yard water tower used for filling locomotive tenders.

Ball locking and bailed, regular packing jars. The lids for the ball lock jars have a red slash which lines up with a mark on the jar to align the lid. The bailed jars were intended to be sealed with wax.

When the United Commercial Travelers held their convention in Red Wing in 1912 the whole business district downtown joined in the revelry. A jail cell was erected in the middle of a street and kangaroo court was held to incarcerate undesirables found not wearing a convention booster pin.

The U.C.T. was a professional fraternity of traveling salesmen and, therefore, the little trinket turned out by the pot shops was a traveling bag, not a doctor's bag as many believe.

The *Red Wing Daily Republican* reported, "One of the prettiest souvenirs of the convention are the miniature traveling bags, manufactured and distributed to U.C.T. delegates only by the Red Wing Union Stoneware Company of this city. A booklet, entitled: "How We Lost Our Best Customer," goes with the souvenir. On the inner pages in deep mourning appear the words: 'He Died'."

It seems certain that the bags became available to other than delegates; some may also have been made later because they lack the U.C.T. emblem.

 0

The Potters' Excursions

The Stoneware Potters' Union, formed in 1895, held an annual riverboat excursion aboard the sternwheel steamer *G.W. Hill*. The vessel had a capacity of 2000 passengers and featured a 30 x 120 foot dance floor, a full orchestra and, of course, a steam calliope. The excursions were highly touted events with a prize, in one case a diamond ring, going to the person selling the most tickets. Proceeds of the event went to the potters' benefit fund.

Some 800 persons attended the inaugural event in 1912 and over 1000 participated in subsequent trips. The newspapers would be full of announcements for weeks in advance and the event itself always received a big write-up. The boat left Red Wing early in the morning and didn't return until near midnight. The pottery declared the day a holiday and shut down entirely. People really knew how to have fun in those days before television.

As a method of drawing attention to the 1915 excursion, special one gallon jugs were made up and displayed in store windows throughout town advising that tickets could be purchased therein. On Sunday, May 16, one of these jugs was dropped into the Mississippi at Prescott, upstream of Red Wing. The lucky finder was entitled to a free admission by presenting the jug to Roxie Nelson. On June 15, too late for the excursion, Chas. L. and C.A. Carlson found the jug near Trudell Slough, downriver. Nelson substituted five gallons of gasoline as the prize and kept the jug as a souvenir. (The excursion tickets cost 75 cents!)

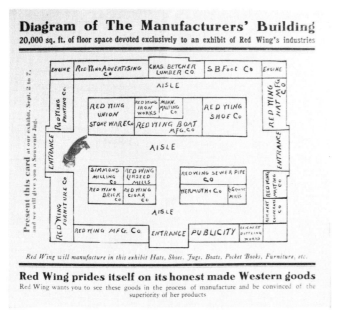

Diagram of The Manufacturers' Building
20,000 sq. ft. of floor space devoted exclusively to an exhibit of Red Wing's industries

Red Wing will manufacture in this exhibit Hats, Shoes, Jugs, Boats, Pocket Books, Furniture, etc.

Red Wing prides itself on its honest made Western goods
Red Wing wants you to see these goods in the process of manufacture and be convinced of the superiority of her products

"Present this card at our exhibit, Sept. 2 to 7, and we will give you a Souvenir Jug" read the card with the layout of the Manufacturers' Building given out by the Red Wing Union Stoneware Co. for the 1907 State Fair. Red Wing industries occupied the entire building.

The potteries, as they had done at many previous fairs, built a small kiln and made the souvenir jugs on the premises. The pictured jug may have been from that or any of a number of later fairs.

State Fairs

Here is an interior view of the Manufacturers' Building from the 1923 State Fair Edition of the *Red Wing Daily Republican.* Large, specially decorated jars similar to the one on page 121 formed the focal point of the many types and sizes of stoneware in the display.

"Three monster jugs, the largest ever made, are creating no end of attention at the fair. They are 70 gallons or 280 quart capacity each, and were turned out by Red Wing Union Stoneware Co."

"One of these jugs is at the Minneapolis entrance to the fairgrounds, another at the St. Paul entrance and a third in the Red Wing building. The jugs are as tall as a man and three men can easily stand up inside of each one." (The 1890's Union catalog had offered turned jugs up to 30 gallons to the trade on special order in salt-glaze with stenciling. A shard of one of these has been found with a handle as thick as a man's wrist.)

Two ounce (one-eighth pint) cone top souvenirs and a very rare one ounce bottle with a wing!

The jug with the oval has a tiny wing on the back, the same size as on the bottle above.

Three more 2 ounce souvenir jugs. The ovoid shaped one is likely from the 1920's.

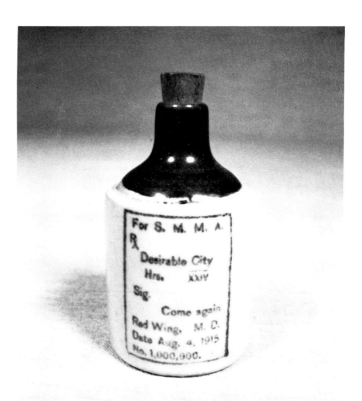

A 2 ounce shoulder jug, souvenir of the Southern Minnesota Medical Association convention in 1915.

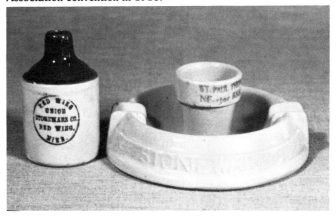

A local liquor bottle with a screw-in stopper. The size was not recorded when photo was taken but it is larger than 2 ounces, maybe one-half pint.

Here is a more modern suitcase; the stamp is the same one used on the bottle on the previous page.

It is not often that an oddity like this double marked 5 gallon jar is found; a collector's dream.

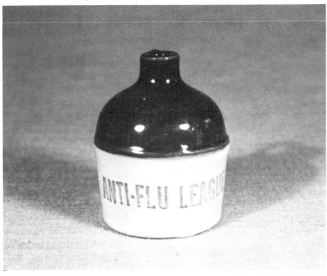

The button handle lids were replaced by a style with a bar handle. This one, marked with a wing, reveals that the old style lasted until at least 1912.

The 2 ounce fancy jug at center left might have been made in the winter of 1918-19 when a flu epidemic struck Red Wing. Schools were closed and public gatherings forbidden; 31 deaths occurred.

Most butter jars were unsigned. Around 1920 Jefferson elementary school sixth grader David Tefft received 10 cents per hundred for fettling the rough edges of these jars as they came from the molds. He could do 300 in his 4 hour shift.

RED WING — "The Jars With Handles"

How Easy to Carry !

Sizes

4, 5 and 6

8, 10 and 12

15, 20

25 and 30

Gallons

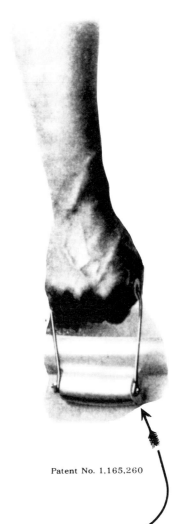

Patent No. 1,165,260

Note the BOLT

An Exclusive Red Wing Feature

On December 21, 1915 E.S. Hoyt, RWUSCo. President, received a patent for the invention of securing a handle to a stoneware jar by means of a lug of clay through which passed a bolt. The use of applied "ear" handles had been eliminated and for a number of years jars with handles were unavailable. The patent date was stamped on or near the lug of one of the handles on jars for the rest of the stoneware production years. A few rare examples have been found with a "Patent Applied For" stamp. These had to have been made between August and December of 1915.

Red Wing Bailed Line

JARS—WITH BAILED SIDE HANDLES

4 gallon size with galvanized steel wire handles.

5, 6, 8, 10, 12, 15, 20, 25, 30 gallon with galvanized wire and pail wood handles.

(Note lugs and bolts on larger sizes—a distinctive Red Wing Feature.)

CHURNS—WITH BAILED SIDE HANDLES

Sizes 2, 3, 4, 5, 6 gallon with galvanized steel wire handles.

WATER COOLERS AND COVERS

Sizes 2, 3, 4, 5, 6, 8 and 10 gallon.

No. 1 Covers for Jars sizes ½ to 12 gallon.

No. 2 Covers for Jars sizes 15 to 60 gallon (note wire handles).

Nos. 3 to 10 High Butter Jars sizes ¼ to 6 gallon.

Nos. 11 to 20 Large Jars sizes 8 to 60 gallon (full measure).

Outside Measurements (diameter under rim)

¼ gallon jars.	4⅜ inches	5¼ inches in height
½ " "	5 9/16 "	6¼ " " "
1 " "	7⅞ "	8⅜ " " "
2 " "	9⅛ "	10⅛ " " "
3 " "	10 1/16 "	10¾ " " "

Outside Measurements (diameter under rim)

4 gallon jars	11⅛ inches	12 inches in height
5 " "	12 "	12¾ " " "
6 " "	12 "	14¾ " " "
8 " "	13½ "	15⅞ " " "
10 " "	14½ "	16¼ " " "
12 " "	16⅛ "	16¾ " " "
15 " "	17¼ "	18⅛ " " "
20 " "	18¾ "	20 " " "
25 " "	18¾ "	24½ " " "
30 " "	20⅜ "	24¾ " " "
40 " "	21⅜ "	30 " " "
50 " "	22½ "	33⅞ " " "
60 " "	24 "	34 " " "

The RED WING LINE

THE CELEBRATED RED WING JUGS

No. 21 Cone top, light and dark glaze ½, 1 and 2 gallon.
No. 22 Round top turned shape, light and dark glaze 2, 4 and 16 oz. and ¼, ½, 1 and 2 gal.
No. 23 Dark top shoulder jugs ¼, ½, 1 and 2 gallon.
No. 24 White glazed shoulder jugs 3, 4 and 5 gallon.
No. 25 Dark top shoulder syrup jugs with lip ½, 1 and 2 gallon.
No. 26 Fruit jugs, 2¼" corkage ¼, ½, 1 and 2 gallon.
No. 27 Bailed fruit jugs, 2¼" corkage ½ and 1 gallon.
No. 28 Bailed jugs, 1¼" corkage ¼, ½ and 1 gallon.
No. 29 Field or Monkey jugs 1 gallon size only.
No. 30 Dark top cone jugs, patent porcelain stopper—1 gal. size only.

We make Imperial measure jugs for Canadian trade - sizes ¼, ½, 1, 2, 3 and 5 gallon.

PRESERVING PACKAGES

No. 31 B. L. Style self sealing jar 3¼" opening ½ and 1 gallon.
No. 32 B. L. Style self sealing jar 3¼" opening 2, 3, and 5 gal. Can furnish 5 gal. size with 5" opening
No. 33 High shape wax seal jar with bail.
    Size   5 lb.   3¼" opening
    Size 10 lb.   3½" opening
    Size 20 lb.   4¾" opening
No. 34 Wax seal jar with bail 3 and 5 gal., 6" opening
No. 35 Low shape wax seal jar with bail.
    Size ½ gal.   3¾" opening.
    Size 1 gal.   4½" opening.
No. 36 Wax seal preserve jar no bail—½, 1 and 2 gal. 3½" opening.

The RED WING LINE

138

No. 37 Boston Bean Pots ¼, ½, 1 and 2 gallon.
Nos. 38 and 39 Bailed Bean Pots ¼, ½ and 1 gallon.
No. 40 Individual Bean Pot, dark glazed 6 and 9 ounce.
No. 41 Nappies or Baking Pans, blue tint 8, 9 and 10" in diameter.
No. 42 Salad or Shoulder Mixing Bowls, blue tint 6, 7, 8, 9, 10, 11 and 12" in diameter.
No. 43 Blue Mottled Mixing Bowls 6, 7, 8, 9, 10 and 11" in diameter.
No. 44 Blue Band Mixing Bowls— 5, 6, 7, 8, 9, 10 and 11" in diameter.
No. 45 Bowls— Size 1 pint and 1 quart.
No. 46 Small Pans— ½, 1 and 2 pint.
No. 47 Milk Pans— ½, 1, 1½, 2 and 3 gallon.

No. 48 Covered Meat Roasters—11 and 13" diameter.
No. 49 Bailed Stew Pans—½, 1 and 1½ gallon.
Nos. 50 and 51 Refrigerator Jars, bailed— 3 and 5 pound.
No. 52 Egg Beater Jar—4½" in diameter, 6" in height.
No. 53 Beer Mugs 12 ounce capacity.
No. 54 Pie Plates 9" in diameter.
No. 55 Pitchers, blue tint— 2, 4 and 5 pint.

CASSEROLES, OR COVERED BAKING DISHES

No. 56 4½" capacity ½ pint.		
No. 57 5½" " 1½ "		
No. 58 7" " 3 "		
No. 59 8" " 4 "		

Nos. 60 and 61 General Utility Hospital Jar, capacity 2 gallon.

Nos. 62 and 63 Hot Water Bottles or Bed Warmers with or without knit covers, capacity 3 quarts.

No. 64 Red Wing Pattern Combinettes blue tint.

No. 65 Red Wing Pattern Combinettes—white.

No. 66 Lily Pattern Combinettes.

No. 67 Ewers and Basins—blue tint.

No. 68 Chambers blue band, 7 and 9" with or without covers.

No. 69 Dark Glazed Cuspidors—6, 7½ and 10" across the top.

No. 70 Removable Top Spittoons 12" in diameter.

The
RED WING
LINE

140

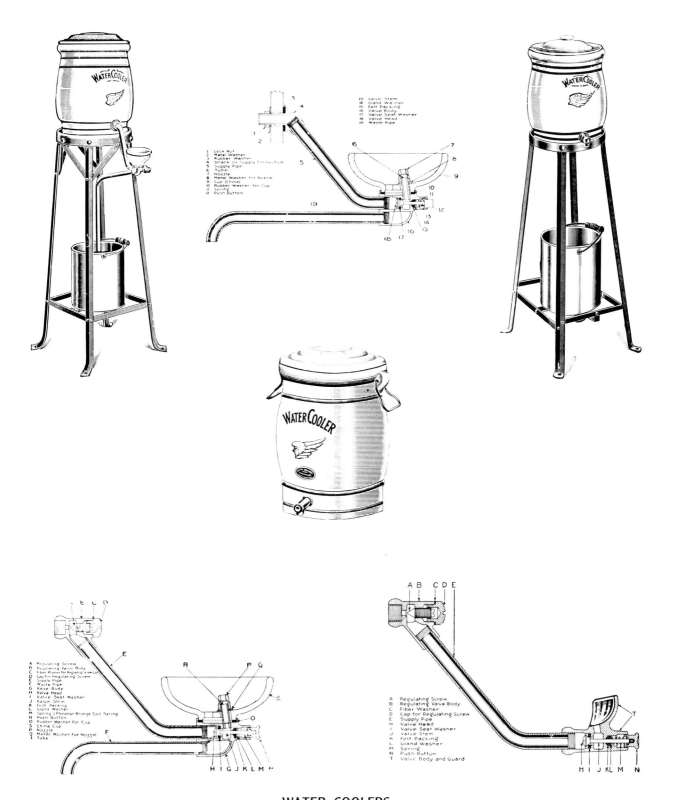

WATER COOLERS

Equipped with Bubbling Founts, for use in Schools

141

No. 71 Cut Flower Jars—red brown glaze.

Diameter	Height—Outside Measurement
7½"	14 "
8¼"	17½"
9¾"	20½"

No. 72 Cut Flower Jar, with handle—5½" in diameter 10" in height.

No. 73 Cut Flower Jar, no handle—5½" in diameter, 10" in height.

No. 74 Umbrella Stand—blue and brown mottled.

No. 75 Porch Pots—with or without saucers, 13 and 15" across the top.

Nos. 76, 77 and 78 Standard Flower Pots, with or without saucers—See list for sizes. (Page 12)

No. 79 Azalea Pots—see list for sizes. (Page 12)

No. 80 Bulb Pots or Pans—see list for sizes. (Page 12)

No. 81 Cemetery Pots, unglazed bisque body, glazed white vitreous body.

No. 82, 83 and 84 Jardinieres—Style 200, red brown glaze, 5, 7 and 9" in diameter across the top.

Nos. 85, 86 and 87 Jardinieres—Style 300, red brown glaze, 5, 7 and 9" in diameter across the top.

No. 88 Hanging Baskets—unglazed bisque body, with or without chains, sizes 8, 10 and 12" in diameter across the top

Nos. 89 and 90 Success Filters best gravity filter made, sold over 60,000 4 and 10 gallons. 10 gallon size has three blocks.

No. 91 Water Coolers sanitary, attractive, white glaze, blue band, (note handle) 2, 3, 4, 5, 6, 8 and 10 gallon. Nickel plated self closing faucets.

No. 92 Red Wing Self Draining Jar 5 and 10 gallon only.

No. 93 Red Wing Self Draining Jar with or without covers, 15, 20, 25, 30, 40, 50 and 60 gallons.

No. 94 Laboratory or Syrup Jar—with faucet opening on side near bottom, with or without covers, 12, 15, 20, 25, 30, 40, 50 and 60 gallons.

No. 95 Same as above with overflow under rim.

Self draining and syrup jars unless otherwise ordered will be equipped with 1" opening.

143

Low Butter Jars and Chicken Drinking Founts

Sanitary Fount—Sizes ½, 1 and 2 gallon.   Eureka Founts—Sizes ½, 1 and 2 gallon.

Red Wing Sanitary Steam Table Jars and Coffee Urn Linings
Bristol White Glaze—Vitreous Body—Standard Sizes

Style A	Steam Table Jar	size 5 inch		Style F	Steam Table Jar	size 9 inch
" B	" " "	" 6 "		" G	" " "	" 10 "
" C	" " "	" 6¾ "		" H	" " "	" 10½ "
" D	" " "	" 8 "		" I	" " "	" 12 "
" E	" " "	" 8½ "				

Size denotes diameter of opening in Steam Table

Coffee Urn Linings, sizes 2, 3, 4, 5, 6, 8, 10 gallon. Opening in bottom 1¾ inches.

MR. MERCHANT:

Mere words count for nothing.

But behind our words is a keen desire and demonstrated ability to look after your requirements in exactly the way you expect.

Our business was founded over forty years ago with the idea that we would make a high grade product and render a distinctive service to the merchants who handle same.

This has always been, and still is, our aim. We fill your orders promptly, carefully, intelligently---that's the kind of service we are giving other merchants. That's the kind of service we offer you.

| Large Production is the basis of satisfactory Service. |

FACTORY-R

FACTORY-M

AMERICA'S GREATEST STONEWARE POTTERIES

RED WING UNION STONEWARE CO.

RED WING, MINNESOTA

HANG ME IN A PROMINENT PLACE FOR REFERENCE

Use the selling price sheet—you will find it both convenient and valuable.

Because of the information in the second paragraph above, "Our business was founded over forty years ago . . . ," we would date this advertisement to right around 1920. This was intended to be a wall hanging catalog like a calendar; it was produced by Red Wing Advertising Co. The backs of the illustrated pages were printed with hints and recipes headed, "Keep it in Stoneware" and the final pages contained an order list but, alas, no prices.

1

5

2

6

7

3

8   9

4   10   11

Here is a study of the ovals used on RWUSCo. winged jars. Numbers 1 through 4 are the "large ovals," 2⅞ in. wide. No. 1, "the ski oval," was also used on leaf decorated ware. Nos. 2 through 4 are not found on bail handled jars, so must date 1909-15. Ovals 5 through 7 are 2¼ in. wide and are all found on hand turned jugs, so all started before 1917-18. Number 7 is so prominent that we call it the "standard oval." No. 8 is 1-11/16 in. and is seen on pieces with smaller than usual wings, which figure to date from the 1930's. There is also a 2¼ in. version of No. 8, of similar age. In collectors' parlance, Nos. 9, 10 and 11 are called "round ovals"; they originated on artware in the 1920's-30's.

We've still not found an example of the 2¼ in. version of oval number 8 on a 2 gallon jar, so we've used one of the unusual "oval-over" varieties to make up an even dozen. The "standard oval" is the one most often seen swapped in position with the wing, but oval No. 6 has also been seen. The wings on the earliest jars were 4⅛. It shrunk to 2¼ and even 1⅝ in later years, as the uranium oxide used to make the reddish-brown color became more expensive in the years prior to WWII. Yes, the wings are radioactive; so is much yellow and red glazed dinnerware and art pottery from the 1930's. The quest for variety can be continued to encompass the odd trio below, missing ovals or even wings.

147

Most of the smaller shoulder jugs produced in the RWUSCo. days had no maker's identification whatsoever. A few, like these, were fancied up with a wing. Because of their scarcity it would be assumed that they weren't made for a great period of time. The wing sizes are always as shown here which leads us to date them in the mid to late 1920's.

One gallon jars with wings are even scarcer than the brown top jugs, but apparently they were made over a span of time. They must have been made special, either by managerial decree or decorator's whim.

A one gallon fancy jug and a two gallon ball lock jar with wings.

What is it? It's a thermos jug liner. Glazed inside and bisque outside, one and two gallon sizes usually. Made by Red Wing and probably several other potteries, they are usually not signed because they were made on contract for the thermos manufacturer.

148

Red Wing Beater Jars were first shown with a single blue band. This signed style was not shown in the literature until later, but the thin, runny glaze often seen on them suggests that they were made early-on as well.

The salad bowls are called "Greek Key" bowls for the classic pattern on their side. They are done in a new glaze style: blue and gray. Light blue was fogged in a band around the top and bottom using a spraygun. These were offered in 7 sizes, 6 through 12 inch.

Two styles of handles can be discerned on the popular mugs; the one on the left looks handmade. The mugs were ultimately offered in 3 sizes.

The short refrigerator jars were made to stack one upon the other in the ice box. The bottoms are stepped to fit inside the rim of the jar below it.

The bean pot began to take on a more modern look; molded, with two-tone glaze. The lids have a "B" on the button.

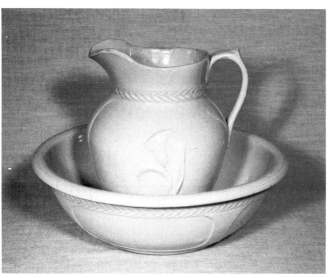

The blue tint Ewer and Basin (bowl and pitcher) has a molded flower to match the "Lily Combinette." This combinette is derived from the one shown on page 124; the flower is changed and now the lid has a less fragile and easier to manufacture bar instead of an applied "suitcase handle." Strangely, the combinette, although apparently related to the pitcher, was never offered in blue tint.

Here are two stoneware hot water bottle bed warmers. The triangular cross sectioned one below is most frequently found. Molded into the bottom is the admonition, "Do not place on hot stove." The style at right is most often seen in brown, is not advertised, but is signed with a circle stamp.

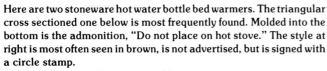

Daisy decor and basket weave canisters and butter pails were shown in 3 sizes in a circa 1915 catalog. They have been found in blue and gray, brown and gray and all white. No signed specimens have been reported.

The "Cherry Band" pitchers are another Red Wing product that have been widely treasured and collected for years with no knowledge of their origin. They are usually in blue tint; a few notable examples are shown here. They are never signed.

Left pitcher is all white; Right is amber with green tint.

August Becker was a Red Wing grocer who believed in promotion. He commissioned these all-white pitchers with an unusual, dated pictorial stamp.

Here is a little pitcher very much like the mug on page 120. This one is in pale yellow with dark green tint. Bottom signed with a RWUSCo. circle stamp.

The Peterson Co. of Winona, Minnesota, used these red and blue mottled cherry band pitchers to advertise their grocery store.

151

The "Dutch Boy and Girl" pitchers are another mystery, they are not shown in any of the known literature and they are unlike anything else that was made at Red Wing. They are highly traditional, the blue and white decoration style comes from Delft pottery of Holland. For some reason they were not produced for long. Consequently they are quite rare. The second tallest one above was done in dark amber and green.

The 20 lb. butter jar became the only one to be customarily signed. And, oh, what a signature! A special stamp was made for it alone.

This curiosity is the same diameter as a 5 gallon jar. It is, however, only 7-1/4" tall. It must have been intended to be a butter jar. Complete with handles it must have proved too costly for continued production.

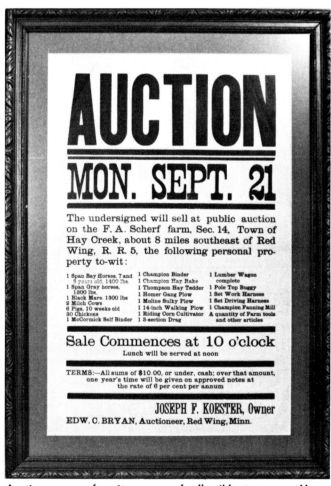

Auctions are our favorite sources of collectible stoneware. Almost every farm auction offers a few "old crocks and jugs," usually under the heading of "lots of other items." Here is an auction bill from 1908. Joseph Koester was my grandfather on my mother's side.

Multiple gallon sized jars with advertising are rare. The company had a strange habit of separating city and state with a hyphen as well as a comma.

Steam table inserts for restaurant or cafeteria use.

This insert must have had some type of hinged lid that fit to the lug on the side. Possibly a chocolate pot.

An uncommon beehive jug with advertising.

AFTER YOU READ THIS FOLDER, TURN

A Noteworthy Characteristic of the RED WING LINE, from a merchant's standpoint, is the steady, dependable business that it insures. Any user of a single RED WING container is not only a logical prospect for others, but one favorably prejudiced in advance.

Since the modern merchant is now a salesman rather than a mere order taker, the value of customers predisposed toward the RED WING LINE is not only measured by the more rapid movement of his stock with less effort; but by the time saved in making sales which can be devoted to pushing less popular merchandise.

In a nutshell: It takes less time to sell a recognized advertised product—and time is the most valuable thing you have. Now, in answer to an appreciable demand, we are stimulating the sale of RED WING jars and crocks for home use by advertising.

Add a line of "Koverwa

RED WING UNION S

America's Greates

RED WINC

The practicability and adaptability of blue and gray pantry jars are well recognized facts. They will beautify any kitchen or pantry. They are easily cleansed or sterilized. They, because of the peculiarities of stoneware, will keep moist foods moist; dry foods dry—every home should have several.

As an added incentive, to boost your sales, we are now making a new combined cover and weight that every housewife will want at canning and pickling time. For preserving foods in brine or other solution, it automatically keeps the contents submerged—insuring uniformity in quality.

This "Koverwate" is made for 4, 5, 6, 10, 15, 20 and 25 gallon containers. It *does* save food. Recommend it! Display it! Sell it!

When you have absorbed the information on this page, this big, double page broadside wants to get to work for you. Display it well—it'll mean profit to you.

Of course you'll want a few of the new "Koverwates" in your next order. We are going to have cars moving in your direction in July, August and September and if you will sign the enclosed card—checking the time you will be ready to buy—we will have one of our salesmen see you and arrange for a pool car at a delivered price.
DO IT TODAY—WE WISH TO SERVE YOU

to your next order to the

NEWARE COMPANY
toneware Potteries
INNESOTA

BLUE and GRAY

LINE OF
PANTRY JARS

for storing:

FLOUR— KEEPS IT DRY
BREAD— KEEPS IT MOIST
CEREALS—KEEPS THEM CLEAN
COFFEE— PRESERVES FLAVOR
SPICES, SUGAR OR ANY FOOD

—AN ORNAMENT IN ANY KITCHEN

THEY are ideal containers for all foodstuffs and provisions. Because they keep bread, cookies and pastry fresher, waste due to staleness is overcome. This means that "baking days" are less frequent, and real economy results. The beauty, practical utility and cleanliness of RED WING Stoneware, make it by far, the housewives' favorite container. Its ability to promote economy in the home, by the elimination of waste thru spoilage, makes it likewise the favorite of the man of the house. Every home should have a complete equipment of types and sizes of RED WING jars, crocks and jugs.

Of the pieces that have been seen, like this complete collection, all have rather small wings. This, and the style of the advertising poster suggest that the Blue-Gray Line came from the mid to late 1920's. All of these are scarce; lids are particularly difficult to acquire because they are special having double rows of blue bands. The 4 gallon lid above has a star around the knob, it is the same as the white lid on page 66 except for the bands.

The Koverwate fit down inside a jar to hold the contents submerged to prevent contact with air. The ad did not include the 3 gallon size; conversely, 6 and 25 gallon sizes are not found.

The lid of the smallest pantry jar sits down inside the rim. This is just the right size for a sugar bowl.

157

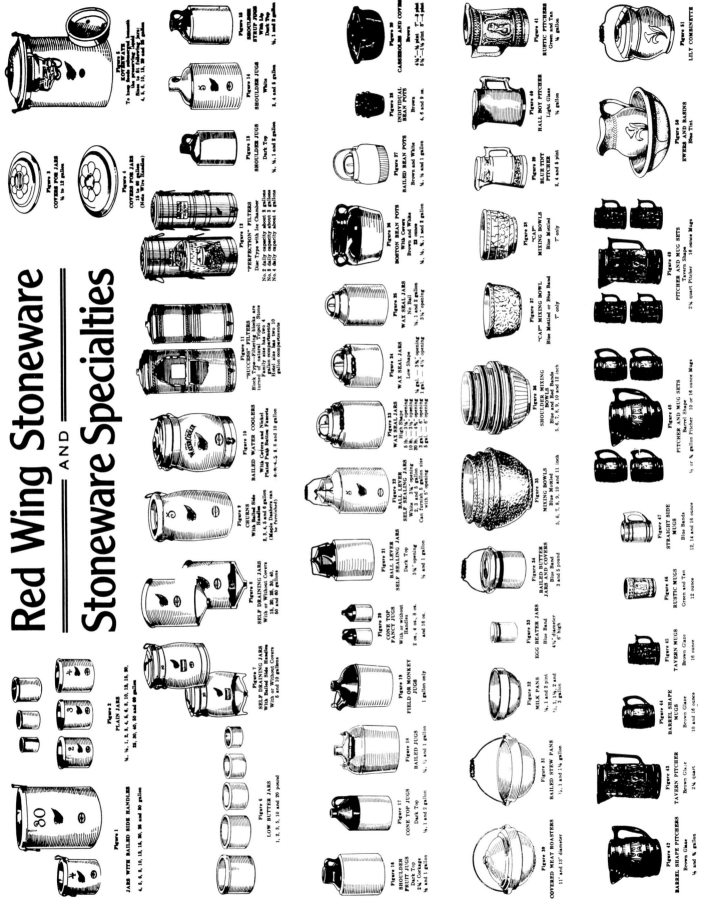

Red Wing Stoneware
AND
Stoneware Specialties

This poster, original size 23 x 35, originated around 1930. Some new items had been added and a few old ones dropped. By this time art pottery

158

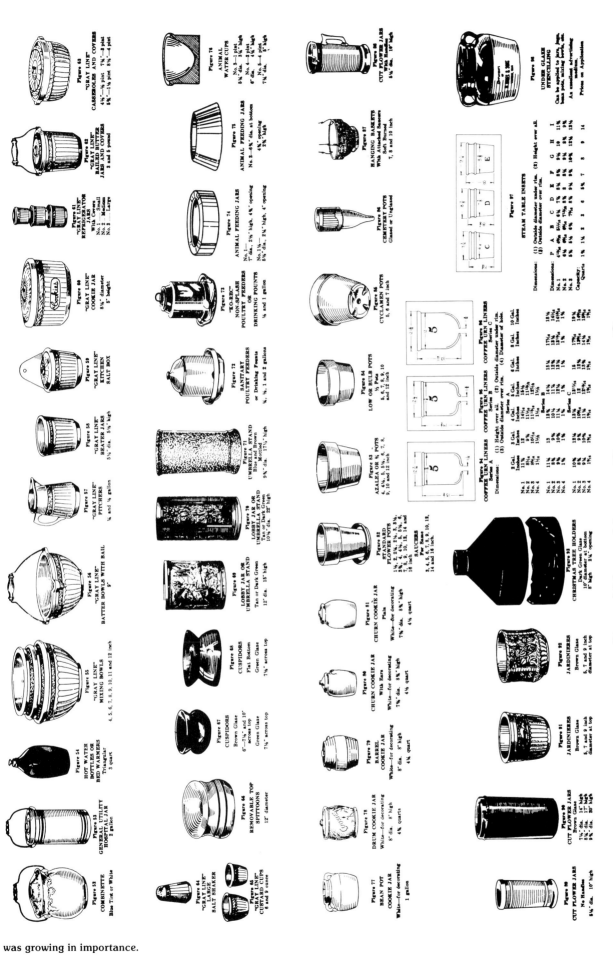

was growing in importance.

RED WING UNION STONEWARE CO.
RED WING, MINNESOTA

159

The prettiest line of kitchenware that Red Wing ever made was "Gray Line." The potteries had often referred to their white-glaze as "gray." These had a band of red daubed between two stripes of blue. The effect is breathtaking. Shown are #3 butter jar, 6 and 9 oz. custards, 1 qt. pitcher, citrus reamer, cake holder and salt shaker.

The Gray Line bailed batter bowl. The red was actually applied with a textured coggle wheel, the "sponged" pattern repeats. Gray Line was introduced in the late 1920's, lasted perhaps 10 years.

Three sizes of covered refrigerator jars. Like their plain forerunners these are made so they will stack; these stack on top of the covers.

Gray Line

The mug was the only piece not to have the "daisy petal" pattern, a theme carried from the salt-glazed lids and flower pots.

Those pieces that are signed bear this circle on their bottom.

The cake stand is the rarest piece, the hanging salt box is also tough to find and is one of the most desirable pieces.

Bowls were offered in 9 sizes, 4 through 12 inch. There were four sizes of covered casseroles, a cookie jar and a beater jar.

Another line which shared many of the same molds as Gray Line was Saffron Ware, a lower firing, yellow ware bodied line. Some pieces were unique to Saffron Ware: casserole lids, the cookie jar and pudding pan. Bean pot was like the later brown and white style.

The slight difference in height between the stoneware bodied Gray Line and the yellow ware bodied Saffron piece is due to the less dense nature of yellow ware; less vitrification/shrinkage in firing.

Another variation from these molds was blue tint. We've seen pitchers, bowls, custards, casseroles and beater jars.

Pitchers are also seen in red and blue sponged decoration. The fired clay is yellow, the overall glaze is clear. Two brown bands split by a band of white. Because it is porous earthenware, Saffron Ware is often discolored from use.

The nest of shouldered sponged bowls on the left are stoneware; on the right, Saffron. Five through ten inch diameter. Below is a rare grape decor Saffron bowl.

This casserole was apparently an experimental piece, glaze notes appear on the bottom.

161

This advertising banner is found inside a 4 inch Gray Line bowl. Bowl has "Made in Red Wing" signature on bottom. See page 121.

More August Becker advertising, this on the final style of bean pot. Banner has also been seen inside a paneled spongeware bowl.

As the demand for traditional stoneware products decreased the company willingly tried whatever way they could to create new

markets. The Christmas tree holder is one of the most notable. Those found in green, as shown on the poster, are not signed.

From the illustration on page 158, a side view, these mugs are not very memorable. But, when viewed head-on the tavern scene reveals why they were called tavern mugs.

An uncle who worked at the pottery around 1930 and later at a funeral parlor confirms that these, indeed, were crematory jars and Red Wing made them.

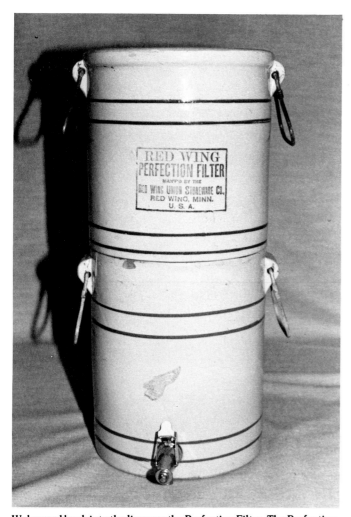

Three versions of this style "cap bowl" are: smooth sided, fluted, and patterned fluted. Molded into bottom is 7A, 7B or 7C; also, rarely, came in 5 inch diameter. Lid with steam hole converts it to a casserole.

Welcomed back into the line was the Perfection Filter. The Perfection name now implied a different filtering mechanism and different sizes. Relationship to Blue and Gray Pantry Line is obvious. This is one of the smaller sizes.

This style with raised circle pattern is not often seen. Cap bowls are sometimes signed, "Red Wing Ovenware."

The projection opposite the pouring lip on this sponged 6 inch batter bowl is a thumb hook so that you don't have to stick your thumb inside the bowl to hold it while pouring.

Red Wing
Union Stoneware
Company

America's Greatest Stoneware Potteries

Red Wing
Minnesota

The Red Wing Line is well and favorably known as it has been on the market for over fifty years. The first ware was made in 1878. The business was started in a small way with one old fashioned up-draft kiln that was fired with wood. All the ware was hand turned—the Potter and his Wheel played a prominent part in the early history of the business.

We now have two modern plants with nine large down-draft periodic kilns and one continuous car tunnel kiln for burning the product and all wares are now made by mechanical appliances.

We have built up an organization of skilled artisans who are experts in their respective lines, thus insuring quality of product.

We manufacture a complete line of:

Food Containers

Jars, 2 ounces to 60 gallon capacity. Jugs, both common and special shapes, 2 ounces to 5 gallon. Preserving jars, wax and self sealing in various sizes, also the Famous Red Wing Bailed Line of Jars with bailed side handles from 4 to 30 gallon capacity.

Kitchen Utensils

Mixing bowls, casseroles, salt shakers, fruit juice extractors, cake stands, pitchers, batter bowls, beater jars, refrigerator jars, custard cups, cookie jars, bread and cake jars.

Art Ware

Vases in various shapes, sizes and colors, jardenieres, pedestals, lamp bases, bird baths, lawn and garden pottery, beautifully designed and finished.

Flower Pots

One inch to sixteen inches in diameter, both plain and decorated for florist and home use, also hanging baskets and cemetery pots.

Restaurant and Hotel Equipment

Steam table insets, coffee urn liners, soup and chocolate pots.

Laboratory Containers

For bottlers and chemical use, including the well known Red Wing Self Draining jars from 5 to 60 gallon capacity.

Special Ware

We are equipped to make clay containers in special sizes and shapes. Bring your problems to us and we will try to render a helpful service.

We have facilities for making 1,200 carloads per annum and carry large stocks in all departments so that we can handle your orders—be they large or small—in a manner we know will please you.

We offer you service and a quality product that we feel sure will be acceptable. We would be glad to tell you more about the wares in which you may be interested, sending illustrations and prices. If we do not serve you now it is our desire to do so. May we?

Continuous Burning Process by Car Tunnel Kiln

The train of loaded cars moves thru the tunnel, which is 385 feet long, at the rate of four and two-thirds feet per hour. It takes 81 hours for a car to make the trip thru the kiln.

A car of unburned ware is put into the charging end of the kiln and a car of burned ware is taken out at the discharging end every 90 minutes, day and night, 365 days a year.

The heat is applied midway between the ends of the tunnel, using oil for fuel. A maximum temperature of 2,390 degrees F. (Cone 9) is maintained at this point for the maturing of the clay and glaze.

Fans are used to secure a gradual increase in the temperature from the charging end up to the hottest zone at center and to secure a gradual decrease in the temperature after it passes the finishing point. By this process the ware passes from room temperature at the charging end thru increasingly hotter zones in the kiln until it reaches the finishing heat at center and then on thru gradually decreasing temperatures until it reaches the discharge end at a temperature of 180 F.

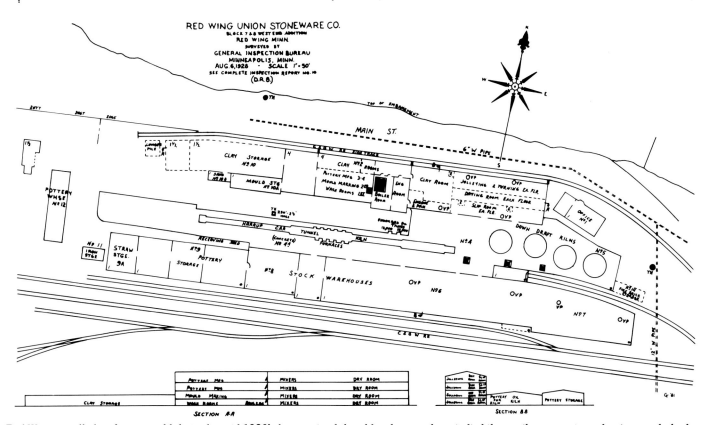

Red Wing installed its first tunnel kiln in the mid 1920's but retained the old style, round, periodic kilns until stoneware production was halted in 1947. This was likely because the efficiency advantage of the tunnel kiln did not apply to large pieces like the multiple gallon jars. This factory plan, redrawn from the original at the Minnesota Historical Society Archives Division, shows Factory M during 1928.

Red Wing Pottery

Price List – August, 1931

GLAZED WARE

PRICES—
Are as per dozen pieces, F.O.B. Red Wing, Minnesota. Crating charge on orders under $30.00.

IN ORDERING—
Specify colors wanted for each piece. Items can be furnished only in the colors noted.

SIZES GIVEN—
For jardin-iers are the diameters. For vases and all other pieces, the heights.

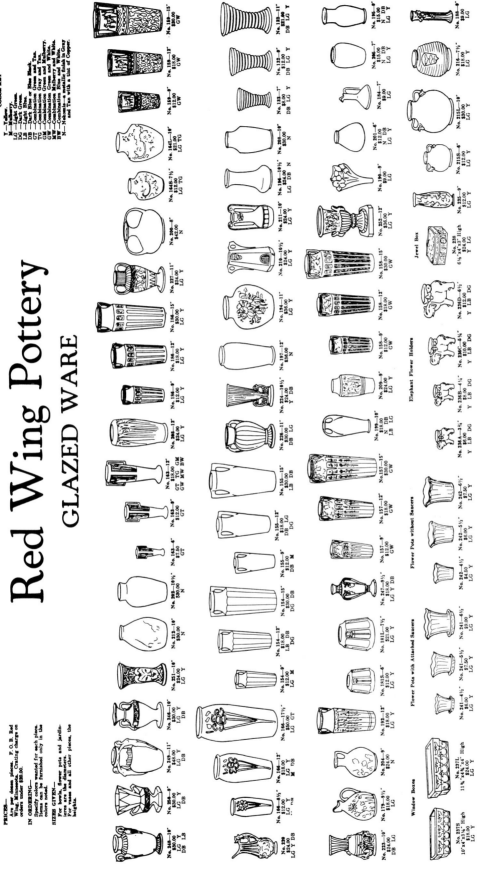

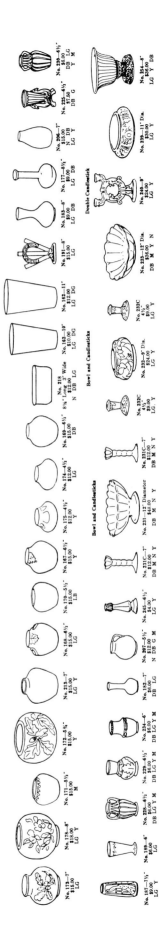

BRUSHED WARE

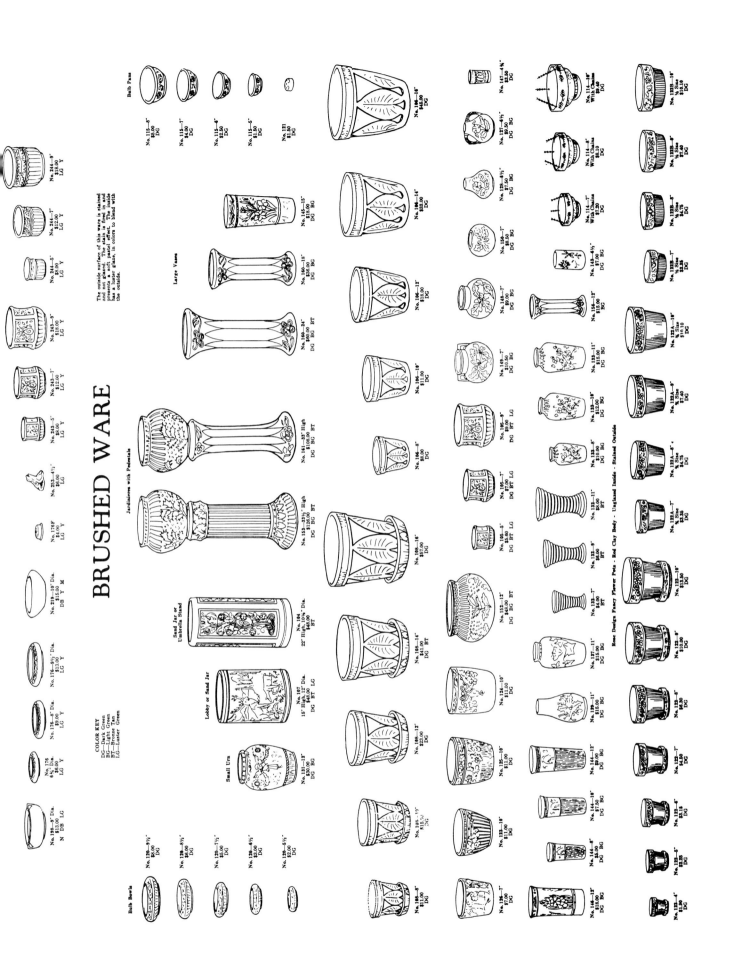

The outside surface of this ware is stained and not glazed. The stain is fired in and presents a soft pastel effect. The inside has a luster glaze, in colors to blend with the outside.

COLOR KEY
DG—Dark Green
BG—Light Green
BT—Bronze Tan
LG—Luster Green

Bulb Pans

No. 115—8"
$5.00
DG

No. 115—7"
$4.00
DG

No. 115—6"
$2.50
DG

No. 115—5"
$1.50
DG

No. 121
$1.50
DG

Large Vases

No. 142—15"
$18.00
DG BG

No. 160—18"
$26.00
DG BG

No. 160—24"
$60.00
DG BT

Jardinieres with Pedestals

No. 161—33" High
$128.00
DG BG BT

No. 153—33½" High
$60.00
DG BG BT

Sand Jar or Umbrella Stand

No. 104
22" High, 10¼" Dia.
$65.00
BT

Lobby or Sand Jar

No. 107
15" High, 12" Dia.
$65.00
DG BT LG

Small Urn

No. 131—11"
$30.00
DG BG

Bulb Bowls

No. 120—9½"
$8.00
DG

No. 120—8½"
$6.00
DG

No. 120—7½"
$5.00
DG

No. 120—6½"
$3.00
DG

No. 120—5½"
$2.00
DG

No. 244—9"
$18.00
LG Y

No. 244—7"
$12.00
LG Y

No. 244—5"
$8.00
LG Y

No. 243—9"
$18.00
LG Y

No. 243—7"
$12.00
LG Y

No. 243—5"
$8.00
LG Y

No. 253—4½"
$6.00
LG

No. 176F
$4.00
LG Y

No. 219—10" Dia.
$15.00
DB Y M

No. 176—9½" Dia.
$13.00
LG Y

No. 176
6¼" Dia.
$6.00
LG Y

No. 176—8" Dia.
$9.00
LG Y

No. 198—9" Dia.
$13.00
N DB LG

No. 106—18"
$45.00
DG

No. 106—16"
$33.00
DG BG

No. 106—12"
$18.00
DG

No. 106—10"
$11.00
DG

No. 106—8"
$8.00
DG

No. 106—16"
$57.00
DG

No. 106—16"
$41.00
DG BT

No. 106—12"
$23.00
DG

No. 106—8"
$11.00
DG

No. 133—18"
$11.00
DG

No. 106—8"
$11.00
DG

No. 147—4½"
$1.50
DG

No. 127—4½"
$2.50
DG BG

No. 128—4½"
$7.50
DG BG

No. 150—7"
$3.50
DG BG

No. 145—7"
$9.00
DG BG

No. 149—10½"
$10.50
DG BG

No. 105—9"
$9.00
DG BT LG

No. 105—7"
$7.00
DG BT LG

No. 105—6"
$5.60
DG BT LG

No. 153—12"
$45.00
DG BG

No. 137—11"
$15.00
DG BG

No. 124—10"
$11.00
DG

No. 125—10"
$11.00
DG

No. 144—12"
$7.50
DG BG

No. 144—18"
$15.00
DG BG

No. 146—18"
$18.00
DG

No. 114—4½"
With Chains
$9.40
DG

No. 114—4½"
With Chains
$7.40
DG

No. 114—4½"
With Chains
$7.20
DG

No. 155—12"
$16.00
DG BG

No. 133—11"
$16.00
DG BG

No. 133—18"
$12.00
DG BG

No. 133—6"
$10.00
DG

No. 133—11"
$8.00
BT

No. 133—9"
$6.00
BT

No. 133—7"
$4.00
BT

No. 132—18"
$10.10
DG

No. 132B—7"
$7.60
DG

No. 132B—6"
$4.75
DG

No. 132B—4½"
$7.40
DG

No. 132A—10"
$10.10
DG

No. 132A—8"
$7.40
DG

No. 132A—6"
$4.75
DG

No. 132A—5"
$3.35
DG

Rose Design Fancy Flower Pots - Red Clay Body - Unglazed Inside - Stained Outside

No. 132—18"
$13.50
DG

No. 133—9"
$10.00
DG

No. 133—8"
$6.30
DG

No. 133—7"
$4.50
DG BG

No. 123—18"
$9.15
DG

No. 123—6"
$2.25
DG

No. 123—4"
$1.90
DG

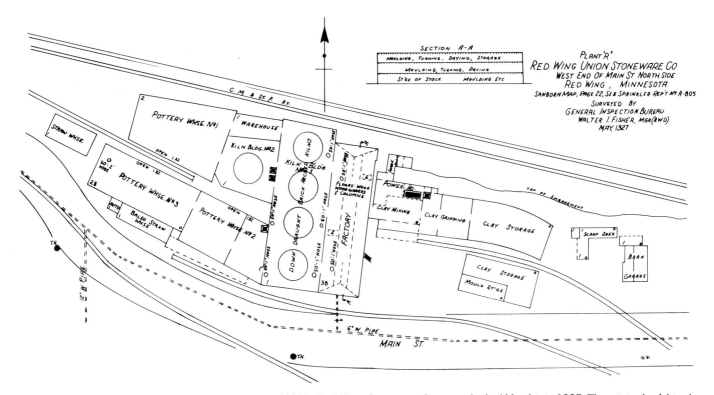

Factory R, the wooden, three story building erected in 1900 by Red Wing Stoneware Company looked like this in 1927. The originals of this plan, held by the Minnesota Historical Society Archives Division, were made to show the fire protection measures of the buildings. The main factory building was the only one equipped with sprinklers.

At right is a loving cup awarded to the Red Wing Union Stoneware Company for having the best exhibit at the 1932 Minnesota Industrial Exposition.　　　Goodhue County Historical Society collection

Below is a view of the office and part of Factory M in the 1930's (note the art pottery displayed in the office window). Except for the chimneys which serviced the old round kilns the view is essentially preserved today.

By now the daisy petal scalloped flower pots had been retired, replaced by fancy molded ones like this above and plain, red clay

pots as on page 142. Below are jardinieres in matte brushed and glossy green.

Two styles of "Rustic Pitcher." These were advertised on pg. 158 in green and in tan; the ones here had a green stain partially brushed away and covered with a clear gloss. When the molds for these pitchers and especially the mugs were worn, the lady holding the lyre can be mistaken for a monk raising a cup to drink. They have been mistakenly called "Monk Mugs."

A gorgeous, covered breadbox. These were done in the brushed, matte green and brushed, glossy green like this one. All are white inside. As big around as a 5 or 6 gallon jar. One of the primary uses of the orignal covered jars was to store bread; this beauty with its "sheaves of wheat" decor could do the job in style.

Derivations of the Cleveland vase lived on into the 1930's, now in brushed ware and even in glazed art pottery. The insides are a glossy green or sometimes blue-green to make them water tight.

One of the marks of "good art" in art pottery is how well the style of the glaze or coloration complements the other elements of the design. The "cat-tails" vases and lamp bases exemplify the ability of these properly executed features to set a mood.

Most of the brushed ware designs were natural or floral subjects. The brushed, matte stain was perfectly, though unexcitingly, in tune with the theme.

Brushed Ware was introduced in the early to mid 1920's and though popular with the florist trade was considered dreary. Glazed art pottery was more spritely, as this "dancing nudes" vase will witness.

The "lion vase" was made in two sizes and at least two glazes: light green as seen here and a blend of bluish greens. The advertising poster says that it also came in blended tan and gray.

This "Egyptian" vase is done in a blue so rich that it appears black except in the strongest light.

A goblet shaped vase. The styles shown here do not reflect the garish or gaudy, overdone styles that unfortunately are part of the trade in commercial art pottery.

Nokomis Ware

A particular style of semi-matte glaze in variegated tones of tan and olive with highlights of copper was called Nokomis. This glaze was customarily limited to a handful of styles; occasionally it will show up on a piece not known to be in the Nokomis line such as the elephant planter. The lion vase on the previous page, when done in the two-tone blended glaze is often mistakenly reported as Nokomis, but none in the true Nokomis have been seen.

———————— 0 ————————

More souvenir jugs; from left to right: commemorating the convention of the Improved Order of Red Men, August 7 & 8, 1927; souvenirs of the state convention of the Elks in 1929 and the Moose Lodge in 1930. The Minnesota 14th Joint Postal Convention jug from 1939 and the Egyptian bottle both bear embossed and printed foil stickers declaring, "Red Wing Art Pottery" and finally the two ounce fancy jug with the unusual "Red Wing Potteries" signature around a star. This signature should be ample evidence that other potteries than North Star used a star in their signature.

The Minnesota-Michigan "little brown jug" college football rivalry dates back to 1903 when the visiting Michigan team left behind a water jug which they had purchased just prior to the game to supply the team with water for refreshment. The Minnesota team challenged Michigan to return to play for possession of the jug which has since become a traveling trophy.

The jug, though neither little nor brown, is probably a 5 gallon, white-glazed Red Wing beehive. We say probably because it is now painted blue and maroon, the two schools' colors. A duplicate jug which resides permanently at the University of Minnesota on careful examination reveals the outline of a wing beneath the paint.

Here are some two ounce souvenirs and a metal badge on a pin which came stuck in the cork of one of these jugs at the 1934 "Little Brown Jug" game. Versions of the souvenir with Minnesota getting top billing were also made, apparently for sale on the "home" side of the stadium. Another version lists the scores of three previous years' contests.

172

Because of the covered wagon, airplane, locomotive and automobile depicted on this set, they are called the "Transportation" pitcher and mugs. The motif actually is symbolic of the theme of the 1933 Chicago World's Fair — "Century of Progress." They are signed with a small circle "Red Wing Potteries, Red Wing, Minn." Though the company name change did not take place until 1936 they referred to themselves in that way earlier.

Barrel shaped pitchers and mugs were made by numerous potteries usually in brown or green; most are unsigned. This white one has a "Made in Red Wing" signature like the one used on Gray Line. The mug has "Gluek Brewing Co." stamped on the bottom in blue.

The "Happy Days Are Here Again" theme would suggest an end of Prohibition, 1933 date for the introduction of this mug.

The ball lock applesauce jar evolved into a two-toned, round shouldered form just before the 1936 company name change. The 5 gallon on the left and the 3 gallon in the center are missing their wings entirely. Wing is small and faint on the 5 gallon on the right.

Red Wing Potteries 1936-1967

When the officers and directors of the Red Wing Union Stoneware Company held their annual meeting in January of 1936, a decision was made to change the name of the company to the Red Wing Potteries, Incorporated. During the preceding year they had introduced their first non-experimental dinnerware patterns, solid color place settings and serving pieces ultimately in four style shapes known collectively as Gypsy Trail.

Art pottery had become much more important to the product line. An extensive quantity of styles marketed by George Rumrill and designed by his wife were produced under the Rumrill signature beginning in 1933. A June, 1933 catalog was titled, "Red Wing Potteries; Red Wing, Minnesota; Manufacturers of RumRill Art Pottery." The relationship with the Rumrills lasted until 1938; many of the designs were continued under the Red Wing signature.

It was for these reasons that the company name had been changed, "stoneware company" no longer represented what they were about. Old building floorplans on file at the Minnesota Historical Society Archives Division show that only one half of the first floor of factory M was devoted to stoneware early in 1947. A plan from later in the year shows that this had then been rearranged and the last of the round, downdraft kilns removed; utilitarian stoneware was no longer being produced. Extensive study of the art pottery or dinnerware lines is beyond the scope of this book.

Later, starting in 1953, a wing ash tray in rich red was produced. The first of these were signed "Red Wing Pottery; 75th; 1878-1953; Anniversary" on the bottom. No collection is complete without one.

The "Pretty Red Wing" ash tray was supposedly a prototype for the 75th Anniversary piece rejected as being too risque . . . the maiden appears to be topless. It was once believed that only six of these were made. We know this to be false because we have seen six in southeast Wisconsin alone.

When asked if you would like a refill you had only to raise your mug which said, "Certainly, the Peterson Co." Mugs flank a 2 gallon Red Wing Potteries, Inc. water cooler.

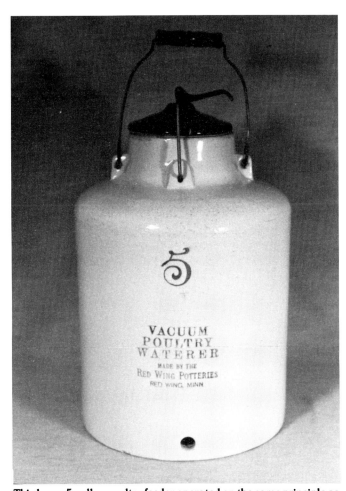

This huge, 5 gallon poultry feeder operated on the same principle as the old, dome top feeders, but it had the advantage of being fillable from the top. It originally had a giant saucer to stand in.

We briefly believed that it was a Michigan wolverine on the center souvenir in the upper photo above. It's the Wisconsin badger; another football rival. The Minnesota gopher was also placed on the stump toothpick holder. (The left to right order between top and bottom views is shuffled.)

175

Here is a collection of souvenir ash trays created by Stenwick. Andy's Pottery Shop and Red Wing Trading Post, which operated at the corner of 7th and Plum Streets in Red Wing between the years 1938-42, retailed these for Albert. The Pottery Shop carried a large selection of artware and had a lifesize polychrome wooden Indian, carved by Stenwick, guarding the door.

An ashtray very similar to the one at upper right in the photo at left, is shown on pg. 93a in the color section with a Red Wing Potteries trademark.

Albert O. Stenwick

On pages 88-89 we presented sculptural pieces made by potter Albert Olson at the turn of the century. Olson later changed his name to Albert O. Stenwick, reportedly because being in Minnesota, there were too many Olsons in town. Support for this is demonstrated in the 1894 city directory which listed nearly 90 Olsons.

He left Red Wing shortly after the turn of the century to study art and sculpture and worked for many years upon his return as a carpenter. Just prior to WWII, he returned to the pot shops as a model maker, an occupation for which he had a well developed talent.

A bust of his daughter Fern done in 1948.

Indian chief and squaw figurines in plaster, signed on the back of the bases.

Appendix

Newspaper References to Red Wing Clay Industry

Here is an index of newspaper references to the pottery industry in Red Wing. Transcribed copies of the complete articles have been placed on file at the Goodhue County Historical Society Museum in Red Wing. They have been collected in our research into the clay industry's history. Scanning this index alone gives a flavor of the events and concerns of the day as they unfolded; the articles themselves provide a warm bond with the past and those who lived it.

Mallory has plans for the new works)
Red Wing Advance   Wed., Sept. 19, 1883
"Red Wing and Vicinity" (manufacture of pottery here is very profitable)
Red Wing Republican   Sat., Sept. 29, 1883
"Our Fair" (about MSCo.'s display at the fair)
Red Wing Advance   Wed., Oct. 10, 1883
"Local Layout" (RWSCo. establishes headquarters in St. Paul)
Red Wing Republican   Sat., Nov. 3, 1883
"Local Squibs" (more on RWSCo.'s warehouse in St. Paul)
Red Wing Advance   Wed., Nov. 14, 1883
"The New Stoneware Works" (MSCo. beings production)
Red Wing Republican   Sat., Jan. 5, 1884
"The Mallory Cooler" (milk cooler patented by T.H. Mallory and made by MSCo.)
Red Wing Republican   Sat., Jan. 26, 1884
"Stockholders Meeting" (RWSCo. stockholders to meet)
Red Wing Republican   Sat., Feb. 2, 1884
"Manufacturing Corporations" (about RWSCo. and MSCo.)
"Statistical" (about RWSCo. and MSCo.)
Red Wing Republican   Sat., Feb. 9, 1884
"Short Locals" (notice of RWSCo. meeting)
Red Wing Sun   Thurs., Feb. 14, 1884
"The Red Wing Stoneware Co." and "Sunbeams" (report of RWSCo.'s annual meeting)
Red Wing Advance   Wed., Feb. 20, 1884
"The Fire Fiend" (fire at RWSCo.)
Red Wing Argus   Thurs., Feb. 21, 1884
Red Wing Sun   Thurs., Feb. 21, 1884
"Local Brevities and Personals" (city council votes to extend water mains to MSCo.)
"Another Disastrous Fire" (fire at RWSCo.)
Red Wing Republican   Sat., Feb. 23, 1884
"Localities" (RWSCo. will rebuild on a larger scale)
Red Wing Argus   Thurs., Feb. 28, 1884
"Local Brevities and Personals" (RWSCo. stockholders vote to rebuild at once)
Red Wing Sun   Thurs., Feb. 28, 1884
"Sunbeams" (about RWSCo. rebuilding)
"Articles of Association of the Red Wing Stoneware Co."
Red Wing Republican   Sat., March 1, 1884
"City Fathers" (6" water main to be laid to MSCo.)
"Localities" (talk of a drain pipe or stoneware company being formed)
Red Wing Sun   Thurs., March 6, 1884
"Sunlights" (new plans for RWSCo. completed)
Red Wing Sun   Thurs., March 13, 1884
"Sunlights" (speculation of a pottery being built by eastern people)
Red Wing Argus   Thurs., March 20, 1884
"Local Brevities and Personals" (building frame for RWSCo. going up)
Red Wing Sun   Thurs., March 20, 1884
"Sunlights" (work on RWSCo. progessing rapidly)
Red Wing Argus   Thurs., March 27, 1884
"Local Brevities and Personals" (J.H. Rich returns from Akron where he purchased machinery)
Red Wing Sun   Thurs., March 27, 1884
"Sunlights" (J.H. Rich visits Akron and buys 2 carloads of stoneware)
Red Wing Argus   Thurs., April 3, 1884
Red Wing Sun   Thurs., April 3, 1884
(working progressing rapidly at RWSCo.)
Red Wing Republican   Sat., April 4, 1884
"Localities" (Densmore Bros. repairing RWSCo.'s engine)
Red Wing Sun   Thurs., April 17, 1884
"Sunlights" (RWSCo. buning ware supplied by MSCo.)
Red Wing Sun   Thurs., April 24, 1884
"Sunlights" (RWSCo. to have 4 kilns; MSCo. enlarging)
Red Wing Republican   Sat., April 26, 1884
"Localities" (our manufacturing corporations continue to boom)
Red Wing Sun   Thurs., May 15, 1884
"Sunlights" (Martin Wilson injured at RWSCo.)
Red Wing Republican   Sat., June 7, 1884
"Localities" (report of RWSCo.'s annual meeting)
Red Wing Sun   Thurs., June 12, 1884
"Sunlights" (RWSCo. expects to start up next month)
Red Wing Republican   Sat., June 21, 1884
"Localities" (RWSCo.'s engine tested)
Red Wing Argus   Thurs., June 26, 1884
"Local Brevities and Personals" (RWSCo. started up this morning)
Red Wing Republican   Sat., June 28, 1884
"A Model" (about the new RWSCo. factory)
Red Wing Sun   Thurs., July 3, 1884
"Sunlights" (RWSCo. started up last Thursday)

Red Wing Republican   Sat., July 5, 1884
"Notice of Stockholders Meeting" (MSCo. annual meeting)
Red Wing Sun   Thurs., July 31, 1884
"Sunlights" (report of MSCo.'s annual meeting)
Red Wing Republican   Sat., Sept. 13, 1884
"Localities" (RWSCo. ships ware down river by barge)
Red Wing Sun   Thurs., Sept. 18, 1884
"The Sun Bulletin" (ad for MSCo.)
Red Wing Sun   Thurs., Sept. 25, 1884
"Second Annual Fair" (about MSCo.'s display)
Red Wing Sun   Thurs., Oct. 2, 1884
"Sunlights" (RWSCo. building fourth kiln)
"Farmers, Take Notice" (RWSCo. has wood for sale)
Red Wing Sun   Thurs., Oct. 9, 1884
"Farmers, Attention" (RWSCo. has coal for sale)
"Sunlights" (N.K. Simmons of RWSCo. traveled thru Iowa)
Red Wing Republican   Sat., Oct. 18, 1884
"Administrator's Sale" ($1,000 worth of MSCo. stock for sale from C. Clauson estate)
Red Wing Sun   Thurs., Oct. 30, 1884
Red Wing Republican   Sat., Nov. 1, 1884
"The City of Red Wing" (early history & manufactories)
Red Wing Sun   Sat., Dec. 6, 1884
"Goodhue's Solid Citizens" (personal property tax assessments)
Red Wing Sun   Sat., Dec. 13, 1884
"Hartland, WI" (Henry English is drawing clay for the pottery)
"The City of Red Wing" (about RWSCo. and MSCo.)
"Sunlights" (about the need for a railroad)
Red Wing Sun   Sat., Dec. 27, 1884
"Sunlights" (employees give J.H. Rich a Christmas gift)
Red Wing Argus   Thurs., Jan. 1, 1885
Red Wing Sun   Sat., Jan. 3, 1885
(J.H. Rich gives a New Year's dance for employees)
Red Wing Argus   Thurs., Feb. 5, 1885
"Local Brevities and Personals" (Wm. Philleo died last Saturday)
Red Wing Sun   Sat., Feb. 21, 1885
"Sunlights" (RWSCo. shuts down, lack of coal)
Red Wing Sun   Sat., March 7, 1885
"Sunlights" (N.K. Simmons will resign from RWSCo.)
Red Wing Sun   Sat., March 14, 1885
"Sunlights" (large amounts of stoneware being shipped)
Red Wing Sun   Sat., March 21, 1885
"Sunlights" (RWSCo. putting up warehouse on the Milwaukee track)
Red Wing Sun   Sat., March 28, 1885
"Sunlights" (RWSCo. has issued a lithograph of its large works)
Red Wing Sun   Sat., May 9, 1885
"Sunlights" (MSCo. intends to build addition)
Red Wing Sun   Sat., May 30, 1885
"The Potters' Strike" (companies reduce wages and potters strike)
Red Wing Sun   Sat., June 20, 1885
"Sunlights" (RWSCo. erects clay storage shed)
Red Wing Argus   Thurs., August 27, 1885
"Local Brevities and Personals" (John Morgan of MSCo. died)
Red Wing Sun   Sat., Sept. 5, 1885
"Industrial Association Fair" (about MSCo.'s exhibit)
Red Wing Sun   Sat., Sept. 26, 1885
"Sunlights" (J.H. Rich & E.T. Mallory attend meeting of stoneware manufacturers)
Red Wing Argus   Thurs., Dec. 10, 1885
"Council Proceedings" (discussion of a fire alarm near the potteries)
Red Wing Argus   Thurs., May 13, 1886
"Local Brevities and Personals" (fire alarm put up near the potteries)
Red Wing Argus   Thurs., Dec. 16, 1886
"Local Brevities and Personals" (pool among potteries of this country ended)
Red Wing Argus   Thurs., March 10, 1887
"Council Proceedings" (discussion of a fire alarm in one of the potteries)
Red Wing Argus   Thurs., May 12, 1887
"Minnesota" (RWSCo. burns a kiln with crude coal oil)
Red Wing Argus   Thurs., June 30, 1887
"Local Brevities and Personals" (crude petroleum oil buring not successful now)
Red Wing Daily Republican   Wed., August 10, 1887
"The Local Pickup" (MSCo. to put up 80 foot addition)
Red Wing Daily Republican   Thurs., August 11, 1887
Red Wing Argus   Thurs., August 11, 1887
"The Local Pickup" (MSCo. increases capital stock from $30,000 to $50,000)
Red Wing Daily Republican   Wed., August 17, 1887
"The Local Pickup" (J.W. McChesney of MSCo. returns from selling trip)

Red Wing Argus   Thurs., August 18, 1887
"Local Brevities and Personals" (MSCo. increases capital stock)
Red Wing Daily Republican   Sat., Sept. 3, 1887
"The Local Pickup" (RWSCo. displays at Minnesota exposition)
Red Wing Daily Republican   Tues., Oct. 11, 1887
"President and Mrs. Cleveland" (about train trip thru town and gift of a vase)
Red Wing Argus   Thurs., Oct. 13, 1887
"Local Brevities and Personals" (more on the Cleveland vase)
Red Wing Daily Republican   Fri., Oct. 21, 1887
"The Local Pickup" (about MSCo.'s addition)
Red Wing Daily Republican   Fri., Oct. 28, 1887
"The Local Pickup" (MSCo.'s addition nearly completed)
Red Wing Daily Republican   Wed., Nov. 9, 1887
"The Local Pickup" (fire alarm to be placed at MSCo.)
Minneapolis Tribune   Wed., Nov. 16, 1887
(MSCo. lithograph)
Red Wing Daily Republican   Fri., Nov. 18, 1887
"The Local Pickup" (RWSCo. purchases more clay fields)
"As Others See Us" (about the *Minneapolis Tribune* article)
Red Wing Daily Republican   Mon., Nov. 21, 1887
"The Local Pickup" J.W. McChesney of RWSCo. returns from selling trip)
Red Wing Daily Republican   Thurs., Dec. 1, 1887
Red Wing Argus   Thurs., Dec. 1, 1887
(thank you from Mrs. Cleveland)
Red Wing Daily Republican   Wed., Dec. 14, 1887
"Stoneware Manufacture" (about the Red Wing potteries)
Red Wing Daily Republican   Thurs., Dec. 22, 1887
"Red Wing's Industries" (about RWSCo. and MSCo.)
Red Wing Daily Republican   Thurs., Dec. 29, 1887
"Goodhue's Prosperous Sons and Daughters" (personal property tax report)
The Advance Sun   Wed., Jan. 4, 1888
"Localities" (Engineer Stedee of MSCo. gives Tams Bixby 2 statuettes)
Red Wing Daily Republican   Thurs., Jan. 5, 1888
"The Local Pickup" (MSCo. shut down for improvements)
Red Wing Daily Republican   Wed., March 30, 1888
"The Local Pickup" (Thomas Mallory quits MSCo.)
Red Wing Argus   Thurs., April 5, 1888
"Local Brevities and Personals" (J.W. McChesney of RWSCo. returns from sales trip)
Red Wing Daily Republican   Tues., April 17, 1888
"Wanted" (teams to haul clay for RWSCo.)
The Advance Sun   Wed., April 18, 1888
"Localities" (stoneware companies short of clay; bad roads)
Red Wing Daily Republican   Wed., May 2, 1888
"The Local Pickup" (RWSCo. and MSCo. shut down; out of clay)
The Advance Sun   Wed., May 16, 1888
"Localities" (RWSCo. and MSCo. expect to resume operations this week)
Red Wing Daily Republican   Thurs., May 17, 1888
"The Local Pickup" (RWSCo. resumed today)
Red Wing Daily Republican   Wed., May 23, 1888
"The Local Pickup" (RWSCo. shut down again; lack of clay)
Red Wing Daily Republican   Fri., May 25, 1888
"The Local Pickup" (stoneware companies unable to fill orders)
The Advance Sun   Wed., June 20, 1888
"Localities" (RWSCo. shut down yesterday)
The Advance Sun   Wed., July 11, 1888
"Red Wing's Charms" (*The Globe* visits RWSCo.)
The Advance Sun   Wed., July 18, 1888
"The *Spectator's* View of Red Wing" (*Minneapolis Saturday Evening Spectator*)
The Advance Sun   Wed., August 1, 1888
"Localities" (J.W. McChesney of RWSCo. returns from sales trip)
The Advance Sun   Wed., August 15, 1888
"Localities" (RWSCo. exhibit at A.W. Pratt's store)
The Advance Sun   Wed., Sept. 12, 1888
"Localities" (RWSCo. exhibits at Minneapolis exposition)
Saturday Evening Spectator   Sat., Sept. 22, 1888
(about RWSCo. and MSCo.)
The Advance Sun   Wed., Sept. 26, 1888
"Red Wing" (F.W. Hoyt's letter about the resources of Red Wing)
The Advance Sun   Wed., Oct. 17, 1888
"Localities" (J.W. McChesney of RWSCo. home from sales trip)
The Advance Sun   Wed., Oct. 31, 1888
"Localities" (potters to give first annual ball)
The Advance Sun   Wed., Nov. 21, 1888
"Localities" (side track will be put into clay fields)
The Advance Sun   Wed., Nov. 28, 1888
"Localities" (MSCo. finishing up improvements)
The Advance Sun   Wed., Jan. 2, 1889
"The Record of a Year" (about RWSCo. and MSCo.)

The Advance Sun   Wed., Jan. 9, 1889
"Important to Red Wing" (on the growth and importance of stoneware manufacture)
The Advance Sun   Wed., Jan. 16, 1889
"Localities" (personal property tax report for RWSCo.)
The Advance Sun   Wed., Feb. 13, 1889
"Localities" (Western Terra Cotta, Tile & Brick Co. of St. Paul interested in locating in Red Wing)
The Advance Sun   Wed., March 6, 1889
"Localities" (J.W. McChesney of RWSCo. returns from sales trip)
The Advance Sun   Wed., April 3, 1889
"Localities" (Emily Willard becomes stenographer and typist for RWSCo.)
The Advance Sun   Wed., May 29, 1889
"Localities" (spur track to clay fields will not be built this season)
The Advance Sun   Wed., June 12,1889
"Localities" (Zumbrota interested in a stoneware works there)
The Advance Sun   Wed., June 19, 1889
"Localities" (MSCo. shut down Saturday for two weeks)
The Advance Sun   Wed., July 10, 1889
"Localities" (MSCo. started up after being shut for three weeks for repairs)
The Advance Sun   Wed., July 17, 1889
"Localities" (RWSCo. and MSCo. order coal from Chicago)
The Advance Sun   Wed., July 24, 1889
"Localities" (tracks to the stoneware works are in)
The Advance Sun   Wed.,August 28, 1889
"Localities" (Cleveland vase to be a prize at National Guard Rifle Association tourney)
The Advance Sun   Wed., Oct. 30, 1889
"Localities" (MSCo. preparing a catalog)
The Advance Sun   Wed., Dec. 4, 1889
"Personal Property Tax Payers" (report of personal taxes paid)
Red Wing Argus   Thurs., Dec. 5, 1889
"Local Brevities and Personals" (ad for pottery superintendent)
The Advance Sun   Wed., Jan. 1, 1890
"Red Wing — The Gem City of the Mississippi Valley" (about the town, RWSCo. and MSCo.)
Red Wing Daily Republican   Wed., Jan. 22, 1890
Red Wing Daily Republican   Fri., Jan. 24, 1890
"The Local Pickup" (potters to give second annual ball)
The Advance Sun   Wed., Jan. 29, 1890
"Localities" (report of the potters' ball)
The Advance Sun   Wed., Feb. 5, 1890
"Localities" (J.H. Rich to travel to Pacific coast; C.D. Jacobi of RWSCo. returns home)
Red Wing Daily Republican   Mon.,Feb. 17, 1890
"The Local Pickup" (J.H. Rich leaves today; J.W. McChesney of RWSCo. left for Kansas)
Red Wing Daily Republican   Tues.,April 8, 1890
The Advance Sun   Wed.,April 9, 1890
(Sheldon returns from Pacific coast)
Red Wing Daily Republican   Fri.,April 11, 1890
"The Local Pickup" (J.H. Rich has returned)
The Advance Sun   Wed., April 23, 1890
"Localities" (stoneware works doing a larger business this year)
Red Wing Daily Republican   Tues., May 27, 1890
The Advance Sun   Wed., May 28, 1890
(MSCo. to build kiln for burning fire brick)
Red Wing Daily Republican   Tues., June 3, 1890
The Advance Sun   Wed., June 4, 1890
(work is progressing on new kiln at MSCo.)
The Advance Sun   Wed., July 16, 1890
"Localities" (report on MSCo.'s annual meeting)
Red Wing Daily Republican   Wed., Oct. 15, 1890
"The Local Pickup" (MSCo. employees challenge RWSCo. employee to a squirrel hunt)
Red Wing Daily Republican   Thurs., Oct. 16, 1890
"The Match Declined" (RWSCo. declines squirrel hunt challenge)
Red Wing Daily Republican   Sat., Oct. 18, 1890
"The Local Pickup" (MSCo. will have a response on Mon.)
Red Wing Daily Republican   Mon., Oct. 20, 1890
"That Squirrel Hunt" (MSCo.'s response about the hunt)
Red Wing Daily Republican   Wed., Dec. 24, 1890
The Advance Sun   Wed., Dec. 31, 1890
(stoneware business is doing well)
Red Wing Daily Republican   Wed., Dec. 31, 1890
"In 1891" (what the Daily Republican would like to see in 1891)
"Red Wing — The Gem City of the Upper Mississippi Valley" (about the town, RWSCo. & MSCo., including lithograph and ad for MSCo.)
Red Wing Daily Republican   Mon.,Sept. 7, 1891
The Advance Sun   Wed., Sept. 9, 1891
"Death of E.T. Mallory" (manager and secretary of MSCo.)
Red Wing Daily Republican   Tues., Sept. 8, 1891

"The Local Pickup" (on the death of E.T. Mallory)
Red Wing Journal   Wed., Sept. 9, 1891
"Death of E.T. Mallory"
Red Wing Argus   Thurs., Sept. 10, 1891
"Death of Edward T. Mallory"
"City Council" (why has MSCo. been stopped from laying a spur track)
Red Wing Journal   Wed., Sept. 16, 1891
"Goodhue" (discusses trip to clay pits)
Red Wing Journal   Wed., Sept. 23, 1891
(John Rehder elected superintendent of MSCo.)
Red Wing Journal   Wed., Oct. 7, 1891
"Articles of Incorporation of the Red Wing Sewer Pipe Company"
Red Wing Journal   Wed., Oct. 14, 1891
(Red Wing Sewer Pipe Co. purchases Red Wing Wagon factory)
Red Wing Daily Republican   Sat., Dec. 5, 1891
"Here and Now" (a new enterprise is being projected)
Red Wing Journal   Wed., Dec. 9, 1891
"City Council Meeting" (complaint about RWSCo.'s buildings infringing on street)
Red Wing Daily Republican   Tues., Jan. 26, 1892
"Here and Now" (land sells for $40 an acre)
Red Wing Journal   Wed., Feb. 17, 1892
"The Pottery Business" (on the beginnings and importance of the pottery industry)
Red Wing Daily Republican   Fri., Feb. 19, 1892
"Here and Now" (new stoneware works locates on John Day farm)
Red Wing Journal   Wed., Feb. 24, 1892
(property in west Red Wing sure to increase in value)
Red Wing Daily Republican   Sat., March 5, 1892
The Advance Sun   Wed., March 9, 1892
(articles of incorporation of the new stoneware co. have been drawn up)
Red Wing Journal   Wed., March 9, 1892
(all stock for new company has been subscribed)
"Articles of Incorporation of the North Star Stoneware Company"
The Advance Sun   Wed., March 9, 1892
"The North Star" (formation of North Star Stoneware Company)
Red Wing Daily Republican   Fri., March 11, 1892
"Here and Now" (E.T. Howard will be involved in new stoneware works in Red Wing)
Red Wing Journal   Wed., March 16, 1892
(more on the formation of North Star)
Red Wing Daily Republican   Thurs., March 24, 1892
"Here and Now" (officers and directors of NSSCo. elected)
Red Wing Daily Republican   Wed., March 30, 1892
"Here and Now" (H.C. Misener preparing plans for NSSCo. building)
Red Wing Daily Republican   Thurs., April 7, 1892
"Here and Now" (contract let for grading site of NSSCo.)
Red Wing Daily Republican   Sat., April 9, 1892
"Here and Now" (John Otterson & Peter Olson to excavate clay for NSSCo.)
Red Wing Daily Republican   Wed., May 4, 1892
"Here and Now" (NSSCo. purchases clay lands for $150 an acre)
Red Wing Daily Republican   Tues., May 10, 1892
"Here and Now" (Gust Lillyblad to put in foundation for NSSCo.; F.H. McClure becomes superintendent and manager of MSCo.)
Red Wing Daily Republican   Tues., May 17, 1892
"Here and Now" (work progressing slowly at NSSCo. due to heavy rains)
Red Wing Daily Republican   Fri., May 27, 1892
"Here and Now" (foundations for 6 kilns put in at NSSCo.)
Red Wing Journal   Wed., July 13, 1892
"Here and Now" (need for continuous train to and from clay pits)
"A Sudden Summons" (F.W. Hoyt, president of NSSCo. dies)
Red Wing Journal   Wed., July 13, 1892
(Duluth road working on clay pit branch)
"Gone to His Reward" (on F.W. Hoyt's death)
Red Wing Daily Republican   Mon., July 18, 1892
"Here and Now" (MSCo. putting in improvements)
Red Wing Daily Republican   Tues., July 19, 1892
"Here and Now" (work progressing at NSSCo.; may be ready by August 20)
Red Wing Journal   Wed., August 17, 1892
"Resolution" (on the death of F.W. Hoyt)
Red Wing Journal   Wed., August 24, 1892
(trains are running to the clay beds)
Red Wing Daily Republican   Fri., August 26, 1892
"Here and Now" (NSSCo. may open middle of September; doubt expressed as to how long clay will last)
Red Wing Daily Republican   Sat., Oct. 8, 1892
"City Council" (NSSCo. requests a spur track)
Red Wing Daily Republican   Wed., Nov. 2, 1892
"Here and Now" (electric light plant for NSSCo. being put in)

Red Wing Journal   Wed., Nov. 30, 1892
"The Big Factory" (about RSWPCo.)
"Local News" (NSSCo. opens second kiln of ware, first was unsatisfactory)
Red Wing Journal   Wed., Dec. 7, 1892
"Chips of Clay" (about the successes of the clay manufactories)
"Western Potteries" (Peoria Journal gives account of the Western pottery industry)
Red Wing Journal   Fri., Dec. 23, 1892
(hydrant left open at NSSCo. and ware was spoiled)
Red Wing Daily Republican   Mon., Dec. 26, 1892
"$448,825!" (building improvements for 1892)
Red Wing Daily Republican   Fri., Dec. 30, 1892
"The Record of a Year" (on the improvements in the clay industries)
Red Wing Daily Republican   Mon., Jan. 9, 1893
"Here and Now" (Albert Olson of NSSCo. was injured)
Red Wing Journal   Fri., Jan. 27, 1893
"Clay Cullings" (about various clay workers)
Red Wing Journal   Fri., Feb. 3, 1893
(John H. Rich Sewer Pipe Works to open February 13)
Red Wing Journal   Fri., Feb. 17, 1893
(MSCo. has new office)
"Klay is King" (on the opening of the JHRSP Works)
Red Wing Daily Republican   Tues., Sept. 19, 1893
(NSSCo. started this morning)
Red Wing Daily Republican   Fri., Sept. 22, 1893
(MSCo. willing to reopen next month if employees take a 10% cut in wages)
Red Wing Journal   Fri.,Sept. 22, 1893
(NSSCo. started up Monday after being idle 3 months)
Red Wing Daily Republican   Mon., Oct. 2, 1893
(MSCo. will reopen tomorrow; clay mills were put into operation today)
Red Wing Daily Republican   Sat., Oct. 21, 1893
(RWSCo., idle for several months, will resume Monday)
Red Wing Daily Republican   Mon., Oct. 23, 1893
(RWSCo. opened this morning)
Red Wing Daily Republican   Tues., Oct. 24, 1893
(J.C. Pierce speaks on the importance of the railroad; spur track goes into NSSCo.'s clay beds)
Red Wing Journal   Fri., Oct. 27, 1893
(spur track goes into NSSCo.'s clay beds)
Red Wing Daily Republican   Mon., Oct. 30, 1893
(MSCo. has started up with full force)
Red Wing Journal   Fri., Nov. 17, 1893
(A.J. Meacham elected president of NSSCo.)
Red Wing Journal   Fri., Feb. 23, 1894
(RWSCo. will start up Monday)
Red Wing Argus   Thurs., June 21, 1894
"Local Brevities and Personals" (NSSCo. shut down for indefinite time; scarcity of coal)
Red Wing Argus   Thurs., July 12, 1894
"Local Brevities and Personals" (report of MSCo.'s annual meeting)
Red Wing Argus   Thurs., August 16, 1894
(report of RWSCo.'s annual meeting)
The Advance Sun   Wed., August 22, 1894
"Local News" (report of RWSCo.'s annual meeting)
Red Wing Daily Republican   Tues., Sept. 11, 1894
"Local News" (announcement of the formation of Union Stoneware Co.)
The Advance Sun   Wed., Sept. 12, 1894
(announcement of the formation of Union Stoneware Co.)
"The City Fathers" (street at NSSCo. to be widened)
"Local News" (NSSCo. has exhibit at State Fair)
"Articles of Incorporation of the Union Stoneware Co."
"Red Wing Needs a Paving Brick Works" (from The Clay Record)
Red Wing Daily Republican   Tues., Sept. 25, 1894
(report on Union Stoneware Co. and how orders will be handled)
Red Wing Daily Republican   Wed., Sept. 26, 1894
(A.J. Meacham's name omitted from yesterday's list of officers)
Red Wing Journal   Fri., Sept. 28, 1894
(report of the stockholders' meeting of USWCo.)
Red Wing Argus   Thurs., Oct. 25, 1894
"Local Brevities and Personals" (USWCo. erects office adjacent to RWSCo.'s office)
Red Wing Journal   Fri., Nov. 9, 1894
(NSSCo. will reopen in a few days)
Red Wing Journal   Fri., Jan. 11, 1895
(NSSCo. started up Monday)
Red Wing Journal   Fri., Jan. 18, 1895
(USWCo. now occupy their new office)
Red Wing Argus   Thurs., Feb. 14, 1895
(employees of stoneware companies accept a 10-15% cut in wages)

Red Wing Daily Republican   Thurs., Feb. 28, 1895
(Northwestern Stoneware Co., headed by T.H. Mallory, opens store at Minneapolis)
Red Wing Daily Republican   Fri., March 8, 1895
(NSSCo. will resume next Monday)
Red Wing Daily Republican   Mon., March 14, 1895
(NSSCo. resumed this morning; MSCo. uses oil for burning ware)
Red Wing Argus   Thurs., March 28, 1895
"Minnesota News" (all manufactories except sewer pipe works are in operation)
Red Wing Daily Republican   Thurs., April 4, 1895
"Doings of a Day" (all manufactories except JHRSP Works are in operation)
Red Wing Daily Republican   Tues., April 9, 1895
"Claybank" (digging resumes at clay pits)
Red Wing Daily Republican   Sat., April 13, 1895
Red Wing Argus   Thurs., April 18, 1895
Red Wing Journal   Fri., April 19, 1895
(MSCo. has small fire caused by oil leak)
Red Wing Republican   Sat., April 20, 1895
"Doings of a Day" (NSSCo. shut down for repairs)
Red Wing Daily Republican   Fri., May 3, 1895
"Doings of a Day" (MSCo. shut down for repairs from fire)
Red Wing Journal   Fri., May 24, 1895
(USWCo. has an office in Chicago)
Red Wing Argus   Thurs., June 20, 1895
"Local Brevities and Personals" (NSSCo. will close for at least a month)
Red Wing Journal   Fri., July 5, 1895
(NSSCo. will resume next week)
Red Wing Journal   Fri., July 12, 1895
(NSSCo. started up Monday)
Red Wing Daily Republican   Thurs., July 12, 1895
Red Wing Argus   Thurs., July 18, 1895
(report of NSSCo.'s annual meeting)
Red Wing Journal   Fri., August 23, 1895
(NSSCo. shut down Monday for engine repairs)
Red Wing Daily Republican   Sat., Sept. 7, 1895
"Doings of a Day" (NSSCo. will resume on Monday)
Red Wing Daily Republican   Wed., Jan. 1, 1896
"$221,875" (improvement record for 1895)
Red Wing Daily Republican   Tues., March 17, 1896
"Doings of a Day" (annual stoneware capacity is 9 million gallons)
Red Wing Daily Republican   Wed., April 22, 1896
"Doings of a Day" (F.J. Fewings of RWSCo. accepts railroad job in Duluth)
Red Wing Republican   Fri., May 22, 1896
"Doings of a Day" (NSSCo. closed down on Wednesday night; annual report of the D.R.W.& S. railroad)
Red Wing Republican   Wed., June 3, 1896
(ads for RWSPCo., JHRSP Works and USWCo.)
Red Wing Daily Republican   Sat., June 13, 1896
"Doings of a Day" (MSCo. shuts down for summer vacation)
Red Wing Daily Republican   Wed., July 8, 1896
"Doings of a Day" (NSSCo.'s annual meeting today; USWCo. will meet tomorrow)
Red Wing Daily Republican   Thurs., July 9, 1896
"Doings of a Day" (MSCo. making improvements)
"North Star Stoneware Company" (report of annual meeting)
Red Wing Argus   Thurs., July 9, 1896
"Local Brevities and Personals" (report of MSCo.'s annual meeting)
Red Wing Daily Republican   Fri., July 10, 1896
"Union Stoneware Company" (report of annual meeting)
Red Wing Journal   Fri., July 10, 1896
(report of MSCo.'s annual meeting)
Minneapolis Tribune   Sun., July 12, 1896
"Northwest News" (report of NSSCo.'s annual meeting)
Red Wing Argus   Thurs., July 16, 1896
"Local Brevities and Personals" (report of USWCo.'s annual meeting)
Red Wing Argus   Thurs., July 30, 1896
"Minnesota State News" (report on Minnesota clay)
Red Wing Argus   Thurs., August 13, 1896
"Local Brevities and Personals" (report on RWSCo.'s annual meeting)
Red Wing Journal   Fri., Sept. 4, 1896
"The City" (MSCo. employees given 2 days off to attend the fair)
Red Wing Daily Republican   Tues., Sept. 22, 1896
Red Wing Republican   Wed., Sept. 23, 1896
(E.S. Hoyt and others purchase 7/8's of NSSCo. stock)
Red Wing Journal   Fri., Oct. 2, 1896
Minneapolis Tribune   Fri., Oct. 2, 1896
(NSSCo.'s new stockholders elect directors)
Red Wing Republican   Wed., Oct. 21, 1896
"Local News" (MSCo. employees buy a flag for political use)

Red Wing Republican   Wed., Nov. 18, 1896
Red Wing Argus   Thurs., Nov. 19, 1896
(JHRSP Works & RWSPCo. form a union called the Union Sewer Pipe Co.)
Red Wing Journal   Fri., Dec. 25, 1896
"Jerusalem in Clay" (George Hehr's [RWSCo.] 78 piece stoneware nativity set)
Red Wing Journal   Sat., March 27, 1897
"Red Wing" (sketch of Red Wing as reported by *The American Land & Title Register*)
Red Wing Daily Republican   Wed., June 16, 1897
Red Wing Republican   Wed., June 23, 1897
"White Ware" (report of full scale production of white ware)
Red Wing Times   Fri., June 18, 1897
"Timely Topics" (stoneware companies now producing white ware)
Red Wing Daily Republican   Tues., July 6, 1897
"Doings of a Day" (MSCo. to hold annual meeting today)
Red Wing Daily Republican   Wed., July 7, 1897
Red Wing Times   Fri., July 9, 1897
Red Wing Argus   Thurs., July 15, 1897
(report of MSCo.'s annual meeting)
Red Wing Times   Fri., July 23, 1897
"Timely Topics" (RWSCo. closed down for a time)
Red Wing Times   Fri., August 6, 1897
"Timely Topics" (RWSCo. to hold annual meeting)
Red Wing Times   Fri., August 13, 1897
"Timely Topics" (report of RWSCo.'s annual meeting)
Red Wing Argus   Sat., Sept. 11, 1897
"Here and Elsewhere" (MSCo. builds new flower pot kiln)
Red Wing Argus   Sat., Oct. 2, 1897
"Pottery Notes" (various notes about the potteries)
Red Wing Republican   Wed., Oct. 20, 1897
"In Days of Old" (about F.F. Philleo and son William making terra cotta flower pots in 1867)
Red Wing Argus   Sat., Oct. 23, 1897
"Here and Elsewhere" (NSSCo.'s shed being torn down)
Red Wing Republican   Wed., Nov. 3, 1897
"The Local News" (NSSCo. is wholly stripped of clay equipment)
Red Wing Republican   Wed., Nov. 17, 1897
"Substantial Citizens" (report on personal property tax)
Red Wing Argus   Sat., Nov. 27, 1897
"Pottery Pickings" (RWSCo. building new kiln)
Red Wing Republican   Wed., Dec. 1, 1897
"Local News" (labor commissioner's report on Red Wing's industries)
Red Wing Argus   Sat., Dec. 18, 1897
"Stoneware Revolution" (use of machinery at Monmouth, Ill.)
Red Wing Republican   Wed., Jan. 5, 1898
"$139,265" (building improvements in 1897)
Red Wing Argus   Sat., Jan. 22, 1898
"Ourselves and Neighbors" (potters union wants assistance in having buyers purchase Minnesota ware)
Red Wing Argus   Sat., Feb. 26, 1898
"Received Painful Injuries" (C.F. Swanson of MSCo.)
Red Wing Argus   Sat., March 12, 1898
"Ourselves and Neighbors" (Joseph Pohl was granted a pension of $10)
Red Wing Argus   Sat., March 19, 1898
"Ourselves and Neighbors" (USWCo. will exhibit at Trans-Mississippi Exposition in Omaha)
Red Wing Argus   Sat., May 7, 1898
"They Struck" (clay pit employees strike for higher wages)
Red Wing Argus   Sat., July 16, 1898
"Stoneware Company Officers" (report of MSCo.'s annual meeting)
Red Wing Argus   Sat., July 23, 1898
"Ourselves and Neighbors" (B.F. Seiz now foreman at MSCo.)
Red Wing Argus   Sat., August 20, 1898
"Ourselves and Neighbors" (RWSCo. stockholders will meet Monday)
Red Wing Argus   Sat., August 27, 1898
"Ourselves and Neighbors" (report of RWSCo.'s annual meeting)
Red Wing Daily Republican   Wed., August 31, 1898
"Lieut. Morley Dead" (was a brother of stoneware employees)
Red Wing Argus   Sat., Sept. 10, 1898
"Ourselves and Neighbors" (John Sell of MSCo. died)
Red Wing Argus   Sat., Jan. 7, 1899
"Here and Elsewhere" (E.W. Brooks funeral was Sat.)
"Ourselves and Neighbors" (P. Peterson of RWSCo. was injured)
Red Wing Argus   Sat., Jan. 28, 1899
"A Miraculous Excape" (Edw. Johnson [RWSCo.] trapped in old clay pit)
Red Wing Argus   Sat., April 29, 1899
"Ourselves and Neighbors" (B.F. Seiz of MSCo. goes to Ft. Dodge Stoneware Co., Ft. Dodge, Iowa)

Red Wing Argus   Sat., May 6, 1899
"Another Raise in Wages" (2 stoneware companies raise wages)
Red Wing Argus   Sat., May 13, 1899
"Ourselves and Neighbors" (urn given to Hastings camp No. 4747 MWA by Red Wing Camp No. 1486)
Red Wing Argus   Sat., May 27, 1899
"Ourselves and Neighbors" (25 stoneware companies east of Mississippi consolidated)
Red Wing Republican   Wed., June 21, 1899
"New Industry" (malting house established in old NSSCo. building)
Red Wing Argus   Sat., July 8, 1899
"Ourselves and Neighbors" (stoneware companies to hold annual meetings)
Red Wing Argus   Sat., Sept. 9, 1899
"City Council" (water mains ordered extended to MSCo.)
Red Wing Daily Republican   Tues., Jan. 9, 1900
"Bones Broken" (Nels Nelson employed at the clay pit was injured)
Red Wing Republican   Wed., Jan. 10, 1900
"Review of Events" (NSSCo. building was sold in June of 1899)
Red Wing Argus   Fri., Jan. 12, 1900
"Annual Meeting" (report of USWCo. annual meeting)
Red Wing Daily Republican   Thurs., Feb. 8, 1900
"Consumed by Fire" (about the fire at MSCo.)
Red Wing Argus   Fri., Feb. 9, 1900
"In Ashes" (about the fire at MSCo.)
Red Wing Daily Republican   Sat., Feb. 10, 1900
"The Local Pickup" (MSCo. employees will be paid next Wednesday at Goodhue County Bank)
Red Wing Daily Republican   Wed., Feb. 14, 1900
"The Local News" (insurance representatives will adjust fire loss at MSCo.)
"Consumed by Fire" (on the fire at MSCo.)
Red Wing Argus   Fri., Feb. 16, 1900
"City Happenings" (west end wants better fire protection)
Red Wing Daily Republican   Mon., Feb. 19, 1900
Red Wing Daily Republican   Tues., Feb. 20, 1900
Red Wing Argus   Fri., Feb. 23, 1900
(settlement of $41,000 made to MSCo. on an estimated loss of $70,000)
Red Wing Daily Republican   Mon., Feb. 26, 1900
Red Wing Daily Republican   Fri., March 2, 1900
(MSCo. will be rebuilt)
Red Wing Republican   Wed., March 7, 1900
"Real Estate Transfers" (NSSCo. to Minnesota Malting Co.)
"The Local News" (potters will give second annual ball)
Red Wing Daily Republican   Mon., March 12, 1900
"The Local News" (MSCo.'s new foundation going in)
Red Wing Daily Republican   Wed., March 14, 1900
"Water Works Tested" (water works tested at the potteries)
Red Wing Argus   Fri., March 16, 1900
"City Happenings" (work progressing at MSCo.)
Red Wing Daily Republican   Tues., April 3, 1900
"Death of T.B. Sheldon" (prime mover and president of MSCo.)
Red Wing Daily Republican   Mon., April 9, 1900
"The Local News" (first story of MSCo. now up)
Red Wing Argus   Fri., April 13, 1900
"City Happenings" (work progressing on MSCo.)
Red Wing Daily Republican   Wed., April 25, 1900
"The Local News" (new plant of MSCo. now enclosed)
Red Wing Argus   Fri., May 11, 1900
"City Happenings" (new 3 [sic] story brick building of MSCo. is splendid)
Red Wing Daily Republican   Tues., May 15, 1900
"The Local News" (C. Ogren, working in the clay pits was injured)
Red Wing Daily Republican   Thurs., May 17, 1900
"The Local News" (RWSCo. clay diggers ask for a raise)
Red Wing Daily Republican   Thurs., June 7, 1900
"Rose Phoenix-Like" (on the new MSCo. plant)
Red Wing Daily Republican   Sat., June 9, 1900
"The Local News" (MSCo. will resume Monday)
Red Wing Daily Republican   Mon., June 11, 1900
"The Local News" (MSCo. started up this morning)
Red Wing Daily Republican   Thurs., July 5, 1900
"The Local News" (RWSCo. has been shut down a few days)
Red Wing Daily Republican   Mon., July 9, 1900
"The Local News" (MSCo. will hold annual meeting)
Red Wing Daily Republican   Wed., July 11, 1900
"Minnesota Stoneware Company" (report of annual meeting)
Red Wing Daily Republican   Thurs., July 12, 1900
"The Local News" (report of NSSCo.'s annual meeting)
Red Wing Daily Republican   Wed., August 22, 1900
"The Local News" (RWSCo. closed due to death of H.S. Rich's only son)
Red Wing Daily Republican   Tues., Oct. 9, 1900

"The Local News" (report of RWSCo.'s annual meeting)
Red Wing Daily Republican Thurs., Oct. 18, 1900
"The Local News" (RWSCo. closed today for repairs)
Red Wing Daily Republican Tues., Nov. 20, 1900
"The Local News" (John Peterson of MSCo. injured)
Red Wing Daily Republican Thurs., Nov. 22, 1900
"Destructive Fire" (on the fire at RWSCo.)
Red Wing Daily Republican Mon., Nov. 26, 1900
"The Local News" (insurance representatives in town to view RWSCo. damage)
Red Wing Daily Republican Tues., Nov. 27, 1900
"Minnesota News in Brief" (on the fire at RWSCo.)
"Will Rebuild at Once" (RWSCo. will be rebuilt)
Red Wing Daily Republican Fri., Dec. 7, 1900
"The Local News" (F.M. Weir of Monmouth potteries visited stoneware and sewer pipe works)
Red Wing Daily Republican Wed., Dec. 12, 1900
"The Local News" (RWSCo. new main building is up)
Red Wing Daily Republican Thurs., Dec. 13, 1900
"These Pay Taxes" (personal property tax record)
Red Wing Daily Republican Wed., Dec. 26, 1900
"The Local News" (MSCo. employees present manager Hoyt with a chair)
Red Wing Daily Republican Sat., Dec. 29, 1900
"Magnificent Record" (building improvements during 1900)
The Minneapolis Journal Sat., Nov. 2, 1901
"The Clay Potteries of Red Wing"
Red Wing Republican Wed., Jan. 3, 1906
"Fine Quality of Their Goods" (about Red Wing potteries display at H.L. Hjermstad's)
Red Wing Republican Wed., Jan. 17, 1906
"Red Wing Building Improvements for 1905"
Red Wing Daily Republican Sat., March 17, 1906
"Articles of Incorporation of Red Wing Union Stoneware Company"
"Local News" (about formation of Red Wing Union Stoneware Company)
Red Wing Republican Wed., March 21, 1906
"The Local News" (story of incorporation of RWUSCo.)
Red Wing Daily Republican Thurs., March 22, 1906
"Local News" (Nels Skramstad sells 10 acres to RWUSCo.)
Goodhue County News Sat., March 24, 1906
"Brief News Notes of the Past Week" (land sells near Claybank)
Red Wing Daily Republican Tues., March 27, 1906
"Local News" (RWSCo. votes to form RWUSCo.)
Red Wing Daily Republican Thurs., March 29, 1906
"Local News" (more on land sale near Claybank)
Red Wing Daily Republican Mon., April 2, 1906
"Local News" (officers of RWUSCo. take over today)
Red Wing Daily Republican Fri., May 21, 1906
"Boys Wanted" (boys needed at Factory M)
Red Wing Daily Republican Thurs., June 21, 1906
"Additional Locals" (Albert Olson home for vacation)
Red Wing Daily Republican Tues., June 26, 1906
"Local News" (Factory R shut down for repairs and inventory)
Red Wing Daily Republican Fri., June 29, 1906
"Local News" (Factory R will reopen Monday)
Goodhue County News Sat., June 30, 1906
"Brief News Notes of the Past Week" (A.A. Page visits home in Galesburg)
Goodhue County News Sat., July 14, 1906
"Brief News Notes of the Past Week" (report of RWUSCo.'s annual meeting)
Red Wing Daily Republican Fri., Oct. 26, 1906
ad — The Bee Hive (souvenir ware made by RWUSCo.)
Red Wing Daily Republican Thurs., Dec. 6, 1906
"Red Wing at the Front" (editorial on Red Wing's display at next year's state fair)
Goodhue County News Sat., Dec. 8, 1906
"Red Wing Manufacturing" (quoting St. Paul Dispatch)
Red Wing Daily Republican Fri., Dec. 14, 1906
"Personal Taxes Exceeding $10"
Red Wing Daily Republican Fri., Dec. 21, 1906
"Red Wing Enterprise Receives Recognition" (on success of Red Wing as a manufacturing town)
Red Wing Daily Republican Wed., Dec. 26, 1906
"Local News" (Ernest Rehder becomes bookkeeper at RWUSCo.)
Red Wing Daily Republican Fri., Jan. 25, 1907
"Statistics of Clay Products" (general report from bureau of census)
Red Wing Daily Republican Sat., Feb. 23, 1907
"Clay Products of Minnesota" (more on bureau of census report)
Red Wing Daily Republican Sat., March 2, 1907
"Car Shortage in Red Wing" (shortage of freight cars causing some factories to shut down)

Red Wing Daily Republican Mon., April 8, 1907
"Goodhue" (clay workers on vacation due to rail car shortage)
Red Wing Daily Republican Mon., May 6, 1907
"Goodhue" (on a search for more clay beds)
Red Wing Republican Wed., May 15, 1907
"Will Make a Great Showing" (on Red Wing display at state fair this year)
Red Wing Daily Republican Tues., June 11, 1907
"Discriminate Against Red Wing" (railroads giving unfair rates to Red Wing potteries)
Red Wing Daily Republican Mon., July 8, 1907
"Local News" (Hilmer Loken injured at stoneware works)
Red Wing Daily Republican Mon., July 15, 1907
"Local News" (area near sewer pipe B and RWSCo. being cleaned up)
Goodhue County News Sat., July 20, 1907
"Red Wing and Vicinity" (McChesney visiting Red Wing)
Red Wing Daily Republican Fri., August 2, 1907
"Local News" (more on forthcoming fair exhibit)
Red Wing Daily Republican Wed., August 7, 1907
"Good Boosts for Red Wing" (editorials and news articles from various other papers)
"Red Wing Exhibits Feature of Fair"
Red Wing Republican Wed., August 7, 1907
"Lake City" (John Phillips taking clay sample to RWUSCo. for testing)
Goodhue County News Sat., August 10, 1907
"Red Wing Exhibits Feature of Fair"
Red Wing Daily Republican Mon., Sept. 2, 1907
(ad — See Red Wing Exhibit at State Fair)
Red Wing Daily Republican Thurs., Sept. 5, 1907
"Story of the Red Wing Exhibits"
Red Wing Daily Republican Fri., Sept. 6, 1907
"They All Talk of Red Wing" (quoting Minneapolis Journal on fair exhibit)
Red Wing Daily Republican Sat., Sept. 7, 1907
"What They Say of Red Wing" (about the fair exhibit)
Red Wing Republican Wed., Sept. 18, 1907
"What the Twin City Papers Say About Red Wing Exhibits"
"Red Wing Manufacturers Consider Important Things"
"Red Wing's Lively Pace" (quoting Commercial Bulletin and Northwest Trade)
Red Wing Daily Republican Mon., Oct. 7, 1907
"Local News" (three new employees at RWUSCo.)
Red Wing Daily Republican Thurs., Oct. 10, 1907
"Local News" (Henry Dack of Farmington works at the pottery)
Red Wing Daily Republican Mon., Oct. 21, 1907
"Local News" (New Ulm laborers have gone to Red Wing clay pits to work)
Red Wing Daily Republican Thurs., Oct. 31, 1907
"Local News" (Pioneer Press has section on Red Wing)
Red Wing Daily Republican Fri., Dec. 6, 1907
"Local News" (F.A. Johnson to demonstrate 'throwing' in Winona)
Red Wing Daily Republican Mon., Dec. 16, 1907
"Crushed at the Clay Pits" (Ole Hagen killed in the clay pits)
Red Wing Daily Republican Fri., Jan. 1, 1908
"Those Who Pay a Personal Tax"
Red Wing Daily Republican Sat., Jan. 11, 1908
"Traces of the Fire Bug" (gasoline can found near MSCo.)
Red Wing Republican Wed., Jan. 29, 1908
"Local News" (F. Busch, director of RWSPCo. and RWUSCo. died)
Red Wing Republican Wed., May 13, 1908
"Red Wing Life 25 Years Ago" (about formation of MSCo.)
Red Wing Republican Wed., July 8, 1908
"Local News" (RWSCo.'s horse runs wild)
Red Wing Republican Sat., July 25, 1908
"Red Wing Life 25 Years Ago" (MSCo. to be ready soon)
Goodhue Enterprise Thurs., July 30, 1908
(clay pit workers take off due to heat)
Red Wing Daily Republican Mon., Sept. 14, 1908
"Local News" (John [sic] Koester to hold auction)
Red Wing Daily Republican Tues., Nov. 3, 1908
Goodhue County News Sat., Nov. 7, 1908
"Red Wing Life 25 Years Ago" (RWSCo. establishes a wholesale department at St. Paul)
Red Wing Daily Republican Wed., Nov. 11, 1908
"To Study Our Clays" (U.S. Geological survey)
"Red Wing's Labor Unions"
Red Wing Republican Wed., Nov. 11, 1908
"Local News" (exhibit of American pottery at Library)
Goodhue County News Sat., Nov. 14, 1908
"Local News" (more on library pottery exhibit)
Red Wing Republican Wed., Nov. 18, 1908
Red Wing Daily Republican Tues., Nov. 24, 1908

"Valuable Exhibit of Pottery" (more on library pottery exhibit)
Red Wing Republican Wed., Nov. 25, 1908
"Local News" (more on library pottery exhibit)
Goodhue Enterprise Thurs., Dec. 17, 1908
"Claybank Jottings" (steam hoist shut down for winter at the clay pits)
Red Wing Daily Republican Mon., Jan. 4, 1909
"Those Who Pay Ten Dollars" (personal property tax report)
Red Wing Daily Republican Sat., Jan. 9, 1909
"Close Call at Stoneware Works" (small fire at MSCo.)
Red Wing Daily Republican Wed., Jan. 20, 1909
Goodhue County News Sat., Jan. 23, 1909
"Almost Half Million Expended for Local Improvements in 1908"
Goodhue Enterprise Thurs., Jan. 21, 1909
"Local News" (C.E. Rucker makes deliveries to clay pits)
Goodhue Enterprise Thurs., Feb. 4, 1909
"Local News" (clay pits shut down due to storm)
Goodhue Enterprise Thurs., March 25, 1909
"Local News" (Zumbrota Clay Co. starts up)
Red Wing Daily Republican Fri., April 2, 1909
"Red Wing Co. Buys Stoneware Plant" (buys Marshalltown, Iowa plant)
Red Wing Republican Wed., June 2, 1909
Goodhue County News Sat., June 5, 1909
"Local News" (electrical storm damages MSCo. building)
Red Wing Daily Republican Thurs., June 3, 1909
"Local News" (McChesney was caller in Red Wing)
Red Wing Daily Republican Mon., June 7, 1909
"Beloved Citizen Falls Asleep" (death of E.H. Blodgett)
Red Wing Daily Republican Wed., June 16, 1909
"Are Please with Red Wing" (State Federation of Labor held 3 day convention in Red Wing)
Red Wing Republican Wed., June 30, 1909
Goodhue County News Sat., July 3, 1909
Red Wing Daily Republican Sat., July 10, 1909
"Local News" (RWUSCo. shut down for inventory and repairs)
Red Wing Daily Republican Wed., July 14, 1909
Goodhue County News Sat., July 17, 1909
"Local News" (report of RWUSCo.'s annual meeting)
Red Wing Daily Republican Tues., August 10, 1909
Goodhue County News Sat., August 14, 1909
"Open Switch, Train Wrecked" (stoneware damaged)
Red Wing Republican Wed., Sept. 1, 1909
"Local News" (A. Olson goes to work for RWUSCo. in Marshalltown, Iowa)
Red Wing Free Press Fri., Sept. 24, 1909
"Facts About Red Wing"
Red Wing Free Press Fri., Oct. 8, 1909
"Red Wing Pottery Works Have Made City Famous"
Red Wing Daily Republican Fri., Oct. 15, 1909
"Clay Products in United States"
Red Wing Free Press Fri., Oct. 29, 1909
"Red Wing's Sewer Pipe Industry"
Goodhue Enterprise Thurs., Nov. 4, 1909
"Local News" (men wanted, clay pits)
Red Wing Daily Republican Sat., Nov. 27, 1909
"Promise in Local Artist" (A. Olson Stenwick)
Red Wing Daily Republican Tues., Dec. 7, 1909
"Our Little Brown Jug"
Red Wing Daily Republican Wed., Dec. 22, 1909
"Encouraging Signs of Clay" (clay exploration near Belvidere Mills)
Red Wing Republican Wed., Dec. 22, 1909
"Local News" (J. Reinboldt hurt at stoneware works)
Red Wing Daily Republican Fri., Dec. 24, 1909
(editorial cartoon — Merry Christmas)
Red Wing Daily Republican Wed., Dec. 29, 1909
". . . Local Improvements for 1909"
Red Wing Daily Republican Fri., Dec. 31, 1909
"Ten Dollars and Upward" (personal property tax report)
Red Wing Daily Republican Sat., Jan. 1, 1910
"Ten Dollars and Upward" (personal property tax report)
Red Wing Free Press Fri., Feb. 4, 1910
"Acquiring More Clay Lands" (RWUSCo. looking for more clay)
Goodhue Enterprise Thurs., Feb. 10, 1910
Red Wing Free Press Fri., Feb. 18, 1910
"Local News" (clay prospectors done for the winter)
Red Wing Daily Republican Tues., March 8, 1910
Red Wing Republican Wed., March 9, 1910
"B.B. Herbert is Honored"
Red Wing Daily Republican Sat., March 26, 1910
"Local News" (feddlers, mold runners ask for more money)
Red Wing Daily Republican Wed., March 30, 1910
"Local News" (feddlers, mold runners can't agree with their employers)

Red Wing Daily Republican Thurs., March 31, 1910
"Local News" (turners report no problems with feddlers and mold runners)

Red Wing Daily Republican Tues., April 5, 1910
"Wages Are Increased" (clay workers get raise)

Red Wing Free Press Fri., April 8, 1910
"The City" (clay industries raise wages $2 per day)

Red Wing Daily Republican Wed., April 13, 1910
(editorial cartoon — clay workers raise)

Red Wing Daily Republican Sat., April 16, 1910

Red Wing Republican Wed., April 20, 1910
"Local News" (display of Red Wing stoneware in Seattle)

Goodhue Enterprise Thurs., April 29, 1910
"Local News" (two clay pit workers fall into water filled pit)

Red Wing Daily Republican Wed., May 11, 1910
"Local News" (potters to give dance May 27th)

Red Wing Free Press Fri., May 13, 1910
"Hold Their Annual Meeting" (Red Wing manufacturers)

Red Wing Free Press Fri., May 13, 1910
"The City" (Geo. Cook returns from Marshalltown — plant shut down)

Red Wing Daily Republican Mon., May 23, 1910
"Local News" (potters to give dance May 27th)

Red Wing Daily Republican Wed., May 25, 1910

Red Wing Republican Wed., May 25, 1910
"Exhibit Products Made At Home" (first mention of new red wing trademark on stoneware)

Red Wing Daily Republican Tues., July 12, 1910
"Local News" (potters' union will meet tonight; report of RWUSCo.'s annual meeting)

Red Wing Free Press Fri., July 15, 1910
"The City" (report of RWUSCo.'s annual meeting)

Red Wing Daily Republican Tues., July 19, 1910
"Local News" (RWUSCo. shut down for inventory and repairs)

Red Wing Daily Republican Wed., August 31, 1910

Red Wing Republican Wed., August 31, 1910
"Local News" (C.E. Sheldon retiring)

Red Wing Daily Republican Mon., Sept. 19, 1910

Red Wing Republican Wed., Sept. 21, 1910

Red Wing Daily Republican Wed., Sept. 28, 1910

Red Wing Daily Republican Wed., Sept. 28, 1910
"Local News" (potters' union to throw benefit for ill member)

Red Wing Republican Wed., Sept. 28, 1910
"Local News" (F.J. Crandell to work as salesman for RWUSCo.)

Red Wing Daily Republican Mon., Oct. 3, 1910
"Local News" (potters' benefit tomorrow night)

Red Wing Daily Republican Wed., Oct. 5, 1910
"Local News" (report on potters' benefit)

Red Wing Republican Wed., Oct. 5, 1910
"Local News" (A. Olson Stenwick returns to school)

Goodhue Enterprise Thurs., Oct. 6, 1910
"Local News" (L. Johnson, clay pit boss retires)

Red Wing Daily Republican Fri., Oct. 7, 1910
"Local News" (report on automobile party touring new clay beds)

Goodhue Enterprise Thurs., Oct. 13, 1910
"Local News" (railroad to clay pits to be done soon; Ole Opsahl new proprietor of clay pit boarding house)

Red Wing Republican Wed., Oct. 19, 1910

Red Wing Free Press Fri., Oct. 21, 1910
"The City" (Williston Rich takes over C.E. Sheldon's job)

Goodhue Enterprise Thurs., Nov. 10, 1910
"Hurt At Clay Pits" (Hubbard Smith injured at clay pits)

Red Wing Republican Wed., Dec. 21, 1910
"Local News" (RWUSCo. shut down; traveling agents home for holidays)

Red Wing Free Press Fri., Dec. 23, 1910
"Local Gleanings" (RWUSCo. shut down)

Red Wing Republican Wed., Jan. 4, 1911

Red Wing Republican Wed., Jan. 11, 1911
"Resume of Local Events During the Year 1910"

Red Wing Republican Wed., Jan. 18, 1911
"Improvements During 1910"

Red Wing Daily Republican Wed., Jan. 25, 1911
"Personal Taxes Over Ten Dollars"

Red Wing Republican Wed., March 15, 1911
"Local News" (potters' union to give ball April 24th)

Red Wing Republican Wed., March 22, 1911
"Decorated Clay in Red Wing"

Red Wing Republican Wed., April 5, 1911
"Local News" (day laborers at RWUSCo. get raise)

Red Wing Republican Wed., April 12, 1911
"Local News" (potters' union to give ball April 24th)

Red Wing Republican Wed., May 10, 1911
"Old Red Wing is a Pretty Good Town"

Red Wing Republican Wed., May 24, 1911
"Clay Beds Found Near Zumbrota"

Red Wing Republican Wed., May 31, 1911
"Local News" (McChesney returns to Kansas)

Red Wing Republican Wed., August 30, 1911
"One to Five Decades Ago" (about MSCo. exhibit at fair)

Red Wing Republican Wed., Dec. 13, 1911
"Clay Workers Elect Officers" (stoneware potters' union)

Red Wing Daily Eagle Thurs., Jan. 4, 1912
"Potters Benefit Association" (association est. to extend sick benefits to members)

Red Wing Republican Wed., Jan. 10, 1912
"Potters Organize Benefit Association"

Red Wing Republican Wed., March 6, 1912
"Local News" (E. Thrano, kiln burner, injured in fall on icy walk)

Red Wing Republican Wed., March 20, 1912
"Local News" (potters to give river excursion)

Red Wing Republican Wed., March 27, 1912
"Local News" (John Nelson to take employment at What Cheer, Iowa)

"Red Wing Clay at State Fair Exhibit"

Red Wing Republican Wed., April 17, 1912
"Local News" (E. Thrano died)

Red Wing Daily Republican Thurs., April 18, 1912
"Local News" (C.L. McGrew to demonstrate 'throwing' at school in Winona)

Red Wing Republican Wed., April 27, 1912
"Local News" (railroad service to clay pits resumed)

Red Wing Daily Republican Tues., May 14, 1912
"Local News" (potters to give river outing)

Red Wing Daily Republican Wed., May 22, 1912

Red Wing Daily Republican Wed., May 22, 1912

Red Wing Daily Republican Sat., June 1, 1912
"Local News" (potteries to close for excursion to Stillwater on June 13th)

Red Wing Daily Republican Fri., June 7, 1912
"Local News" (U.C.T. convention in Red Wing, souvenir is a stoneware traveling bag)

Red Wing Daily Republican Thurs., June 13, 1912
"Potters Enjoy Big Excursion" (on the potters excursion to Stillwater)

Red Wing Daily Republican Fri., June 14, 1912

Red Wing Republican Wed., June 19, 1912
"Man is Shot by his Friend" (intoxicated pottery employee shot entering wrong house)

Red Wing Republican Wed., July 10, 1912
"Local News" (report of RWUSCo.'s annual meeting)

Red Wing Republican Wed., August 21, 1912
"Found Dead on Couch at Home" (N. Stedee, engineer at MSCo. died)

Red Wing Republican Wed., August 28, 1912
"Buried Alive in Bed of Clay" (Anton Mown aka Anton Nick died)

Red Wing Republican Wed., Nov. 6, 1912
"Resigns Presidency of Sewer Pipe Co." (John Rich resigns)

Red Wing Republican Wed., Nov. 13, 1912
"Local News" (R.J. Steffa died, was foreman at USCo.)

Red Wing Republican Wed., Nov. 20, 1912
"Retires After Thirty Years" (on J. Rich's retirement)

Red Wing Republican Wed., Nov. 27, 1912
"New President of Sewer Pipe Co." (E.S. Hoyt elected)

Red Wing Republican Wed., Dec. 11, 1912
"Tiedeman Heads Potters' Union"

Red Wing Republican Wed., Dec. 25, 1912
"Fine Business Year in Sight"

Red Wing Daily Republican Mon., June 9, 1913
"Local News" (potters to travel to Stillwater)

Red Wing Daily Republican Tues., June 10, 1913
"Local News" (potters excursion postponed, G.W. Hill is held up down stream)

Red Wing Daily Republican Wed., June 11, 1913
"Local News" (potters outing to be held August 21st)

Red Wing Daily Republican Mon., August 18, 1913
"Local News" (potters outing this week)

Red Wing Daily Republican Tues., August 19, 1913
"Potters' Excursion Takes Place August 21"

Red Wing Daily Republican Wed., August 20, 1913
"Potters' Outing to be Big Event"

Red Wing Daily Republican Thurs., August 21, 1913
"Potters Biggest of Excursions"

Red Wing Daily Republican Fri., August 22, 1913
"Potters' Trip Greatly Enjoyed"

Red Wing Daily Republican Thurs., March 18, 1915
(suit between RWUSCo. and A. Knoll)

Red Wing Daily Republican Mon., May 17, 1915
"Local News" (free excursion ticket to the person finding the potters' excursion advertising jug)

Red Wing Daily Republican Thurs., June 10, 1915
"Tomorrow is Date of Potters' Event"

Red Wing Daily Republican Fri., June 11, 1915
"Hundreds Enjoy Potters' Outing"

Red Wing Daily Eagle Fri., June 11, 1915
"Splendid Day For Potters' Excursion"

Red Wing Daily Eagle Sat., June 12, 1915
"Potters' Outing is Big Success"

Red Wing Daily Eagle Sat., June 12, 1915
"Potters' Excursion Most Lucky Event"

Red Wing Daily Republican Tues., June 15, 1915
"Potters' Prize Jug Found Down River"

Red Wing Daily Eagle Tues., June 15, 1915
"Jug Found Too Late"

Red Wing Daily Eagle Wed., August 4, 1915
"Hoyt's Clever Red Wing Boost" (about S.M.M.A. souvenirs)

Red Wing Daily Eagle Mon., Dec. 27, 1915
(E.S. Hoyt granted patent on a jar [bail handle])

Red Wing Republican (State Fair Edition) Sept. 1923
"Red Wing Union Stoneware Company"

"Monster Jugs Made in Red" (3-70 gallon jugs made by RWUSCo.)

Red Wing Daily Republican Wed., July 1, 1925
"Barney Seiz, Prominent Figure, Dies"

Red Wing Daily Republican Wed., August 12, 1925
(ad — RWUSCo. welcomes 13th Minn. volunteers)

Red Wing Daily Republican Fri., August 14, 1925
"Reunion of Veterans is Big Success"

Red Wing Daily Eagle Mon., August 8, 1927
"250 Visitors Here for Redmen Convention"

Red Wing Daily Eagle Wed., August 21, 1929
"Red Wing Far Famed Manufacturing City"

Red Wing Daily Republican Wed., Sept. 7, 1932
"Red Wing Clay Working Industries"
(ads for RWUSCo. and RWSPCo.)

Red Wing Daily Eagle Wed., Jan. 15, 1936
"Stoneware Company Re-Elects" (report on annual meeting and name change to Red Wing Potteries, Inc.)

Red Wing Daily Republican Eagle Fri., Feb. 27, 1942
"Little Brown Jugs for Distillery Now Being Made at Red Wing Pottery"

St. Paul Pioneer Press Sun., April 13, 1947
"Minnesota Pottery Plant 70 Years Old"

Red Wing Daily Republican Eagle Thurs., Feb. 21, 1952
"Veteran Red Wing Potter to 'Throw' on Wheel at Art Show" (C.L. McGrew to give pottery demonstration)

Red Wing Daily Republican Eagle Tues., July 10, 1956
"Charles L. McGrew, Veteran Employee of Pottery, Dies"

Red Wing Daily Republican Eagle Fri., May 24, 1957
"Red Wing Potteries in Major Battle for Its Industrial Life"

Red Wing Daily Republican Eagle Fri., Sept. 20, 1957
"Home Industry Starts Pottery Business Here"

Red Wing Daily Republican Eagle Mon., July 6, 1959
"Rites Held for Otto Hartnagel"

Minnesota Stoneware Co. Blueprints

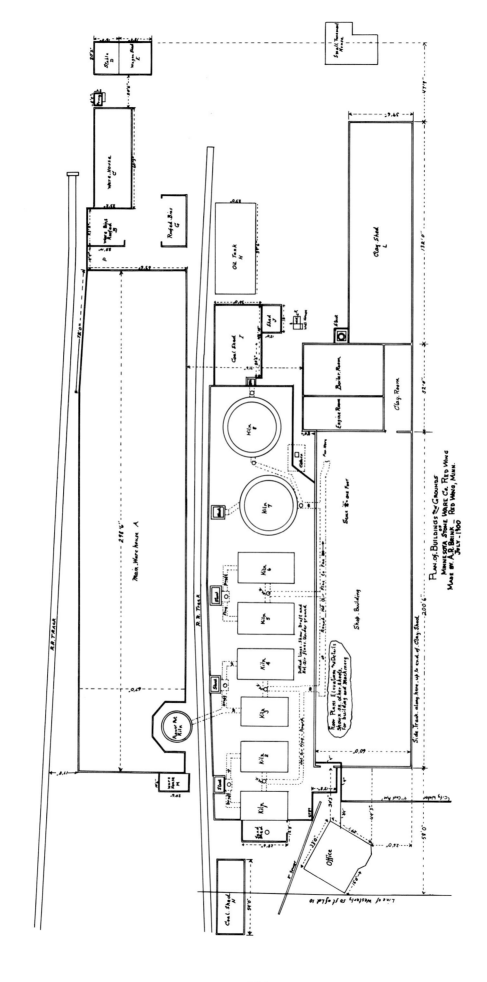

These plans were drawn up for Minnesota Stoneware Company's new plant after the original factory was destroyed by fire earlier in 1900. Original blueprints are on file at the Minnesota Historical Society's Division of Archives and Manuscripts. From these plans an understanding can be formed of the scope of the operations and perception gained of what it was like to work in the shops. They have aided in pinpointing the locations of several of the old interior photographs. Although the building has been gutted of its pottery equipment and converted to other uses; evidence of the old machinery, benches and power shafts can still be found.

Exterior-Elevation of West-Gable-and-Section
below First-Floor-Dat-on-Line-B
Scale ¼"= one foot

Section of Shop-West of Line A
Shown on First Floor-Plan
¼"= one foot

The main factory building, engine and boiler rooms are the only structures remaining. The main building was roughly doubled in length not long after being built. That addition occupies the location of the clay shed in the plan on the previous page.

185

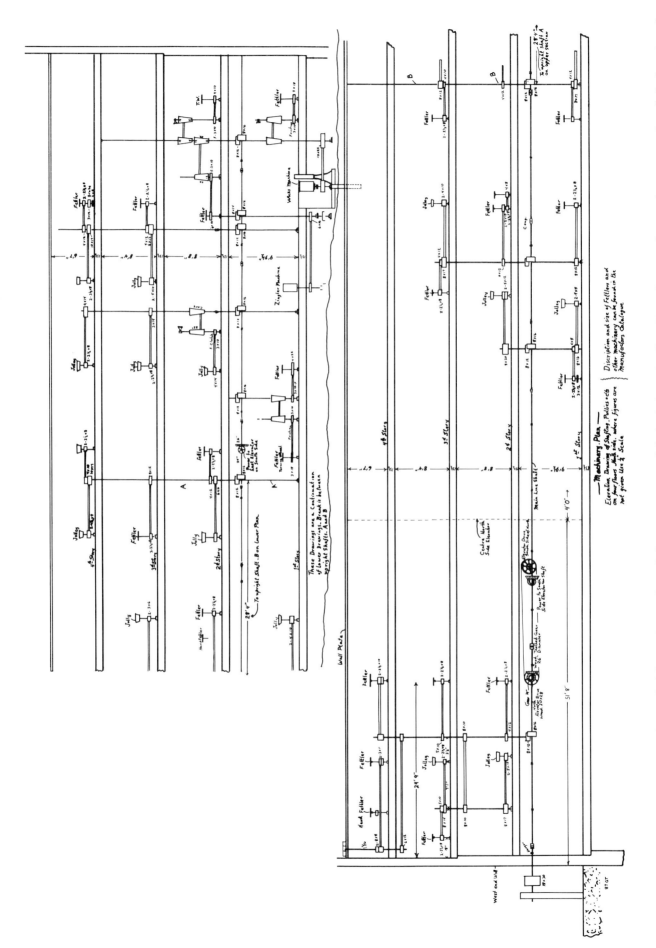

A single 200 horsepower steam engine drove all of the machinery through this arrangement of shafts, belts and pullies. From these machinery plans we can identify the location of the bottom left photo on page 18 as the east end of the second floor. Even today the brick walls bear grease stains where the speed regulating cone mechanism used to be. The hole through the ceiling remains where the vertical shaft passed.

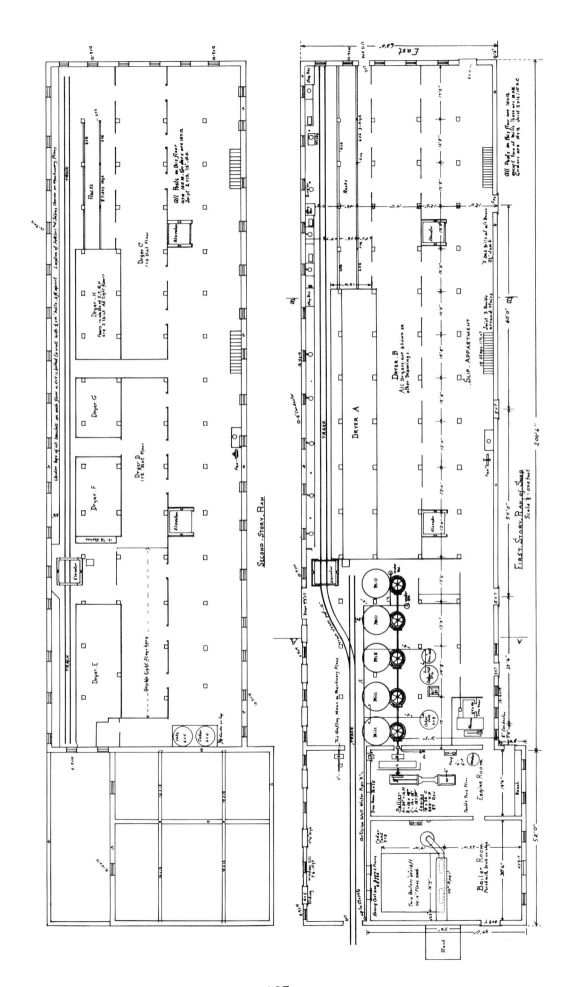

187

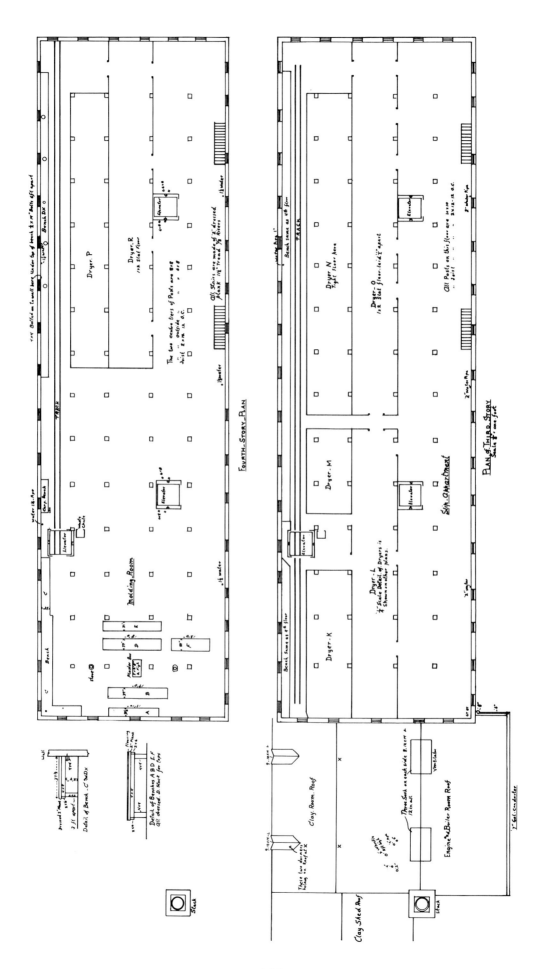

188

This scene appeared on a picture postcard titled "Makeing [sic] Large Ware; Union Stoneware Co.; Red Wing, Minn.", apparently dating from the same time as the ones shown on pages 24 and 26. The photo was taken on the first floor of the Minnesota Stoneware Co.'s 1900 brick building. The worker second from the right is standing in a pit while operating the Wicks Machine, which turned out large ware. A round wooden pallet was placed in the bottom of the cylinder; a piece of heavy cardboard (which can be seen rolled up on the left) lined the machine's cylinder. Clay was thrown in and pressed against the walls by a mechanical arm. A piston then drove the jar out on the pallet, the cardboard was stripped off and the piece fettled.

Goodhue County Historical Society photo

This photo shows handle lugs on the jars, so the date is after 1915. It was taken in "Factory R", the four story, wooden building which had been built by Red Wing Stoneware Co. in 1900. It appears to have been taken in the same location as the center-right photo on page 18, which was published in 1905. On right is Carl Edquist, left is Gustaf Pearson.

Photo courtesy of Phil Revoir

Also taken in Factory R, this seems to be the same work area shown in the top right photo on page 190, but at a somewhat later date. Lining the shelves overhead are molds for articles made in two pieces, such as the jugs on the cart. The door on the left leads into a drying room where the ware, still inside the mold, was dried overnight. The mold would be emptied the next day and the ware transferred to another dryer; meanwhile, the mold would be refilled and the process repeated.

Photo courtesy of Phil Revoir

189

"The Clay Potteries of Red Wing"

On pg. 102-103, we excerpted text from a November 2, 1901 *Minneapolis Journal* newspaper story about the pot shops. Here are reproduced the photographs which accompanied that article. Photos courtesy of Minnesota Historical Society Audio Visual Dept.

Mills for crushing the clay

Potters at work, with clay piled up beside molder

Showing big "jolly" and potters molding

Showing big "jolly" at end and entrances to kilns

Slip or glazing room — showing man at glazing tank

Slipping or glazing butter crocks

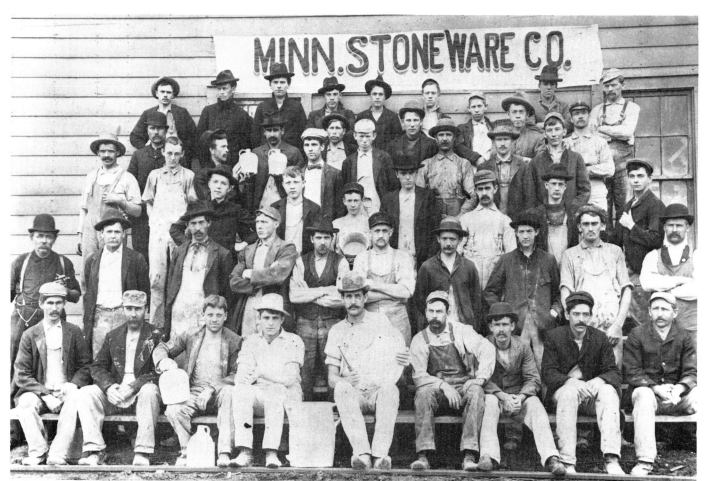

Here is a pre-1900 photo of the Minnesota Stoneware Company's employees. Precise date is unknown, but appears to be from near the turn of the century based upon the styles of the molded jugs displayed. The large pitcher-like vessel front and center is a curious item; its purpose is unknown.
Photo courtesy of Phil Revoir

This previously unpublished exterior view of the Minnesota Stoneware Company shows the original, unexpanded shop between 1885-1887. In the foreground are several cords of firewood which were used for firing the kilns.
Goodhue County Historical Society Photo

In the fall of 1887, an 80 foot addition was built onto the original MSCo. building. Soon afterward this section was increased to three stories in height; in 1892 the entire structure was expanded to three stories. Goodhue County Historical Society Photo

Jar lids were being molded in this section on the day this photo was taken. The observations made by Helen Gregory Flesher (see page 103) regarding the attire of the workers and their clay daubed appearance was certainly accurate. The third floor of Factory R seems to be the location.
Photo courtesy of Phil Revoir

At left are stacking rings used to make efficient use of the space inside the kiln. These are clay rings which fit perfectly to the shoulder of jugs. Here a one-half gallon jug is set upside down on the top of a one gallon jar; another jug could be set on the top of this one and the pattern reversed. The slipped interiors and jug tops would be protected and the exterior surfaces exposed to the salt vapors.

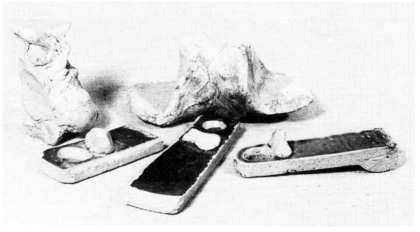

Above are temperature test pieces and "dinosaur dung," lumps of clay squeezed between pieces in the kiln to aid in stacking and prevent collapse during firing. These squeezings became fired and salt-glazed along with the ware. The dump is full of them. The "try pieces" were hooked out of the kiln to check on progress of the burning. More sophisticated "Segar Cones" which melt and bend to indicate when the proper temperature has been reached are still used as the most reliable "thermometer."

This is a "rib"; the thin, wooden tool used by turners to smooth the outside contour of hand thrown pieces.
Goodhue County Historical Society collection

A worker adding handles to molded jugs.
Red Wing, the Desirable City, Argus Press 1903

193

Lou McGrew at the 1952 Art Association Open House. In the 16 mm film McGrew turned a small jug and demonstrated how a pulled handle is applied.

This hand modeled umbrella stand was donated to the Goodhue County Historical Society Museum by McGrew. The broad leaves and cattails were familiar old Red Wing themes.

Lou McGrew

Though he had been retired since 1947, McGrew returned to the pot shops in 1953, the 75th Anniversary year, to turn a vase in the model shop. The Art Association had a close relationship with the pottery and had a workshop in the factory. A cousin of mine was taught turning in this studio when he was six or seven years old. The teacher; McGrew. Minnesota Historical Society photo

The Sheldon Patent

UNITED STATES PATENT OFFICE.

BENJAMIN FRANKLIN SHELDON, OF RED WING, MINNESOTA.

POTTER'S WHEEL

SPECIFICATION forming part of Letters Patent No. 337,632, dated March 9, 1886.

Application filed October 17, 1885. Serial No. 180,168. (No model.)

To all whom it may concern:

Be it known that I, BENJAMIN FRANKLIN SHELDON, a citizen of the United States, resident at Red Wing, in the county of Goodhue and State of Minnesota, have invented certain new and useful improvements in Potters' Wheels; and I do declare the following to be a full, clear, and exact description of the invention, such as will enable others skilled in the art to which it appertains to make and use the same, reference being had to the accompanying drawings, and to letters or figures of reference marked thereon, which form a part of this specification.

Figure 1 of the drawings is a representation of this invention, and is a vertical section. Fig. 2 is a bottom view of the butt-ring. Fig. 3 is a top view of the wheel-head.

This invention relates to potters' wheels; and it consists in the construction and novel combination of parts, as will be hereinafter fully described, and particularly pointed out in the claim.

Referring by letter to the accompanying drawings, A designates the wheel-head, and B the butt-ring, which is provided with recesses C in its bottom, which fit over the lugs D on the wheel-head A. The wheel-head A is provided with openings A' in its bottom, to prevent it from being filled with clay and water. The butt-ring B is of iron, and is to be filled with plaster the diameter of the article to be turned.

The operation of my improved potter's wheel is as follows: Place the butt-ring, constructed as above described, in the wheel-head, and turn the pot or other article desired, and then set the butt-ring with the article turned away to dry. By this construction and method of procedure I dispense with the use of lifters, and obviate the danger of marring or getting the article out of the shape in taking it off the wheel, as is now done; besides, I save time in finishing.

Having described this invention, what I claim, and desire to secure by Letters Patent, is—

The combination, with the wheel-head A, provided with the lugs D, of the butt-ring B, provided with the recesses C in its bottom, substantially as specified.

In testimony whereof I affix my signature in presence of two witnesses.

BENJAMIN FRANKLIN SHELDON

Witnesses:
J. C. McCLURE,
FRANK H. COLE.

(No Model.)

B. F. SHELDON.

POTTER'S WHEEL.

No. 337,632.   Patented Mar. 9, 1886.

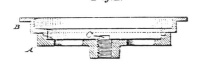

Fig. 1.

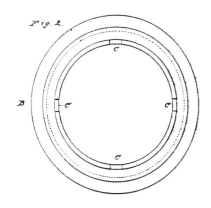

Fig. 2.

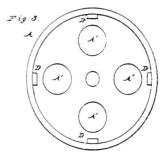

Fig. 3.

WITNESSES
Villette Anderson.
Ben. Fugett.

INVENTOR
B. F. Sheldon.
Anderson & Smith
ATTORNEYS

The principle behind Benjamin Sheldon's patent was really quite important to mass production, especially of large pieces. Previously, when a hand turned item was completed it was cut from the wheel head with a twisted piece of cord. This cord would leave a characteristic swirl on the bottom that looks like it had been made with a comb. Using Sheldon's interchangeable wheel pallet eliminated the need to cut the piece free; the pallet would be removed to a shelf for the piece to dry. Meanwhile, more and more pieces were being made. Upon drying the shrinking clay would release cleanly from the plaster leaving the bottom of the piece smooth.

195

INDEX

197

198

200